C000138639

CHRIST, CHURCH AND SOCIETY

CHRIST, CHURCH AND SOCIETY: ESSAYS ON JOHN BAILLIE AND DONALD BAILLIE

Edited by
DAVID FERGUSSON

T&T CLARK
EDINBURGH

T & T CLARK
59 GEORGE STREET
EDINBURGH EH2 2LQ
SCOTLAND

First Published 1993

ISBN 0 567 09617 3

British Library Cataloguing-in-Publication Data
A catalogue record for this book is available from the British Library

Typeset by Buccleuch Printers Ltd, Hawick
Printed and bound in Great Britain by
Biddles Ltd, Guildford and King's Lynn

CONTENTS

Preface   vii

I Biography

1 The Baillie Brothers: A Biographical Introduction   3
   Alec C. Cheyne

II Theology and Christology

2 Faith, Doubt and Moral Commitment: 41
   An Analysis of D. M. Baillie's *Faith in God*
   Ray S. Anderson

3 D. M. Baillie: A Theology of Paradox   65
   George B. Hall

4 The Christology of Donald Baillie in Perspective   87
   John McIntyre

5 Reflections on Donald Baillie's Treatment of the Atonement 115
   Donald M. MacKinnon

6 John Baillie: Orthodox Liberal   123
   David A. S. Fergusson

7 The Sense of the Presence of God   155
   George M. Newlands

III Church and Society

8 The Baillies' Churchmanship   173
   Alec C. Cheyne

9 John Baillie and 'The Moot'   199
   Keith W. Clements

10 God's Will In A Time of Crisis: 221
    John Baillie as a Social Theologian
    Duncan B. Forrester

11 Church and Society in the Thought of John Baillie   235
    James A. Whyte

IV Personal Reminiscences

12   John Baillie at Prayer   253
    Thomas F. Torrance

13 John Baillie – As a student saw him   263
    John C. Lusk

14 John Baillie on Eternal Life   269
    George S. Hendry

15 Donald M. Baillie – A Witness to Grace   273
    Jan Milič Lochman

16   D. M. Baillie – As a student saw him   281
    Murdo Ewen Macdonald

Notes on Contributors   289

Bibliography of the Principal Writings of   293
John Baillie and Donald Baillie

Index   297

PREFACE

John Baillie (1886–1960) and Donald Baillie (1887–1954) were the leading Scottish theologians of the mid-twentieth century whose significance extended far beyond their native country. While academic theologians the Baillies were also churchmen, preachers and social commentators, their work forming an organic unity which influenced many in their generation.

In 1986–7, centenary conferences held in St Mary's College, St Andrews and New College Edinburgh, indicated a continuing interest in the contribution of the Baillies not only amongst their former students but also amongst a younger generation who had never known them personally. At that time it also became apparent that a number of people had been working on their writings but that very little material had been published. The present volume of essays goes some way towards remedying this lack of literature by assessing the influence of both theologians in the light of the contemporary scene. The various contributions from outwith Scotland register the Baillies' international significance, while the scope of the essays recalls the range of their interests and expertise.

I am grateful to my fellow contributors and to many others who have encouraged and guided me in the gathering of this collection. A particular debt is owed to my former teachers John McIntyre and Alec Cheyne without whose advice and encouragement the project would never have commenced. I am also grateful to Ian and Sheila Baillie for their assistance with biographical material, to the staff of New College Library for their unfailing patience and helpfulness, and to Ute Fleming, Iain McCafferty and Rachel Hart for their contributions to the editing of the text.

David A. S. Fergusson,
King's College,
Old Aberdeen, 1992.

I
BIOGRAPHY

Chapter 1

THE BAILLIE BROTHERS: A BIOGRAPHICAL INTRODUCTION

Alec C. Cheyne

During the penultimate decade of last century three sons were born to the Reverend John Baillie, Free Church minister in Gairloch, Ross-shire, and Annie Macpherson, his wife. All eventually entered the full-time service of the Church. Peter, the youngest, trained as a medical missionary, but at the age of 25 was accidentally drowned soon after his arrival in India. The other two – John, born in 1886, and Donald Macpherson, born in 1887 – followed their father into the Christian ministry, and by the middle decades of the twentieth · century they were among the most influential and highly-regarded theologians of the English-speaking world.

After her husband's death, Mrs Baillie took the family first (in 1890) to Inverness and then (in 1905) to Edinburgh; and throughout the years down to the end of World War I the careers of John and Donald followed almost identical paths. From Inverness Royal Academy both went to the University of Edinburgh, where they gained distinguished Firsts in Philosophy, John in 1908 and Donald in 1909. Both held temporary assistantships in the Philosophy Department under their old teacher, Professor Pringle-Pattison. Both then spent another 4 years in training for the ministry at New College, Edinburgh, the premier theological seminary of the United Free Church of Scotland. Both undertook summer vacation study in Germany, John at Jena and Marburg, Donald at Heidelberg and Marburg. Both became assistant ministers in Edinburgh congregations, John at Broughton Place Church, Donald at North Morningside. On the outbreak of War, both saw service with the Y.M.C.A. in France, John for the duration, Donald quite briefly before returning to Scotland to take temporary charge of a vacant congregation in the Borders at St Boswells near Melrose. Only with the coming of peace did their ways really diverge.

From 1919 (when he married Florence Jewel, a remote descendant of the celebrated Elizabethan bishop) to 1927, John held the Chair of Christian Theology at Auburn Seminary, New York; from 1927 to 1930 the Chair of Systematic Theology at Emmanuel College, Toronto; and from 1930 to 1934 the Roosevelt Chair of Systematic Theology at Union Seminary, New York. While in North America he published, *inter alia*, *The Roots of Religion in the Human Soul* (1926), *The Interpretation of Religion* (1929), *The Place of Jesus Christ in Modern Christianity* (1929), and *And the Life Everlasting* (1933) – works which gave evidence of his mastery of both philosophical and dogmatic theology.

Meanwhile, Donald remained in Scotland and in the pastoral ministry. In 1919 he was called to the little United Free congregation at Inverbervie in Kincardineshire, where he remained until 1923. Thereafter, he held the charges of St John's, Cupar (from 1923 to 1930, by which time the congregation had entered the re-united Church of Scotland) and of St Columba's, Kilmacolm (from 1930 to 1934); and in 1927 he published his first and for long his only book, *Faith in God and its Christian Consummation*.

Not until 1934 did the brothers' careers at last come together again. In that year Donald's increasing reputation as a scholar secured his appointment to the Chair of Systematic Theology at St Mary's College, St Andrews. There he taught until his death in October 1954 – by which time he had achieved international recognition as the author of *God was in Christ: An Essay on Incarnation and Atonement* (1948) and as one of the leading figures on the Faith and Order Commission of the World Council of Churches. Three collections of his writings appeared posthumously, further enhancing his reputation: *The Theology of the Sacraments and other papers* (1957), and two volumes of sermons, *To Whom Shall We Go?* (1955) and *Out of Nazareth* (1958).

The year which took Donald to St Andrews also brought John back to Scotland as W. P. Paterson's successor in the Chair of Divinity at Edinburgh. There he remained until his retirement in 1956 – though there was a break for war service with the Y.M.C.A. (again) in 1940.

Between 1940 and 1945 he presided over the deliberations of the Church of Scotland's formidable 'Commission for the Interpretation of God's Will in the Present Crisis'; and in 1943 he was called to the Moderatorship of the General Assembly; and in 1950 he became Principal of New College and Dean of Edinburgh's Faculty of Divinity. He was named one of the six Presidents of the World Council of Churches at Evanston in 1954, was appointed a Companion of Honour by the Queen in 1957, and served on the joint Committee of Anglicans and Presbyterians which produced the controversial 'Bishop's Report' in 1957. His many publications during those productive years included *A Diary of Private Prayer* (1936), *Our Knowledge of God* (1939), *Invitation to Pilgrimage* (1942), *The Belief in Progress* (1950), and *The Idea of Revelation in Recent Thought* (1956). After his death in Edinburgh in September 1960 three further volumes made their appearance: his undelivered Gifford Lectures, published under the title of *The Sense of the Presence of God* (1962); *Christian Devotion* (1962); and *A Reasoned Faith* (1963).

In the remainder of this paper, an attempt will be made to indicate the significance of the Baillies' theology, first, by a consideration of their intellectual and spiritual inheritance, and second, by an assessment of their distinctive contribution to the religious life and thought of their time.

I
THEIR INHERITANCE

(a) Highland theology and piety
John Baillie's *Our Knowledge of God,* his first substantial publication after returning to Scotland in 1934, contains the following auto-biographical sentence: 'I was born into a Christian home, and God's earliest disclosure of His reality to my infant soul was mediated to me by the words and deeds of my Christian parents.' The home referred to was, of course, the Free Church manse at Gairloch in Wester Ross; and it is not without significance that the writer's father and mother were Christians of a very special kind. Like nearly all their West Highland contemporaries outside Arisaig and Moidart and the southmost islands of the Outer Hebrides, they were Celts by race and Calvinists by conviction; and these two influences – the Celtic and

the Calvinist – were clearly evident not only in their lives but in the lives of their children.

When John retired from the Divinity Chair at Edinburgh in 1956, his fellow Invernessian, John A. Mackay (one-time President of Princeton Theological Seminary), contributed to the *Scottish Journal of Theology* a 'Lyrical Appraisal' which referred, in passing and half-humorously, to 'the curious circumstance' that the first Scottish President of the World Council of Churches should have come from a region which the ancient Romans did not consider to be in any way part of the 'oikoumene', or civilised world. Despite Rome's contrary belief, of course, there was (and still is) a rich and distinctive Celtic culture; and Mackay was surely right when he suggested that the Celtic strain in the Baillies' make-up was at least partly responsible not only for the quite exceptional clarity and grace of all that they wrote but also for their life-long commitment to the essential unity of piety and learning. 'The fact,' he observed, 'that to a greater extent than any [other] professional theologian of our time John Baillie's work [and we should include Donald's name here too] combined the finest scholarship with a deep devotional spirit harks back to Highland religion at its best.' According to the same writer, John's *Diary of Private Prayer* – and, we may add, the early *Daybook of Prayer* for which Donald was largely responsible – had its roots deep in West Highland soil; and one suspects that this may also be said of both brothers' interest in religious experience.

But if the Celtic influence is clearly perceptible in various aspects of the Baillies' life and thought, it was the Calvinist orthodoxy and Evangelical fervour of the late-Victorian Free Church that played the most prominent part in their religious upbringing. The father of the family, who arrived in Gairloch from a charge at Moy and Tomatin (Inverness-shire) in 1875, was once described by his oldest son as a 'Calvinist divine of strong character and courtly bearing'. The mother, though perhaps less severe and more flexible in outlook, shared her husband's loyalties to the full, and was 'not only conversant' with the intricacies of the Westminster Standards but also 'well able to answer any objections that might be brought against them'. The atmosphere they created and the teaching they gave made an indelible impression on their sons. One early tribute to their influence may be found in the article entitled 'Confessions of a

Transplanted Scot' which John contributed in 1933 to an American compilation, *Contemporary American Theology: Theological Autobiographies*, that was edited by Vergilus Ferm of Wooster College, Ohio. Drawing attention, with characteristic lucidity and stylishness, to what we might call the doctrinal and the devotional ingredients in Highland Calvinism, the writer declares: 'I have never, since those days, had the good fortune to live in a community that was, generally speaking, so well acquainted with the contents of the Bible or so well able to explain and defend what it professed to believe.' And he adds that 'Not many systems of thought have been devised which (once certain initial premises are granted) hang together in so coherent a whole, or in which the vulnerable Achilles' heel is so hard to find.'

Interestingly enough, a complementary passage in *And the Life Everlasting*, published next year (1934), fills out these remarks in a slightly off-taking but nevertheless impressive way. 'Among the very earliest pictures my memory provides' (so John tells us) 'is one which, though I see it but dimly, has come back to me again and again during the preparation of the following pages. I am sitting on my father's knee in the day-nursery of a manse in the Scottish Highlands, contentedly gazing into the fire which burns brightly on the hearth. My father asks me what is the chief end of man and I reply, with perfect readiness, that man's chief end is to glorify God and to enjoy Him forever. This is, of course, the first question and answer of the Shorter Catechism which, having been agreed upon by a notable body of divines assembled at Westminster, was prescribed by the General Assembly of the Kirk of Scotland at its meeting in Edinburgh in July 1648, as a "Directory for catechising such as are of weaker capacity." My own infant capacity must have been very weak indeed, for "chiefend" was to me a single word, and a word whose precise meaning was beyond my imagining. But I did grasp, I think, even then, something of the general teaching that was meant to be conveyed, and I grew up understanding and believing that only in the everlasting enjoyment of God's presence could my life ever reach its proper and divinely appointed fulfilment.'

On what might be called the devotional (rather than the strictly doctrinal) side of Highland orthodoxy, John's 'Confessions' waxes even more eloquent. Alongside adherence to the official symbols, he maintains, should be set 'as deep and sincere a development of personal religion as could, perhaps, anywhere be pointed to in the Christian world.' And he continues, in a paragraph or two which call for extended quotation: 'The practice of prayer, private, domestic and public, was given a primary place in the daily and weekly round and was a deep reality for men's thoughts. There was a strong evangelical note, so that one's mind was constantly being turned upon the necessity of regeneration, and yet any kind of sensational or over-emotional "evangelistic" movement was looked at askance. For never in any type of religion was there a greater sense of solemnity than in this one. Nowhere else, however imposing and fitting may have been the ritual, have I ever been so aware of the *mysterium tremendum* as in these rare celebrations of the Lord's Supper. Here, if ever, *das Numinose*, "the sense of the holy", was found prevailing; the comparative rarity of the occasion giving to the sacramental feast that very same acuteness of emphasis which in another tradition (that which I have since learned to prefer) is fostered rather by the opposite rule of frequency. In recent days and in certain other parts of the world to which Scottish influence has penetrated, Presbyterianism has on occasion become a markedly unsacramental religion, the "coming to the Lord's table" being sometimes regarded as not very much more than a pleasant piece of old-fashioned sentiment and therefore an optional addition to one's central religious duties. Nothing, however, could be a greater departure from *original Scottish religion* as I knew it in my youth. The whole year's religion then seemed to me to revolve round the two half-yearly celebrations, together with their attendant special services stretching from the "Fast Day" on Thursday . . . until the following Monday evening. The Scottish sacramental doctrine is a very "high" one, though not in the sense of conformity to the too crude theory that developed within the Latin countries. . . .'

Out of this rich soil flowed the subtle theology of *Our Knowledge of God* and *God was in Christ*, the restrained but fervent piety of the *Diary of Private Prayer* and Donald's lectures on the Sacraments. It has often been argued that Scottish religion during the last two centuries or so has ever and again been revitalised by blood-transfusions from the Gaelic-speaking North-West. The advocates of such a view could hardly find a better example of the vivifying power still present in the Highland religious tradition than the contribution made to twentieth-century life and thought by those sons of a Ross-shire manse, John and Donald Macpherson Baillie.

(b) Humanist culture

Alongside the insights supplied by Highland theology and piety there existed in the minds of the youthful Baillies the very different, and at times frankly inimical, inheritance of humanist culture.

A glimpse of the encounter between these contrasting views of human nature and destiny is provided by John in the biographical sketch of his brother which he published in 1957 as an introduction to Donald's *The Theology of the Sacraments*. Having referred to the sharpening of mind that was brought about by their 'home training in theological dialectic', he continues: 'The sharpening, however, would have been much less had it not been for our growing doubts about some of the premises on which the [Calvinist] system rested. These, as I can now see, were first generated in our minds by the considerably different climate of thought to which we were introduced by what we learned at school.'

The school in question was Inverness Royal Academy, then passing through one of the best periods in its long and distinguished history; and the intellectual climate alluded to has been increasingly dominant in the Western world since the Renaissance. 'Our minds', the elderly professor recalled, 'were awakened and our imaginations stirred by what we heard there, and we were given the keys of what to us, brought up as we had been, was something of a new intellectual kingdom – even if our own independent reading and our eager discussions with some of our fellow-scholars had as much to do with the actual unlocking of the doors as what our masters (several of whom were very remarkable men) had to tell us.' It was an exciting time. 'Together we explored the riches of European literature. Together also we served our apprenticeship in the literary art, especially in the making of what we thought was poetry.'

But along with the enrichment and the exhilaration came problems and perplexities, for it was exceedingly difficult – indeed, well nigh impossible – to reconcile the Calvinist *Weltanschauung* with that to which they had now been admitted. Just how difficult is made plain by one of the more arresting paragraphs in John's reminiscences of those days. 'I have often reflected', he observes, 'that parents who

dutifully bring up their children in a traditional orthodoxy which has
never subjected itself to the challenge of Renaissance and Aufklärung,
and who then send them to a school whose whole ethos is of
humanist inspiration, seldom realise the extent of the spiritual stress
and strain to which they are then subjecting them. Our minds, for
example, were soon set afire by the reading of Shakespeare, but there
was no room at all for Shakespeare within the Puritanism of our early
upbringing; no room for theatre of any kind; but no room especially
for Shakespeare's large and generous and delicately discriminating
appreciation of the human scene. Again, we were trained at school to
develop a fastidious sense for the weighing of historical evidence, and
for distinguishing fact from legend; but our training at home did not
allow us to practise this skill on the Bible stories. Or once more, we
were abruptly introduced to the world-view of modern science, and
we could not make it square with the up-and-down, three-storey, geo-
centric universe of the Biblical writers and our Catechisms, or with
their assumptions about the natural history of the human race.'

There is considerable room for debate about the details – and even
the desirability – of the reconciliation which the Baillies later sought
to effect between humanistic culture and traditional theology. What
cannot be disputed, however, is that neither John nor Donald was in
any doubt as to the need for such a reconciliation; and that if they
eventually attained an eminent place among the Christian thinkers of
their time they were also, without any equivocation, men of the
modern world. Their understanding of the Faith was deeply affected
by the intellectual revolution we associate with the Renaissance, the
Age of Reason and the scientific advances of the nineteenth century.
And it is significant that when the Baillie family migrated to
Edinburgh in 1905 they attended, not the local Free Church (as
apparently they had done in Inverness, even after the split of 1900),
but South Morningside United Free church – and that when John
and Donald embarked a few years later upon theological study it was
to New College (by then a seminary of the liberal United Free
Church) and not the inflexibly Calvinist Free Church College next
door to it that they gravitated. A great divide had been crossed.

No change quite só basic as that which has just been chronicled
took place in the brothers' overall outlook during their sojourn in
Edinburgh as students of philosophy. The tensions already alluded to

were, however, by no means entirely resolved. Indeed, it was in the years between, say, 1905 and 1910 that John and Donald were forced as never before to come to grips with the most negative aspects of modern thought, so far as Christian faith was concerned: the exuberant belief in evolutionary progress; the continuing influence of the Comtian system of atheistic humanism; the mechanistic materialism which at the beginning of this century seemed to be carrying all before it. Looking back on the pre-War period from the vantage point of the nineteen-thirties, John opined that 'he must indeed have been a bold man, and must have risked the sneers of all the emancipated and knowing ones, who dared to speak a word against the principle of universal causation or the invariability of natural laws or the conservation of energy or the conservation of matter or the non-inheritance of acquired characteristics or the point-for-point correspondence of mind with brain.'

Yet in all their struggles with the difficulties created for traditional orthodoxy by recent developments in European thought the Baillies never allowed themselves to draw a sharply divisive line between faith and culture. What they did, rather, was to counter un-believing humanism with the weapons of the mainstream humanist tradition of the West. In that battle three distinct influences above all seem to have enabled them to keep their footing – the remarkably healthy atmosphere (as they saw it) of church life in Edwardian Edinburgh; the steadying effect of their new-found delight in literature and the arts, and their continuing sensitivity to the beauties of the natural world; and the middle-of-the-road attitude of their honoured mentor in philosophy, Professor Pringle-Pattison.

Describing (in the *Confessions of a Transplanted Scot*) the prevalent temper of Edinburgh's religious life in the last decade before the War, John remembered how 'Robert Rainy and Marcus Dods were then well-known and venerable figures in its streets. Alexander Whyte and John Kelman . . . were at the height of their powers. During several winters I was a keenly interested member of Dr Whyte's famous Bible class . . . And who that ever heard or saw John Kelman can forget the fine manliness of his spirituality or the breeze of fresh air that he carried with him wherever he went?' And he continued: 'Moreover, one was of an age to become deeply interested in the various arts, and to begin to entertain dreams of travel such as might give these interests greater opportunity of development. And one's exploration of general literature was as eager as ever, and one's own scribblings as frequent. Thus there was not likely to be any entirely sharp cleft between one's general spiritual life and the philosophical conclusions that were gradually taking shape in one's mind.'

Finally, what John called his 'progress towards a more secure mental outlook' was greatly aided, not only by 'the two great philosophers of ancient and modern times respectively, Plato and Kant', but by the teaching of Professor Pringle-Pattison, that stalwart opponent of the extreme Hegelian Idealism represented by F. H. Bradley and Bernard Bosanquet. 'I was more and more becoming convinced', he tells us, 'of the essential wisdom of my honoured teacher (and later my very dear friend), Pringle-Pattison. These were the days of high (and now almost historic) debate between Pringle-Pattison and Bosanquet. I wonder if there are many who now doubt that the former, whether or not his own position be ultimately acceptable, at least carried off the honours.' According to his admiring pupil, Pringle-Pattison contended that 'our experience does not reveal itself all on one plane, but on a variety of planes', and that 'it is the business of a comprehensive philosophy to assign to each level of experience its true place and measure of importance, according to the degree of value and ultimacy which it finds it to possess.' In agreement with this view, the Baillies took to New College three basic principles or convictions which (John suggests) they never really abandoned. These were: (i) 'interpret by the highest', (ii) consider religious faith as 'a way of knowledge which is at least equal to any other in point or reliability and which leads us into the presence of a Reality that is not discoverable by any other means', and (iii) discern 'an organic connection between faith and morals'. Before entering upon the study of Divinity, the brothers had travelled quite a fair distance along the road to a reconciliation of the two principal elements in their intellectual and spiritual inheritance, Highland religion and humanist culture.

(c) Liberal Evangelicalism

John and Donald entered New College in immediately successive years, John in 1908 and Donald in 1909. All the evidence we have indicates that their religious views and attitudes differed in no important respect from those of the United Free Church generally and of their theological teachers in particular. Between 1860 and 1910 (roughly speaking), a revolution had taken place in Scottish religion. Its effect had been to give a predominantly liberal tone and temper to what until then was a very conservative form of Presbyterianism; and by the Baillies' time all New College's best-known professors – men like Alexander Whyte (Principal), H. R. Mackintosh (Systematic Theology), H. A. A. Kennedy (New Testament) and Alexander Martin (Apologetics and Pastoral Theology) – were both inheritors and proponents of that revolution. The new orthodoxy which these men represented, and to which John and Donald gave their carefully-considered allegiance, was marked by three outstanding characteristics: commitment to the use of literary and historical criticism in the study of the Bible, wariness of what seemed to be undue emphasis on credal and confessional statements, and respect for the methods of natural science.

Apropos the first, in his 'Confessions' of 1933 John tells us that 'the historical study of the New Testament' was one of the new worlds that opened up to him at New College. He then goes on: 'During my first year as a student of theology a small group of us – most of whom were "philosophers" – made a habit of meeting together once a week for the study of the Greek text of Mark. The following year we received much stimulus from the lectures of the very distinguished scholar [Harry Kennedy] who then occupied the Chair of New Testament in our college. And in the summers I listened to the lectures of two equally distinguished New Testament scholars in Germany. I have never since lost my interest in these studies.'

What the Baillies found both at New College and in Germany was a fairly general consensus on the 'assured results' of the literary and historical criticism of the Bible, Old and New Testaments alike. Theories concerning the non-Mosaic authorship of the Pentateuch, the non-Davidic authorship of many of the Psalms, and the non-apostolic authorship of the Gospels were widely accepted – theories soon to be canonised in Peake's famous *Commentary*, which first appeared in 1919. It seems probable that an evolutionary interpretation of Israel's religion became the rule rather than the exception. Many Biblical narratives ceased to be understood literally, and the existence of diverse attitudes among the New Testament writers was either tacitly assumed or openly asserted in most scholarly circles.

Extremer versions of the new approach aroused little enthusiasm at New College; but there were relatively few dissenters when Marcus Dods, whose brief Principalship ended in the year when Donald Baillie became a divinity student, declared in his 1890 inaugural lecture as a professor that the doctrine of verbal inspiration was a theory 'which has made the Bible an offence to many honest men, which is dishonouring to God, and which has turned inquirers into sceptics by the thousand – a theory which should be branded as heretical in every Christian Church.' Dods eventually became an honoured figure in his own communion and beyond, earning praise from Alexander Whyte for his 'noble catholicity of mind and heart'. And of course Whyte himself (who was Principal of New College during the greater part of the Baillies' sojourn there) had told the audience at Dod's induction as a professor that 'The historical, exegetical and theological problems connected with New Testament study in our day are not the ephemeral heresies of restless and irreverent minds; they are the providential result of that great awakening of serious thought, and of scholarly and devout inquiry, which began at the Reformation and has been in steady progress in the best schools of Christendom ever since.' It was not without significance for the Baillies' general development that men of such markedly liberal views should set the tone of New College in the last decades before the War. Indeed, the convictions they then formed remained with them to the end of their days.

As late as 1956, for example, John wrote as follows in *The Idea of Revelation in Recent Thought*: 'The intelligent reading of the Bible – "in the Spirit, but with the mind also" –, and the reading of it so as to understand how it *Christum treibt*, depends entirely on an ability to distinguish what is central from what is peripheral; to distinguish its unchanging truth from its clothing in the particular cultural and cosmological preconceptions of the times and places in which it was written; to distinguish also between its essential message and its numerous imperfections – historical inaccuracies, inaccurate or conflicting reports, misquotations or misapplied quotations from the Old Testament in the New, and such like; and withal to distinguish the successive levels of understanding both within the Old Testament and in the transition from that to the New. We must be as frank in our acknowledgement of this as is, for example, Dr. [C. H.] Dodd when, having quoted some passages from Isaiah, he goes on: "Any theory of the Bible which suggests that we should recognise such utterances as authoritative for us stands self-condemned. They are relative to their age. But I think we should say more. They are false and they are wrong. If they were inevitable in that age – and this is a theory which can neither be proved nor disproved – then in so far that age was astray from God. In any case the men who spoke so were imperfectly harmonised with the will of God".'

In perhaps the very last autobiographical statement which we have from him – 'Some Reflections on the Changing Theological Scene', which appeared in the *Union Seminary Quarterly Review* in 1957, – John recalled how in the battle of the nineteen-twenties between fundamentalists and modernists he had been very ill at ease with the latter, who seemed to him 'to be using their new-found freedom in order to read their own very nineteenth-century predilections and philosophy of life into the Biblical teaching, and thus to be corrupting the true and original Christian message.' Yet he had 'scant enough sympathy' with the fundamentalists. They, he tells us, 'thought of themselves as defending the tradition of their Puritan forefathers, and so in a sense they were, but their defence was inevitably tempered very differently from the original formation of that tradition. The Puritans might be said to have been naive fundamentalists, because up to that time the plenary inspiration of Holy Scripture and the reliability of Biblical history had never been challenged. But in endeavouring to occupy the self-same position the fundamentalists of 1919 were belligerently repudiating the whole development of modern documentary criticism and scientific historiography which had grown up in the intervening period, and I had no doubt at all in my mind that in doing this they were defending a lost cause.'

The second distinguishing mark of pre-War Liberal Evangelicalism – a wariness of undue emphasis on all credal and confessional statements – had brought about the great Declaratory Acts of 1879 (in the United Presbyterian Church) and 1892 (in the Free Church), as well as the Church of Scotland's Act on the Formula of Subscription in 1910. In 1903, Professor W. A. Curtis's inaugural

lecture from the Chair of Systematic Theology at Aberdeen asserted
that the doctrinal details of the Westminster Confession could 'no
longer be claimed to represent the spontaneous beliefs of the great
majority of our preachers and teachers'. Four years later, Curtis's view
found support in an important compilation entitled, *Creed Revision
in Scotland: its Necessity and Scope*. No teacher at New College was
among the authors, who included such fine scholars as James Moffatt,
E. F. Scott, R. H. Strachan and John Harkless; but J. H. Leckie later
became one of Donald's close friends, and neither of the brothers
would have quarrelled with *his* analysis of the situation in the year
before John began the study of theology. 'The fact of dominant force
today', observed Leckie, 'is that the professed creed of the Church
does not any longer, *as a system,* have any particular relation to its
religious life. The Westminster Confession is not expounded in our
theological colleges. You may search the libraries of many divines and
find no copy of it there. It was read for the first time by many official
Presbyterians when the decision of the House of Lords in the Church
case gave it a new and painful interest. No man writes his sermons
with conscious regard to its venerable propositions, nor does any
theological professor compose his books in the light of its authority.
The central thoughts, also, of the Confession are no longer the central
thoughts of living faith. The doctrine of Predestination, which is the
keystone of the Westminster arch, holds no vital place in the belief of
modern man; while, on the other hand, the idea of the Divine
Fatherhood, though it is the centre of real faith today, finds no
adequate expression whatever in the ancient creed of the Presbyterian
Church.'

Leckie was perhaps an exceptionally forthright expositor of the
view then prevailing. Yet even the briefest scrutiny of John Baillie's
earlier works suggests that he was in general sympathy with it. *The
Roots of Religion* (1926) contains a reference to 'the many who have
lost their way in [Christianity's] maze of doctrines and of sects', and
goes on to declare: 'We must make re-discovery, and help others to
make re-discovery, of the true centre of gravity in this accumulated
mass of tradition.' And in *The Place of Jesus Christ in Modern
Christianity* (1929), while affirming that 'the Christian epic'
(Santayana's phrase) 'reflects and embodies the most profoundly
important truth that has ever presented itself to the mind of man',

Baillie also opines that 'to a large number of men and women of our day this great drama reads, not like a history, nor yet like a philosophy, but . . . like a chapter from the world's mythology.' He then adds: 'And you and I understand these feelings of theirs well enough, and even share them ourselves in no small measure. The fault, we feel, is at least not all on our side. We cannot think that all this modern estrangement from the traditional epic of salvation' – the epic to which Westminster bore witness – 'is *wholly* due to spiritual obtuseness and corruption of heart on the part of our eagerly-seeking contemporaries. We are ready to acknowledge that in part at least it is due to some serious defect in the epic itself.'

Their later works undoubtedly show the brothers reverting to a much more central position on the theological spectrum than is discernible in these early pronouncements. 'I am convinced, and have long been convinced,' said Donald in a lecture to his fellow-ministers which eventually found its way into *The Theology of the Sacraments,* 'that we ought to be preaching Christian doctrine much more than we are'. But his own published sermons, while unashamedly doctrinal, are marked by a simplicity – and a catholicity – which devotees of the Westminster tradition, and old-fashioned dogmatists in general, could hardly have found congenial. As for John, though his last publication, *A Reasoned Faith,* contains a whole series of addresses on 'The Substance of the Faith' which proclaim the Christian gospel in unequivocal fullness, there is no evidence that he sought to return to the iron-clad Calvinism of his Presbyterian forbears. Even in such a mature work as *Our Knowledge of God* he was concerned to point out that 'the members of that Assembly [he meant Westminster] were too intellectualistic in their interpretation of Christian faith, too much in love with credal orthodoxy, too ready to understand revelation as consisting in communicated information.' In so saying, he gave evidence of his continuing indebtedness to the mood that had been so powerfully active in the Scottish Churches during his student days.

Liberal Evangelicalism's deference to the methods and findings of natural science (the third strand we have detected in its pre-War outlook) must not be understood as meaning that Scottish theologians in the Edwardian period were disposed to make extreme claims for science and to ignore the dangers attendant upon exclusive absorption in its pursuits. 'Science', declared H. R. Mackintosh, New College's formidable professor of Systematic Theology from 1904 to 1936, 'is irrelevant to the convictions by which the religious man lives and could make nothing of them one way or the other. There is no scientific way of discovering or proving the love of God, the redeeming power of Christ, the forgiveness of sins, the hope of immortality. In short, there are more kinds of knowledge than one.' At the same time, as apologists for the Faith they frequently affirmed their belief that the discoveries of biology, chemistry and physics, if properly understood, could only reinforce the Christian interpretation of the universe; and few if any of them were inclined to repudiate the main principles of evolutionary theory. New College actually had a Chair of Natural Science. The Baillies shared the prevailing attitude, though in their maturity they perhaps expressed it with greater caution than their predecessors had done.

Having devoted a good deal of attention in the early 'fifties to the relations between science and religion (witness his 'Philosophical Discourse' on *Natural Science and the Spiritual Life,* delivered before the British Association for the Advancement of Science in 1951), John came to the conclusion that science, though of inestimable value – not least to religion – could nevertheless be dangerously misused. His argument was that it had a three-fold service to render to 'the things that matter absolutely'. First, it exposed the manner of nature's operations, and so enabled us to harness these operations for the attainment of ends which we spiritually discern to be worth seeking. Second, it revealed to us the instrumentality by which God worked out His purposes. Third, it helped to provide 'that element of otherness and conflict which is so necessary a part of our spiritual discipline'.

In the article just quoted, which bore the title 'Relating Science to Faith' and was written for a little volume on *Science and Faith Today,* (1958), John then went on to declare that 'it is to our Christian advantage to pursue our scientific researches with unabated vigour. No good will ever come of setting any limit to the advance of scientific knowledge. The relations of science and faith are not such that faith comes in where science stops, or comes in to fill up the gaps and supply the missing links. God is not a stop-gap. He is not to be discerned through the cracks of our experience but as giving meaning to the whole. Or, to put it more abstractly, purpose is not to be called in where mechanism fails, or primary causes where no secondary causes can be discovered. Rather is mechanism everywhere, and is everywhere the servant of purpose. The two conceptions are not alternatives but complementary.' At the same time, he warned against an even more fatal error than 'curtailing scientific enquiry to make room for faith': namely, 'to allow our faith to be stifled by our science'. And so to his concluding observation on the subject: 'When the two kinds of knowledge appear to conflict, or when we have most difficulty in seeing how they dovetail into each other, it is quite unreasonable, and in the end it is as unscientific as it is faithless, to cut the Gordian knot by abandoning either in order to abide by the other, by abating either to give the other greater room, or by whittling down both so that they may be more easily mortised. What we must rather do is to accept this strain as inherent in our human situation, resolutely resisting the temptation to resolve it in a premature way, living with it humbly as befits us, and profiting by the discipline it imposes, until such time as a maturer wisdom brings its own better solution.'

Shaped by their inheritance of Highland theology and piety, Humanist culture and Liberal Evangelicalism, John and Donald Baillie were by 1912–13 ready to embark upon the careers for which they had long been preparing. One further influence, however, was about to take a hand in their development – an influence whose impact can only be described as cataclysmic. The outbreak of the First World War in August 1914 did more than postpone the brothers' entry into settled employment: it helped to deepen many of their most firmly-held convictions, and gave an added urgency and passion to the ministry which they were henceforth to exercise. For nearly all who took part in it, or came in contact with it, the 'Great War' constituted the most memorable experience of their lives. Even for intellectuals, who tend to march to a different drum from other people, it was profoundly important – and the Baillies were no exception to the general rule. John, in particular, found his whole way of life transformed and his range of experiences immeasureably widened. 'The years – not much less than four – which I spent in France during the War', he reported nearly two decades later in his 'Confessions of a Transplanted Scot', 'were fallow years for me, as for so many others. I hardly read a page either of divinity or of metaphysics, and I had little time or opportunity for consecutive thinking. Yet the period brought with it a very great broadening of experience and, above all, such an understanding of the mind and temper, the spiritual needs and capacities, of average (perhaps I should rather say of *normal*) humanity as I at least had not before possessed.' Referring to a character in E. M. Forster's *The Longest Journey* who was 'only used to Cambridge, and to a very small corner of that . . . more skilled than [his companions] were in the principles of human existence, but . . . not so indecently familiar with the examples', Baillie added this revealing sentence: 'When I turned again to my old pursuits after the War was over, the khaki figures still seemed to keep their place in the background of my mind, and in much of what I have written since these days a clairvoyant reader may find them haunting the margins of the page.'

His experiences during the War clearly strengthened John's already very considerable desire not only to grasp but also to communicate what is *real* in religion. *The Roots of Religion*, his first book, bears ample testimony to that. At its outset, he examines 'the main features of the situation that is at present confronting the Christian Church' and calls to his help the numerous books and articles which were written during, or immediately after, the Great War about the religion of the men who were engaged in it. His researches lead to a two-fold conclusion. First, the soldier was deeply concerned for *reality*, not least in matters of faith. 'Not only . . . was the army's religion the religion of the nation's prime manhood, but it was the religion of that manhood when face to face with the most searching and testing experience that had come to it for long centuries. In their own vernacular, these men were "up against it" as they had never been before. They were thrown back upon the roots of their being, and there was in consequence among them – as one can testify not only from the literature but from one's own long experience among them – a most remarkable and hardly-to-be-exaggerated sense for reality and for the difference between reality and sham. No word indeed appears more commonly in the literature of which I am speaking than just this word *reality.*' Second, however, and most disturbingly, Baillie had to report the general impression that the Churches failed to satisfy this passion for reality. 'If we put all the evidence together', he told his readers, 'one main charge stands out in the very boldest relief, and that is that there is a lack of reality about the religion of the Christian Church, and a conspicuous unrelatedness to the real problems of human life.'

The Roots of Religion was a preliminary attempt to uncover the reality of the Christian faith and to demonstrate its relevance to the problems of life – but it might be said, without overmuch exaggeration, that the whole course of John's career, and Donald's also, was devoted to the same endeavour.

II
THEIR DISTINCTIVE CONTRIBUTION

Neither of the Baillies founded a theological school, though many of the most famous Chairs in the English-speaking world were, from the nineteen-forties onward, occupied by scholars who had studied under them. They had no desire to turn out little replicas of themselves, and they did not do so; but their teaching by no means lacked distinctiveness. Much could be said on this subject, and elsewhere in the present volume attention is directed to the strongly church-centred character of all their activity, as well as to their interest (much greater than had perhaps been customary among Scottish theologians since the days of Thomas Chalmers) in social questions. Here, however, there is space only for a very selective consideration of three aspects of the brothers' work which marked them off from quite a number of their contemporaries, and for which we still have reason to be grateful.

(a) Apologetic concern
The Reasonableness of the Christian Faith: the title of a little book which David Cairns senior published in 1918, might serve as a kind of motto for much if not all of what John and Donald Baillie stood for, and strove to demonstrate, in the years between 1926 (when *The Roots of Religion* made its appearance) and 1963 (when *A Reasoned Faith,* a posthumous collection of John's addresses and sermons, closed the long list of their publications). Whatever else may be said about them, the brothers were pre-eminently apologists for the Faith, and their life's work was dominated from beginning to end by an

apologetic concern. In our consideration of this theme, some valuable help is provided by the remarks which Professor John McIntyre, John Baillie's successor in the Divinity Chair, made at a conference held in New College to mark the Quatercentenary of the foundation of Edinburgh University – remarks to be found in the September 1983 number of *New College Bulletin*.

Among Professor McIntyre's observations may be noted the following:

(i) He suggests that it was what he calls 'theology's compresence in the University with other disciplines' which challenged John Baillie (whose entire career was spent either in a university or in theological colleges closely associated with their university neighbours) to explore the relationship of theology to other branches of learning.

(ii) He highlights one of the key-phrases in *Our Knowledge of God* – 'a mediated immediacy' – as being especially characteristic of Baillie's understanding of that relationship. According to Professor McIntyre, the concept implies 'a rejection of the idea that we know God directly and intuitively, by means of some sixth sense, which some have and some do not have. It is awareness of God which occurs, as [John Baillie] sometimes said, borrowing Lutheran language, "in, with and under" other entities, such as other selves, the world, human history.' And he continues: 'The university setting is not irrelevant; for God is thought to be known in those fields in which other disciplines operate. In fact, a religious awareness is often presented as an alternative interpretation of phenomena already within the range of those other disciplines.' It is not difficult to see how such an understanding enabled John Baillie to relate sympathetically to the world of culture around him and to pursue the task of persuading his colleagues in Arts and Science that the theological quest was less alien from them than they had been inclined to think.

(iii) He argues, most interestingly, that while what we might call the apologetic enterprise spanned the whole of John Baillie's career its underlying presuppositions changed quite markedly in course of time. 'In the earlier years, he had worked on the assumption that any apologetic that is to be relevant and effective today has to be directed at people who are thought of as sharing the Christian heritage, and whose awareness of other traditions is only second-hand. That assumption informed his *Invitation to Pilgrimage* which though published in 1942 summed up his attitude for some time previously. My impression is that by the time of this writing *The Sense of the Presence of God* [published posthumously in 1962] he had widened the target of his apologetic thrust, directing it as much at those who actively rejected the Christian tradition, or had never at any time stood within it, as at those who lived on its dividends without declaring their capital.'

(iv) He draws attention to the fact that 'One special feature of the kind of apologetic which John Baillie practised was that he not only endeavoured strenuously to understand those who objected to the Christian faith or some aspect of it, but set himself to state the faith or aspects of it as lucidly as he could.' Observing that 'Faithful statement is worth more than many refutations', he continues: 'A good example of this purpose is to be seen in the way in which he dealt with variant forms of the interpretation of history across the centuries in his *The Belief in Progress*. He did so in a manner which dealt with the problem in hand, which also however anticipated the˙ intense discussion of the nature of hope which was to come some twenty years after that book was written'.

All this, in Professor McIntyre's estimation, made John Baillie 'one of the most distinguished practitioners of the discipline of theology as it occurs in and is affected by the situation within a university.' The same could equally be said about his brother Donald, as anyone will agree who has read the tributes paid to him at the time of his death by Principal Knox of St Andrews University and Principal Taylor of Aberdeen, as well as Rudolf Bultmann of Marburg's assessment of *God was in Christ* as 'a model of versatile and understanding dialogue with other theological and religious outlooks.'

The Baillies' dedication to the apologetic task was almost inevitably bound up with a concern for the maintenance or improvement of standards in theological education. It was at least in part through its seminaries that the Church confronted the intellectual world. One of John's most interesting pronouncements, therefore, was a lecture entitled 'The Fundamental Task of the Theological Seminary', which he delivered at the Conference of Theological Seminaries of the United States and Canada held in Toronto in June, 1922. He was then in his earliest professorial appointment (at Auburn), and at the very outset of his long teaching career; but it would seem that the convictions he then expressed were never departed from, and indeed continued to motivate him throughout the remainder of his life.

At the heart of the lecture lies a careful consideration of the ever-recurrent question, what kind of training do our future ministers require, vocational and practical or scholarly and intellectual? Baillie's answer begins with an assertion that the modern theological school had its origin in two very diverse but confluent sources: Jesus' teaching of the Twelve, and the education provided in the philosophical schools of Athens. Historians like Harnack may have believed that the fusion of rational criticism (derived from Greece) with the allegedly simple Galilean gospel was a retrograde step, but the young professor does not agree. 'One of the things that mark off Christianity from all other religions', he avers, 'is precisely this – that though having had its rise, like nearly every other great religious force, in an entirely popular movement among a primitive and backward people in a half-forgotten corner of the world, it yet has had the spiritual vitality to graft into itself the best fruits of the most advanced culture that the race has known, and to develop in the process into being the greatest spiritual force in the modern world'. In the light of this fact of history, Baillie is moved to remark that the question with which he began is really a superficial one. 'Priests or scholars? Of course, if we must choose, we will say priests. But if history has taught us anything, it has taught us that within Western civilisation the priest is not likely to be effective if he is not a scholar too. And is not contemporary experience teaching us the same thing?'

But there is still more to be said. Observing that 'the great problem facing the Christian Church at the present moment is the defection or alienation, to a very serious extent, of two classes in the community – the intellectual class and the masses', Baillie considers that this is in large measure a problem of the Church's making. 'It seems to me clear that *one* reason why the intellectuals in our midst sit on the whole so very loosely to the Church is that the Church itself is not, as it once was, at the forefront of intellectual attainment, nor are its ministers, as they lately were, the intellectual leaders of their communities. I can testify with personal experience to cases in which it is very generally assumed by even the leading business and professional men of a city that the ministers who represent the

Church in their city are second-rate men with second-rate minds. And I know also that an even more extreme view is constantly taken by students and teachers of other subjects of the student body of certain theological seminaries.' As for the average person, reports brought back from the Western front of religious attitudes incline Baillie to suspect that '*at last* the mass of men have begun to do their own thinking, instead of letting the priest think for them', and that 'a far greater proportion of the disloyalty of the masses than is commonly allowed is due to intellectual dissent or doubt or puzzlement.'

'What we have to explain', adds the professor, 'is why so many . . . were and are entirely sceptical as to the ability of the accredited representatives of the Christian Church to help them, and so ready to assume that the chaplain's philosophy was a ready-made affair, or, in their own vernacular, a "put-up job".' And his conclusion is that 'there has never been an age in which it is more necessary than it is now for the Christian minister to be alert mentally and well-equipped intellectually. The minister who fulfils the priestly function only, and is neither prophet nor thinker, may succeed in ministering effectually to the small circle in his community who are already completely loyal to the Church; and one cannot help remarking a certain tendency among us to rest content with that as the main part of the minister's work. Surely, however, the minister's effectiveness can be measured in one way only – by his success in meeting the religious needs of the whole community. In a modern community he can have no such success unless he be able, among other things, to inspire general confidence in himself as a keen-minded, fearless and well-equipped seeker of the truth about God and Man and Life and Destiny.'

The general thrust of Baillie's argument is therefore clear. It is the seminary's task to equip men who can provide the leadership he has described. 'Here is something which we teachers of divinity *can* do – we can (according to the measure of our native ability and theirs) teach the young men to *think* – to think fairly, to think deeply, to think boldly, to think humbly. I believe that there are no questions that should be more in our minds about the students we graduate each year than these: Do they clearly know exactly what they are recommending when they recommend Christianity? And do they clearly know, and profoundly feel, why it is more worthy to be recommended than any other solution of the great riddle of life?' So he concludes: 'The problem of Christianity in the coming years will not be solved by turning out men who (in addition to being devoted servants of their race, for that must go without saying) are good speakers, experts in homiletic form and illustration, able organisers and administrators, diligent pastors, and the like. It can be resolved only if it is represented in our communities by men who can answer, in such a way as to inspire trust, the often very independent questionings of the modern mind. I believe that what the men of today are looking to the Church to provide is above all things *guidance* – not comfort, not good fellowship, not even religious exaltation and inspiration, and certainly not either oratorical thrills or social evenings, but light on the great puzzle of life. And I believe that if the Church will but realise in a really enterprising way her role as teacher, she has a magnificent future before her in our generation.'

Imbued with convictions such as these, and calling upon his contemporaries to 'reflect . . . whether it is likely that Christianity can continue her influence undiminished if our ministers cease to be looked up to as leaders of thought as well as of worship', John Baillie strove as few of his generation did to present a clear and cogent case for Christian faith, to strengthen the ties which by tradition have bound Church and University together, and to raise the standards of theological education not only in his homeland but throughout the English-speaking world.

(b) Sensitivity in the treatment of doubt and unbelief

There are some arresting sentences in John Baillie's *Invitation to Pilgrimage* where he advises the Christian apologist always to bear in mind that 'the debate between belief and unbelief is by no means a debate between himself who believes and another who disbelieves. It is also in large part a debate within himself, who both believes and disbelieves, and who must ever continue to pray humbly, "Lord, I believe; help Thou mine unbelief".' And he continues: 'When we who are within the visible Church of Christ reason with those who are without, we are ever in the position of feeling that there is in our interlocutors no disposition to believe, and in ourselves no disposition to doubt . . . We still do not find faith easy, and hence our *apologia* is always in some sort addressed to ourselves as well as to our neighbours ... The most moving and persuasive arguments are always those in which the arguer is felt to be holding high debate with himself ... When one looks back over the road oneself has travelled, anything like dogmatism appears very much out of place; anything also like a fencing method or a parade of dialectical skill or the desire to score merely a plausible victory over the opponent.'

Elsewhere in the same volume John is even prepared to say of believers and unbelievers that 'in our outlook on *everything*, in our response to *all* life's alarms, there is something that we have in common and again something that divides us. And I am sure that the bit of the road that most requires to be illuminated is the point where it forks. If we could only discover why it is that, when a certain stage is reached, we take different turnings and begin to walk apart, we should perhaps be doing all that we can humanly do. The rest is not in our hands, but in the hands of Something or Someone not ourselves; for faith is not an achievement but a gift.'

Behind such candour and sensitivity there lay, in the case of both brothers, a history of personally-experienced scepticism and anguish. In the course of an address before the British Association in 1951, Donald referred to the difficulties which 'sincere and honest souls' have with belief, and commented: 'far be it from me to speak of these difficulties with anything but respect and sympathy'. There is evidence that he was haunted from an early age by doubts which his brother subsequently diagnosed as due to the conflict then raging in his mind between traditional orthodoxy and the humanist ethos. Even during his schooldays they caused him considerable distress; but at university their impact was still greater. As John tells us in the biographical essay which introduces *The Theology of the Sacraments*, 'Donald was afterwards to be a valiant defender of the faith ... but he had to pass through a long struggle from which only slowly was he able to emerge. It brought with it nervous strain of an acute kind. He could not coerce himself to the methodical reading of the texts required for the approaching examinations, but would rather concentrate his thought for hours at a stretch on a single page, or even sentence, in one of them which seemed to promise some possible relief of his problem. And how often did I see him sit for a whole evening, staring at a book but not seeing it, and turning no page of it, while his mind kept reverting in spite of himself to a spiritual predicament concerning which the book had no real enlightenment to offer!'

By the time he got to New College, Donald's struggle for faith had 'measureably eased'. But it was by no means altogether a thing of the past, and his brother's memoir of him suggests that perhaps the shadow never entirely dissipated. 'Even in his latest years', we read, 'he had periods of depression, in which life seemed to be emptied of its divine meaning. He was in the poorest possible health then, a martyr to a long-standing asthmatic condition, and the depression was physical as well as mental. He would put to himself and to me the question as to whether the extreme bodily lassitude was the cause or the result, or merely the accompaniment, of the darkness of the soul. But one thing was always clear to him – that without God and Christ human life was without significance of any kind, devoid of all interest. He would say, "When the darkness is on me, I walk down the street, and see people walking aimlessly about, and shops and cars and a few dogs, and it all seems to mean nothing, and to matter not at all!" It was Pascal's *misère de l'homme sans Dieu.'*.

Nor was John altogether exempt from the same *Anfechtungen*. In *The Idea of Revelation* he recalls a conversation he once had with a lawyer in the States whose expression of elemental doubt brought back the memory of his own youthful agonisings. '"You speak", he said, "of trusting God, or praying to Him and doing His will. *But it's all so one-sided.* We speak to God, we bow down before Him and lift up our hearts to Him. But He never speaks to us. He makes no sign. It's all so one-sided." Nor was it without real understanding and fellow-feeling that I heard him speak thus, for there had been a time when I used to say the same things to myself . . . I can remember, during my student years in Edinburgh, walking home one frosty midnight from a philosophical discussion on the existence of God, and stopping in my walk to gaze up into the starry sky. Into those deep immensities of space I hurled my despairing question, but it seemed to hit nothing, and no answer came back . . . The stars that night did not seem to say to me, "The hand that made us is divine".'

Against the background of experiences like these, the Baillies spent a great deal of time and energy in tackling the religious difficulties of their contemporaries and in suggesting how – despite such difficulties – a return to faith might be made. An illuminating (and very typical) passage from Donald's first book, *Faith in God and its Christian Consummation*, published in 1927, well illustrates their approach, and merits quotation *in extenso*. 'What counsel', he asks, 'would the wise counsellor give to a man in the modern world who professed himself perplexed by universal doubt regarding the truth of religion?' His answer runs as follows: 'Instead of simply arguing with the doubter and endeavouring to prove religion, or telling him to make up his mind to believe, by an effort of will, or even advising "religious practice"' (references, these, to notions first publicised by William James at the end of the nineteenth century), *the wise counsellor would probably say something like this,* "Underneath your doubt, don't you feel at least a basal kind of certainty about the meaning of your life in the universe? You may feel uncertain about all the dogmas of religion as you have been accustomed to conceive them. But, to go down to something much more simple and elemental, can't you find in the bottom of your heart an ineradicable conviction that the universe is not without a purpose of good, which makes it worthwhile for you even to face your doubts and play the man; that all is not blind chance, but that there is a meaning and principle of good at the heart of things?"'

Commenting on this answer, Donald adds: 'You are appealing to a conviction which you think he has even underneath his doubts. And if you are successful, and he confesses to such a conviction, you will tell him that he is not so entirely devoid of belief as he had miserably supposed; that this is already the beginning of faith, though it looks so different from the dogmas he had been doubting; and that this faith is enough to begin with, enough to live on for the time, until, through faithfulness to it, he gradually finds it growing into something more explicit. It may be no more than what R. L. Stevenson calls

"The half of a broken hope for a pillow at night
That somehow the right is the right
And the smooth shall bloom from the rough."

Stevenson cries out, "Lord, if that were enough?" and again, "God, if this were faith?" Well, you would tell your doubter that it *is* enough to begin with; it *is* faith, though he does not realise it. And it is to this deep, fundamental, unrealised faith . . . that you make your appeal.'

There is a not dissimilar passage in John's first book, *The Roots of*

Religion, published just a year previously. Addressing 'the needs of those who have difficulty about the acceptance of religious belief', he writes: 'I may be in the direst uncertainty about the nature of this "scheme of things entire", about its constitution and construction, about its origin and destined end; but I *know* that love is better than hate, that courage is better than cowardice and honour than treachery, and that it is right to help one's fellow-traveller out of the ditch and to pour oil and wine into his wounds. There may be little to know, and little assurance in the knowing of it, but there is always plenty to do, and for the man who looks it straight in the face, plenty of assurance that it is worth doing.' And so the argument moves, by way of quotations from Carlyle ('Do the duty which lies nearest to thee') and the Baillies' early favourite, F. W. Robertson ('It must be right to do right') to this conclusion: our method of dealing with doubt 'should consist simply in the attempt to bring to clear consciousness, and to express in precise language, the nature of the compulsion which in every age has led earnest seekers after righteousness to trust in an Eternal Righteousness, and his inspired devoted workers to believe that they are working for a more-than-human Cause . . . It is agreed that there is nothing of which I am more certain than that an absolute obligation is laid upon me to do the right and eschew the wrong. But what is it that this obliges me, if it be not some larger order of things to which I stand related? How can values like truthfulness and unselfishness and courage have any claim upon me, if they are not grounded in the all-enclosing System to which I belong? How can the Ultimate Reality demand Righteousness in me, if itself be not righteous?'

How such argumentation translated into the language of the pulpit may be seen in a sermon broadcast by Donald more than a quarter of a century later, on Low Sunday 1954. Offering 'some simple bits of encouragement and counsel for those times when [like the prophet Elijah in I Kings 19:4] you are under the shadow of the juniper tree', the preacher summarised his message in the following 'heads': '(1) Remember that *this is part of the common experience of the Christian life* . . . (2) Remember that *what really matters in the Christian life is not our feelings, our emotions, our moods, but how we live,* with dedicated wills, in faith and love . . . (3) In your bad hours, remember *the fellowship of your fellow Christians,* and lean upon it' – this last point being driven home by a beautifully apposite quotation from Bunyan's *Pilgrim's Progress*.

Before leaving this subject, notice should be taken of some interesting comments that John had to make on the subject of creditable and discreditable doubt and the origins of the former. 'Part of the reason why I could not find God', he writes in *Our Knowledge of God*, 'was that there is that in God which I did not wish to find. Part of the reason why I could not (or thought I could not) hear Him speak was that He was saying some things which I did not wish to hear. There was a side of the divine reality which was unwelcome to me, and some divine commandments the obligatoriness of which I was most loath to acknowledge. And the reason why I was loath to acknowledge them was that I found them too disquieting, involving for their proper obedience a degree of courage and self-denial and a resolute reorientation of outlook and revision of program such as I was not altogether prepared to face . . . For some of what God would say to me I had a very ready ear, and I was therefore greatly disquieted by my doubts as to whether He was really addressing me at all. But because there were other of His words to which I turned a deaf ear, my deafness seemed to extend even to that for which I was most eagerly listening.' He then remarks: 'It seems to me that this is very commonly the case . . . We seek God "carefully with tears". But because we are so loath to find Him as He is, sometimes we cannot find Him at all. We have conceived our own idea of God, but it is an idea in the formation of which our sloth and selfishness have played their part; and because there is no God corresponding to our idea, and because we are looking for none other, we fail to find the God who is really there . . . We cannot be assured of His care if we reject His claim. Before religion can be known as a sweet communion, it must first be known as an answered summons.'

There is, however, another side of the matter, and a few lines further on the writer seeks to deal with it. 'But is *all* our doubt of God', he asks, 'to be explained in this way? Are we sometimes led to doubt God's reality by thinking which, however mistaken, is nevertheless quite honest, and which, though crooked intellectually, is straightforward enough morally?' The reply is without hesitation. 'Plato would answer this latter question in the affirmative . . . Doubt may sometimes spring, not from the corruption of sin, but from the limitations of finitude' – and if there is no recognition of this in Paul we must simply realise that while 'honest doubt' may have been absent from the society in which the apostle lived it is undeniably present in ours, as it was in ancient Athens.

And so we come to the final query in this connection, and to Baillie's response: 'How then are we to account for such honest doubt and denial of God's reality? The answer is perhaps twofold. First, there is the circumstance that our conviction of God first forms itself in our minds in close association with a wide context of other beliefs. In the course of our later intellectual development, however, many of those other beliefs are seen by us to be false and are quite rightly surrendered. The effort of dissociation that is then required to separate our deep-seated belief in God from that part of its original context which we have now been forced to reject, is an effort to which our mental powers are not always equal, so that we are faced with the difficult alternative of keeping our belief in God and keeping with it certain other beliefs the falsity of which seems quite obvious to us, or else surrendering these false beliefs and surrendering with them our belief in God also. Secondly, however, we must consider the appeal of arguments that are directed, not against the original context of our belief in God, but against that belief itself. In ancient Greece, and again in Western Europe since the Renaissance, but especially in the nineteenth century, there have been current a number of philosophical outlooks which found their starting point elsewhere than in belief in God – that is to say either in external nature or in man . . . Not having set out from the reality of God, not only have they (as indeed we should have expected) failed to arrive at any conviction of His reality, but they have conducted us towards a conception of universal being from which God seems to be definitely excluded. Many men of our time are therefore in the position that, while they do (as I should contend) believe in God in the bottom of their hearts, they cannot think how to answer the arguments which certain prevailing philosophies direct against His reality, and are thus led to doubt Him "with the top of their minds".'

The present-day reader may well find much of what the Baillies had to say on doubt and unbelief either old-fashioned or unconvincing – or both. Their reliance on Kant is probably greater than ours would be; their indebtedness to Carlyle and

F. W. Robertson (and Ritschl?) does not impress us as it did our fathers; their assumptions about the continuing existence of a lively Christian culture seem oddly optimistic in the nineteen-nineties. Yet their candour, their genuine if unassertive piety, and their refusal, in the spirit of Isaiah's Servant, to 'break a bruised reed' or 'quench the smoking flax' can still evoke our admiration.

(c) Resistance to the Barthian onslaught

As the nineteen-twenties gave place to the 'thirties, and the storm-clouds of another World War began to gather, new influences from the Continent of Europe gradually transformed the theological scene. In particular, churchmen became acquainted with the names of Karl Barth and Emil Brunner and their associates, and with what has at different times been called 'the Theology of Crisis', 'the Dialectical Theology' and 'the Theology of the Word of God'. They were thereby introduced to a temper and attitude very far removed from that which had prevailed among them for something like half a century. Dogmatic rather than apologetic, it started not from humanity – its predicament, its virtues, its self-consciousness – but from God and the divine Word of judgment and salvation. It asserted a complete discontinuity between the Christian revelation and human life even at its best. Supernaturalistic, authoritarian, strongly church-centred, it was given to paradox and contemptuous of the unredeemed intellect; stressed the transcendence rather than the immanence of God; and violently opposed a number of modern 'isms', including psychologism, historicism and subjectivism. In short, it was bent upon questioning, if not reversing, the dominant tendencies of Christian thought as they had developed in the West throughout the nineteenth century.

Scotland, like other Protestant countries, was very deeply divided in its response to the new movement. As I have suggested elsewhere, its theologians fell, roughly speaking, into four main groups: the first, those who were only superficially influenced and in consequence continued the liberal tradition without much change; the second, those whose entire outlook was affected but who in the end withheld their whole-hearted approval; the third, those who may be described as real if cautious admirers; the fourth, those in whom we can discern the unqualified zeal of out-and-out converts. To the first group may be assigned David Cairns (senior) of Aberdeen; to the third, H. R. Mackintosh; and to the fourth, George S. Hendry, later of Princeton. The Baillies belong fairly clearly in the second group, and both of them – John in particular – had much to say in their writings about Barth and Barthianism.

Though he responded with considerable enthusiasm to the ebullient pre-War liberalism of New College, John always had his reservations about it. On going to the Chair of Systematic Theology at Auburn Seminary, New York, therefore, he seems to have decided to act as a mediator between two extremes, what a contemporary called 'a conservative biblicism which is suspicious of all modern scientific conclusions', and 'a liberal modernism which is equally eager to assimilate every new scientific suggestion as the messianic deliverer of religion from its bondage to custom and tradition'. The consequence was that while in America he appeared a conservative among liberals, in Scotland some years later a liberal among conservatives. Yet the general movement of his thought – at least after the publication of this first three volumes, *The Roots of Religion, The Interpretation of Religion*, and *The Place of Jesus Christ in Modern Christianity* – was fairly steadily towards a greater traditionalism. Of the years around 1930 he wrote later: 'I remember being vaguely haunted by the feeling that, exhilarating as the thought of this period had been, it was now approaching something like a dead end. It seemed as if there were nowhere much further to go along the paths we were then pursuing. As things fell out, however, we had not long to wait before we found ourselves being headed off in a totally different direction. . . . The turning-point is most conveniently marked by the publication of Karl Barth's *Epistle to the Romans* in 1918.' By 1931, influenced by Kierkegaard, Buber, Brunner and Tillich, among others, Baillie could publish an article with the revealing title, 'The Predicament of Humanism'.

Despite all this, however, it is obvious (as one of his students at Union Seminary, Dietrich Bonhoeffer, noted regretfully) that John never gave his complete allegiance to the new Swiss and German fashions. In 1933 he told the readers of his 'Confessions of a Transplanted Scot' that 'the so-called Theology of Crisis seems to me, as regards one side of its teaching, to have grown out of precisely those aspects of Ritschlianism which I found myself from the first rejecting' (he means, particularly, its 'narrow Lutheran Christocentrism', its 'inhospitable attitude toward whatever religious insight stands outside of the Christian tradition' and its 'extreme opposition to mysticism'), 'and this in spite of the fact that the Ritschlian system is in other respects the object of its direct and very bitter attack. Professor Barth listened to Herrmann's lectures at Marburg very nearly at the same time as I was listening to them, but we must have been attracted and repelled by very different sides of our teacher's thought.'

In that same article, Baillie spelled out in some detail his agreements and disagreements with the new theology. On the positive side; 'Its protests against our over-weaning humanism, our cheap evolutionism, our smug immanentism and our childish utopianism have been most challenging; and in what it has to say about our human insignificance as over against God and about our utter dependence on Him for our salvation it is difficult to do anything but rejoice. In debate with my theological friends in this country [America] I have, more often than otherwise, found myself defending the Barthian positions against the very opposite principles which are professed by perhaps the majority of them.' On the negative side: 'Yet even here I am unwilling to follow Professor Barth all the way. There are indeed many things which he might have been the first to teach me, and in which I might be ready to follow him more unsuspectingly, had I not learned them first from Von Hügel – and learned at the same time to beware against understanding them in too one-sided a fashion. Barth and Von Hügel have very much the same medicine to administer to our erring modernism, but only Von Hügel is careful to provide also a suitable antidote against an overdose.

So – bearing in mind Justin Martyr's assertion that 'whatever things have been rightly said by anyone belong to us Christians', as well as Von Hügel's aphorism that '"In my flesh abideth no good thing" will somehow have to be integrated with "the spirit indeed is willing but the flesh is weak"', Baillie kept his balance even in the headiest days of the Barthian challenge; and although practically all his references to Barth in *And the Life Everlasting* (1934) were favourable, this was no longer the case in what may be his most important work, *Our Knowledge of God* (1939).

Nor did the further passage of time remove his misgivings. In the years immediately after the Second World War he began (as one commentator has said) 'to move beyond his earlier neo-orthodoxy, on the basis of a renewed confidence in reason'. The closing pages of the posthumously published Gifford Lectures, *The Sense of the Presence of God*, therefore contain not only the last but also perhaps the strongest expression of his resistance to Barthian teaching. 'That it provides a much-needed corrective to certain errors into which we have been lately inclined to fall', writes the elderly professor, 'I cannot doubt; but it administers this medicine in so brusque and defiant a way, and in such merciless overdoses, that in the end I find myself not only refusing to swallow it but at the same time suspecting that something is wrong with the prescription.' He quotes from Gustav Wingren's 'cogent and indeed merciless refutation of Dr Barth', in which the Swedish theologian had remarked that 'Barth has the ability to a very large degree of being able to employ the language of Scripture in a system that is totally foreign to the Bible', and comments: 'I should probably not myself have been quite so outspoken as Dr Wingren, but I am in full agreement with him none the less.'

Despite all his indebtedness to the great Swiss master, John was never really an adherent of the Barthian school, and his most memorable utterances seem always to have been of a mediating kind. 'I believe', he declared in the late 'fifties, 'any effective and significant post-Barthian movement must go *through* Barthianism, not repudiating the remarkable contribution it has made to all our thinking but entering fully into its heritage, while at the same time correcting its deficiencies and also recovering for us much that was of value in those early ways of thought that were too brashly jettisoned.' There is reason to believe that his brother shared these views. Though *God was in Christ* exhibits considerable indebtedness to the Movement, approval is mixed with criticism. At one point, Donald comments on its 'curious combination of theological dogmatism with historical scepticism'; at another, he 'almost ventures to say that it does not take the Incarnation quite seriously'; and in the end the impression he gives is of rather cautious detachment.

Now that the Barthian tide has receded, arousing less enthusiasm – and less revulsion – than in former days, it is possible to regard the Baillies' open but critical attitude to it as not the least of their many services to the Christian thought of our time.

This brief and very impressionistic introduction to the life's work of the Baillie brothers must not close without mentioning what in the end of the day was perhaps their greatest strength. Quite unconsciously, John drew attention to it in his early lecture on 'The Fundamental Task of the Theological Seminary'. 'The ideal required for our theological schools', he affirmed, 'is that we, the teachers, should be the kind of men who, without knowing how, and whatever be the subject of our discourse, inspire and awaken and change men. The greatest chapters in the history of education are those that tell of individual magnetic personalities, of men whose power lay as much in any counsels they gave'. Many who were their students either in North America during the nineteen-twenties and early 'thirties, or in Scotland at St Mary's College, St Andrews and New College, Edinburgh in the late 'thirties, the 'forties and the 'fifties, would testify that in so saying the young professor foretold with remarkable accuracy what would be the final verdict on the teaching careers of John and Donald Macpherson Baillie.

II
THEOLOGY AND CHRISTOLOGY

Chapter 2

FAITH, DOUBT AND MORAL COMMITMENT: AN ANALYSIS OF D. M. BAILLIE'S 'FAITH IN GOD'

Ray S. Anderson

If one were to mention the name of Donald Baillie amidst serious theological discussion with North American divinity students and, I suspect, with most theologians, he would be remembered without hesitation for his work in Christology and, in particular, for his book, *God Was in Christ – An Essay on Incarnation and Atonement* (1948). I remember well during my own student days the discovery of this book as an oasis of refreshing and stimulating reflection upon the mystery and reality of Christ, compelling in its clarity if not also controversial in its creative use of the power of paradox to grasp the depth of divine love in the miracle of the cross.

I must confess, and I am sure that I speak vicariously for the majority of my fellow students, that the title of his earlier book, *Faith in God and its Christian Consummation,* warranted at best a bibliographic citation. This, I suspect, was more to demonstrate faithfulness in research methodology than to acknowledge indebtedness to its contents.

Only in later years, when Christological polemics were displaced by the more pressing issues of the crisis of faith among those to whom I was called to serve in parish ministry, did I began to see the relevance of the question of faith as of psychological as well as of theological concern. Not least in this agenda shift from the analysis of **what** faith believes, to the **reality** of faith, was a personal struggle and pilgrimage from faith through doubt and to faith again.

During those early years of pastoral ministry, I wrote in my personal journal:

Fear – doubt – and impatience are no friends of the spirit. They make life into an ogre of duty – a distorted, grotesque wilderness where every pathway is a mockery of hope and every spring a pool of sweat. It is bad enough for the world to career its way through a desperate existence – but when the Christian fights the same ghosts, the heart looks for reality and leaves heaven to the weary and impatient. (June, 1962)

Having discovered that truths can so easily become 'untruthful' to the heart, and being confronted by others with questions more honest than my answers, I inwardly risked more than I dared outwardly to acknowledge at the time by writing:

"You will seek me and find me; when you seek me with all your heart." (Jeremiah 29:13) It is strange that we are so easily led astray by a promise such as this. The quest for God is a universal quest, though few will acknowledge the object of their pursuit, and even fewer claim much success. The pathos of life is not so much that so few are successful in their seeking of God, but that so many take this as their first responsibility. Our problem is not finding God but finding all of our heart. (July, 1963)

The key to this pilgrimage was a search for the grounding of faith in God in a structure of reality which, when doubted, would reveal itself as incapable of being denied, compelling faith to arise, as it were, from the dead, and to live again. Later I wrote:

A Point of Reference for Reality. Inevitably every reason gives way to unreasonable circumstances. The first principle is doubt. Doubt of self that routs dignity with scorn and achievement with bitterness. There is nothing that can stand before this scathing storm – ridicule leads to grotesque shadows upon the wall, cast by plans that were once carefully set in the soil of new beginnings. Even that soil is suspect, for it was ground from the rock of failure by the sharp edge of regret.

Ultimately every belief gives way to unbelievable pain. The second principle is realism. Now we recognize the matter for what it is – folly. To have not only believed but to have had faith in the believing! Twice fooled – but now this pain bears us on the crest of truth – realism churns the sand into foam, our eyes sting even as our heart surrenders all claim to truth and every taste is grit between our teeth.

Finally every hope gives way to hopelessness. The third principle is death. Even realism was endurable for the hope of some new thing churned up out of the depth. But now that changelessness is infallibly locked into the order of the days, there is no longer reason to deny the thought that has often tempted us into oblivion – death. An imperceptible joining of the crowd – lest they be frightened by the sudden deadness and reject our corpse.

The logic is unassailable. Doubt brought realism and realism justified death. Not even love can conquer such wisdom . . . unless . . . love dares to include doubt as the first principle of faith. And then moves through its own logic, but now forced to move doubt into relationship finds that it is more important to doubt the one whom we have loved as the greater doubt. For how shall we be secure in doubt if someone yet accepts our love? . . . But love does not fear doubt, for love springs not from reason but from reality. (February, 1964)

In begging the reader's indulgence for this sharing of my own faith pilgrimage, let me say that I find no better way to approach Donald Baillie's book on *Faith in God* than by making connection with his own struggle for faith through doubt as a context for reading and appreciating what he has written in this regard. Professor Cheyne has reminded us that Donald Baillie was 'haunted from an early age by doubts,' and in support of this, cites his brother John, as saying that 'Donald had to pass through a long struggle from which only slowly was he able to emerge. It brought him nervous strain of an acute kind.'[1]

One is reminded of another Scottish theologian, Ronald Gregor Smith, whose life and theology is haunted by the same kind of melancholy of spirit, and who wrote during student days at New College, Edinburgh, of his own struggles to perceive the reality of Spirit amidst the shadows of faith fleeing from the light.

There are dark times in everyone's life, times when the terror of being alive comes swooping down like an evil thing, compassing the poor mind with unimaginable tortures, shaking questions from its wings before which the established habits cower and shrink away, and leaving the victim exhausted and apathetic. If these times come only once or twice in a person's life then it is possible still to continue with the accustomed things, or if that time first breaks through the crust of routine at the crucial moment of death, it does not matter that the routine is smashed for ever. But to one who is studying for the ministry these times come not once, or twice, but again and again, storming like a black wave breaking on an island fortress, till his defences are battered in and he is utterly exposed to the mercy of the attack. . . . it is a fight whose strength is weakness, whose life is the utter nonentity of the person. For the life of it is the Spirit, always and only the Spirit.[2]

---

[1] *In Divers Manners: A St. Mary's Miscellany,* ed. D. W. D. Shaw, (St. Andrews, 1990) p. 105
[2] 'Preparing for the Ministry' *Collected Papers,* (Glasgow University, 1938)

As we shall see, these accounts of spiritual struggle for the reality of faith are not to be dismissed as melancholy murmurings from troubled souls, as though we could stand with detached interest, accounting for them as curious psychological anecdotes. This would be a mistake. We know too much, in our day, of the intricate and complex interplay between the so-called subjective and objective aspects of a single structure of reality. Our knowledge of reality, as Michael Polanyi has reminded us, is 'participatory knowledge.' 'Our believing is conditioned at its source by our belonging.'[3] We can hardly grasp the reality of God through faith when faith has itself become alien and unreal.

If we attempt to understand Baillie's book as an attempt to see faith as the religious element in universal moral conviction, we should have to agree with the criticism of Professor John McIntyre in his introduction to the 1964 re-issue of *Faith in God*. In our contemporary world, McIntyre suggests, the idea that one cannot adopt moral principles without also having faith in God, however embryonic, is untenable. As an attempt to provide an apologetic for faith in the existence of God based upon human moral commitments, the argument of the book will not be convincing for modern persons. To this extent, McIntyre concludes, Donald Baillie's attempt has already become obsolete and irrelevant, despite the intriguing existential undertones which he sees emanating from the work.

My approach in this essay is from quite a different perspective. I will suggest that it was never Donald Baillie's intention to provide a moral rationale for faith as an apologetic for religion, or for the existence of God. I do not understand his purpose as making an argument from unbelief to belief based on moral criteria intrinsic to the human heart. Quite the contrary, I see his intention as more Anselmic than Thomistic. By this I mean, Baillie took the reality of God as an ontological 'given' within the dialectic between belief and unbelief as an existential experience of 'being in the world.' He chose this approach rather than seeking to establish a kind of Thomistic 'analogy' between morality and religion. As a result, there is more of a Kierkegaardian sense of paradox in his thinking than a Hegelian attempt at synthesis.

---

[3] *Personal Knowledge*, 1958, p. 322

In re-reading the book, *Faith in God,* I was struck by the inner connection between Donald Baillie's own life and ministry as a pastor and the writing of this book. He clearly wrote out of the search for reality in his own heart as well as his attempt to understand and speak the mysteries of God to the reality of the world.

I will not attempt an extensive exposition of *Faith in God.* The book itself is so clearly written, with a precis at the beginning of each chapter, as to be expository by its own nature. Instead, I will draw forth, fairly I trust, the assumptions on which his thesis is built and examine this thesis within the context of his understanding of faith as a dialectic between a gift of God and an essential core of human moral life. In so doing, I hope to capture the creative insights of this book so as to show the significance of his contribution for the contemporary reader. Having done this, I will contrast and compare Baillie's work with that of the North American theologian, Edward John Carnell, who followed his own somewhat tormented pilgrimage from belief as a set of intellectual propositions to a faith which finds an anchor in the moral convictions of the heart. A look again at the problem of evil in light of these two theologians will provide an opportunity to show how contemporary and universal is the issue of faith.

The impetus for the book, *Faith in God,* came out of the Kerr Lectures which Baillie gave at Glasgow in 1926, while pastor of St. John's, Cupar. After only seven years of parish ministry, he was able to produce this scholarly work which eventually led to his appointment to the chair of Systematic Theology at St. Mary's College, St. Andrews.

In choosing the subject of faith for the lectures and the book, Baillie acknowledges that this came about through a long process, as he puts it, of 'blundering reflection' on the nature of religion, concluding that the vital concept at the core of the religious experience was that of faith, 'which had been so embarrassingly obtrusive in the pages of the New Testament' (pp. vii–viii). The book is organized into two parts, with an extensive introduction on the idea of faith and its historical emergence. Part One, then examines the idea of faith under the headings of authority and reason, religious experience, the will-to believe, moral conviction, and knowledge of God. Part Two contains two chapters, Faith and the Historical Jesus and Faith and the Gospel of Jesus.

In introducing his discussion of faith, Baillie shows in a wide-ranging survey, that the concept of faith as we understand it today as comprising an intellectual belief rooted in God's revelation of himself was not clearly developed either by the Greeks or by Israel. For Israel, the central element was trust in the God who was known to them, rather than belief in the existence of God as an object of knowledge. The concept of trust carries implicit moral connotations, so that whatever we mean by faith, Baillie argues, cannot be mere intellectual assent to truth without regard to the moral relation of trust. In the New Testament, he concludes, 'these two sides of faith – belief and trust – are simply inseparable' (p. 51). What emerges out of this study, is a definition of faith: 'an attitude of mind, a temper, a disposition, a resolution, and yet also a cognition with an objective reference to truth and reality; . . . a moral and practical thing, and yet more than moral and practical, taking us into still deeper mysteries, and being indeed identical, with the essence of religion' (p. 51).

The centerpiece of the book for our consideration is Chapter Five, 'Faith and Moral Conviction'. Having argued that faith is the human conviction which produces an orientation toward reality on which both religious experience and the 'will to believe' rest, he now moves into his positive thesis that both faith and moral consciousness are central to and indispensable for authentic human existence.

While allowing for the influence of both Kant and Ritschl on his thinking, he charges Kant with attenuating the religious life to the 'ought' of the moral imperative. What Kant is willing to leave as mere 'postulate' – the idea of God – Baillie insists must be affirmed as the practical content of the moral life. Otherwise, he argues, God becomes an inference and faith shrivels to 'mere morality' (pp. 171, 176). While Ritschl is cited approvingly for his influence on Herrmann and the uniting of faith and trust in a unity of the self's orientation to God (p. 98), he is also criticized for making moral consciousness prior to religious consciousness (p. 172). For his part, Baillie wishes to set religion squarely within moral consciousness, and make moral consciousness the embryonic seed of religion.

Here is where we find Baillie's thesis: every person has a moral ideal and thus has an 'unconscious faith' (p. 185). It is faith, therefore, which is the real 'religious a priori.' It is the 'elemental sense of the Divine which expresses itself in all our values . . . ' (p. 186). Because

God's holiness is inseparable from God's moral goodness, there can be no mystical apprehension of God in the form of 'awe' (the *mysterium tremendum,* R. Otto), without it also being a sense of God as the source of all moral reality, without which human life (faith) would be devoid of meaning and value (pp. 211ff).

Baillie becomes so confident that he has discovered the 'point of contact' by which faith as moral consciousness and faith as apprehension of God emerge out of the same elemental core of life, that he can affirm that moral consciousness includes all that is real in life – and reaches out to God. 'God is what we really desire in every simple, spontaneous, disinterested choice of the ideal in our daily lives. God is what we really love whenever we truly love our fellows' (p. 223).

The uncritical assurance with which Donald Baillie used the language of 'moral consciousness,' 'the voice of conscience,' 'moral ideals,' 'moral goodness,' and 'ultimate meaning in life,' as all being somewhat equivalent to 'the voice of God,' presents the contemporary reader with formidable problems. As Professor McIntyre has pointed out, the assumption that knowledge of one's moral duty is *ipso facto* an embryonic knowledge of God is not accepted by many contemporary theologians, and certainly not by many ethicists. I am not sure that Baillie himself would be comfortable with the attempt to make out of his thesis some kind of moral argument for religious faith. In his later unpublished lectures on *Beyond Morality,* he continued to speak of the connection between morality and religion, and yet, in his book, *God Was in Christ,* he wrote concerning Kant's moral argument:

> ... if it is taken as an inferential argument from our moral convictions, as premises, to God the Moral Governor of the universe as conclusion, it does not give us what Christians mean by God. ... To accept it would be to forget that there is a sense in which the Christian secret transcends morality altogether. It is Christianity that has discovered and exposed what we may call 'the paradox of moralism' – that the attempt to be moral defeats itself, leads to 'Pharisaism' instead of real goodness. (pp. 120–121)

I think that it would be safe to say that Donald Baillie never abandoned his attempt to trace out the intrinsic connection between morality and faith. At the same time, I am sure, he intended to suggest by the word 'moral,' not ethical or religious behaviour, but a perception of self as bounded by a 'moral presence' of such personal, unavoidable, and transcendent reality that he could only call it 'moral goodness.' If faith is necessary to perceive God, then Baillie held that each person, by accepting to some degree the value and goodness of life itself, was close to the 'presence of God.'

Not all persons have faith in a religious sense, and not all persons who have moral convictions have religious faith. Baillie readily accepts this observation. What Baillie does observe in people, regardless of their religious convictions and even with religious persons who experience doubt, is that there remains a core of faith in the essential meaning of life. In the scenario he creates with a religious doubter he suggests an approach which avoids argument against doubt but which seeks to uncover a hidden faith.

> Underneath your doubt, don't you feel at least a basal kind of certainty about the meaning of your life in the universe? You may feel uncertain about all the dogmas of religion as you have been accustomed to conceive them. But, to go down to something much more simple and elemental, can't you find in the bottom of your heart a purpose of good, which makes it worth while for you even to face your doubts and play the man; that all is not blind chance, but that there is a meaning and principle of good in the heart of all things? (pp. 139–40)

In reading this one has the feeling that this dialogue with a doubter has its origin in a soliloquy in Baillie's own heart. As a religious doubter himself, he has pressed through to find a depth of conviction that is existentially grounded in his own 'will to live.' This 'will to live' is the source of a 'will to believe.' This is enough to begin with, Baillie assures us, and it may be at first no more than what the poet, R. L. Stevenson calls:

> The half of a broken hope for a pillow at night
> That somehow the right is the right
> And the smooth shall bloom from the rough.

As Baillie tells it, Stevenson goes on to cry, 'Lord, if that were enough?' and again, 'God, if this were faith?' 'Well,' Baillie responds, 'you would tell your doubter that it *is* enough to begin with; it *is* faith, though he does not realize it.' (p. 140)

But, we protest, *how* does one even begin if the doubt has seeped so deeply into that existential core of the self that one doubts, not finally, the goodness of the universe, but the goodness and worth of the very self? Is this embryonic faith then 'self generated?' And if so, what does one do when it cannot be discovered within the self and cannot be generated by the self?

A clue to Baillie's response can be found in an earlier section of the book when he argued that this core of faith is not due to the authority of 'custom' or the power of one's own tradition. Nor is faith due to the power of suggestion, as though it can be stimulated by another. Not even 'auto-suggestion' accounts for the presence of this faith, as though we could 'create it' where it did not exist. No, says Baillie, this core element of faith as a commitment to the value and goodness of life is due to 'inspiration.' The reason why faith can be found in people who have had no religious training and who have no outward circumstances which would promote it, observes Baillie, is due to it being inspired by God within the core of the self. This, he suggests, was the deep insight of George Fox, the Quaker, who held that the same inspiration of the Holy Spirit which produced the Scriptures can be found in every believer's heart (pp. 65–6).

This faith cannot be 'willed,' as William James suggested. Rather, Baillie tells us that this faith which comes by inspiration is a gift of God, and that when it appears to be lacking, one must *wait* for it to appear, as it surely will to the one who lives *with* the doubt, and does not attempt to change it into faith. After citing the testimony of F. W. Robertson who tells of his own struggle with doubt and finally began with what little reality he could find, Baillie comments: 'There is something unmistakeably self-authenticating about that advice, arising out of the depths of a personal experience; and it takes us very near the heart of the whole matter. For one thing, it shows us the sense in which a man may have to *wait* for the coming of faith as a gift of God which he cannot achieve immediately at will.' (p. 146)

Indeed, we are near to the heart of the whole matter with regard to Donald Baillie's concept of faith in God. He has told us *where* it is to be found, and that every person can find it there, where commitment to life belies the lack of evidences which produces doubt. But now he tells us *how* it can be received and experienced as a gift. In a way that can only be understood when we appreciate the Kierkegaardian dialectic in his thought, rather than doubt being an enemy of faith, like the 'dread' (*Angst*) which Kierkegaard described, its purpose is to 'educate faith.' Without dread, Kierkegaard wrote, there can be no spirit in the self, and without spirit there can be no faith. So, the spirit which inspires faith is produced by the 'dread' which comes upon the person who becomes conscious of the 'terror' of life.[4]

What makes *Faith in God* read deceptively like a treatise on morality or as an apologetic for faith in God, is that the dread has been concealed behind the less threatening form of intellectual doubt. Donald Baillie, unlike Kierkegaard, does not permit us to peer directly into the abyss where moral reasoning and religious dogma alike collapse. But it is out of this abyss that the self emerges, inspired to live by some mysterious inner connection with God, and this inspired *trust* in the outcome of that risk and venture has both moral and religious content.

In the conclusion to Part One, Baillie tells us plainly that faith is born and lives in the dialectic of contradiction and trust.

> [Faith]. . . can never see each step of its way, or escape from contradiction. When we endeavour to think it out, as we must needs do, we lose ourselves in paradox. We raise our human values and ideals to the point of infinite perfection, as our one clue to the Divine; but our imaginations cannot follow them. Then our baffled minds realize that their highest ideas about God can be no more than symbolic of an Ineffable Reality whose 'ways are past finding out,' but whose meaning we can trust as better than the best we can conceive. We do not know the method of this Divine Love in any detail. But we know whom we have trusted, and persuaded that He is able to keep what we have committed to Him . . . and it is only 'by Faith' . . . only by 'being rooted and grounded in love' that we can 'know that which passes knowledge' and 'be filled with all the fulness of God.' (p. 224)

When faith has lost its confidence in the intellectual postulates offered as a form of divine truth, it is confronted by divine *love* which, as Francis Thompson tells us out of his own experience, is a relentless *Hound of Heaven* which pursues us until we are beaten, conquered, and then transformed. One cannot help but think of a similar experience in the life of the German pastor and theologian, Dietrich Bonhoeffer, who had many deep crises of faith, and who revealed his own struggle in a sermon preached in London in 1934, on the text: Jeremiah 20:7 'O Lord, thou hast deceived me, and I was deceived; thou art stronger than I, and thou has prevailed.'

---

[4] *The Concept of Dread,* (Princeton University Press, 1944)

"God, you began with me. You sent after me, confronted me suddenly and continuously in my path, tempted and deluded me, made my heart indulgent and willing; you spoke to me about your longing and everlasting love, about your faithfulness and strength. When I sought strength, you strengthened me; when I sought footing, you steadied me; when I sought forgiveness, you forgave my guilt. I did not want it, but you overcame my will, my resistance, my heart; God, you tempted me irresistibly, so that I surrendered. You laid your hands on me as on one unsuspecting, and now I cannot escape any more. Now you pull me like your booty, bind me to your victory chariot, and drag me along so that, maltreated and tortured, I 'participate' in your triumphal procession. How could I know that your love is so painful and that your grace is so pitiless. You became stronger than I and prevailed. When my thoughts about you grew strong, I grew weak. When you defeated me, I was lost. Then my will was broken, my strength diminished, my path the way of suffering with no return, the decision about my life made, I did not decide; you did. You bound me to you, in fortune and misfortune. God, why are you so terribly near to us?"[5]

In Part Two, Baillie addresses the specific nature of *Christian* faith as faith grounded in the historical Jesus and faith as a life lived by the power of the gospel of Jesus Christ. It is of interest to the purpose of this essay to note that what receives Baillie's attention in this section is not a theory of the atonement nor of Christology itself as a doctrine. Rather, he is concerned to explore how Christian faith responds to the contradiction between the goodness and power of God in the face of the presence of evil and suffering.

In a sense, one could say that those whose faith is grounded in God and in the Kingdom of God as revealed through the power and presence of Jesus Christ, find it more difficult to sustain faith than those who cut the cloth of their faith to fit a world shrunk to less than divine proportions. In a comment that carries deep significance for Baillie's concept of faith and offers a suggestion as to the contemporary relevance of his work, he says: 'It has been said that one of the differences between the medieval and the modern spirit is that nowadays people think more about pain than about sin; and this seems relevant to our question.' (p. 276) The 'mystery of pain' is what faith must confront, not only guilt over sin.

---

[5] cited by Jorgen Glentho, "Dietrich Bonhoeffer's Way Between Resistance and Submission," in *A Bonhoeffer Legacy*, edited by A. J. Klassen, p. 172

In Christopher Fry's play, *The Boy With a Cart*,[6] Cuthman, the shepherd boy, who believes that God guards his sheep, is informed of the sudden death of his father. His faith is tormented by this drenching pain. He feels that he has 'stolen God' away from his father to guard his sheep. In the manner of a Greek chorus, the 'People of South England' chant a derisive challenge to his faith:

> Where is your faith now, Cuthman? . . .
> Pain is low against the ground
> And grows like a weed.
> Is God still in the air and in the seed? . . .
> Cold on the roads,
> Desperate by the river,
> Can faith for long elude
> Prevailing fever?

His story then unfolds as a story of faith discovered and recovered in what Donald Baillie would call the working out of a 'moral' commitment to make out of his life an instrument of good.

This is the arena in which Donald Baillie wanted his voice to be heard. While the lectures were given in the comfort and security of the University, and trimmed to fit the 'Procrustean Bed' of academic discourse, he spoke from personal knowledge of the pain and torment of doubt but also from the depths of a faith which survived. Yes, Baillie concluded, 'Christian faith has always claimed to deal, not only with our pains and sorrows, but, above all, with our sins.' (p. 297) But he also added, 'How can there be a real forgiveness of sins, which will be of any real comfort to the penitent, unless he can by faith rise up to lose himself in the love of a God who is not simply a great Comrade, but in some sense the very Source of the moral law which has been broken?' (p. 298)

There is a sense in which the pain of grieving a loss is a deeper threat to the well-being of the self than guilt due to sin. In the biblical account of sin there is indeed guilt incurred due to the breaking of God's law, for which atonement must be made. But the consequence of sin is death, not merely guilt. Sin breaks the fragile bond between the human self and the presence of God. The loss of this 'presence' is not healed simply by having guilt removed. For Donald Baillie, it was

---

[6] *The Boy With a Cart* (Oxford University Press, 1959)

the moral presence of God, not just the moral law of God which he perceived to be the core of faith. This is why the pain of all deep loss affects the vital organs of our religious life. At the same time, if one can grieve this loss without losing faith in the goodness of God's presence, faith can be discovered and restored.

In my re-reading of Baillie's book, *Faith in God*, I was reminded over and over again of the life and teaching of my own theological mentor, Edward John Carnell, Professor of Philosophy of Religion at Fuller Seminary in Pasadena, California until his untimely death in 1968. Carnell often shared with me his own tortuous faith pilgrimage from his early fundamentalist church background, through the corridors of a rationalist philosophy under the teaching of Gordon Clark, touched by the power of grace in the lectures of Reinhold Niebuhr, and finally teased and tormented by the existential passion of Søren Kierkegaard. At the end, he attempted a work in apologetics that scandalized his rationalist friends and stimulated a new evangelical ethos among his students. His book, *Christian Commitment – An Apologetic*[7] marked the culmination of this journey, though he himself hoped it would be a threshold to a renaissance of orthodoxy under the healing and transforming power of love.

In the preface to this work, Carnell wrote:

> An approach to God calls for an exercise of spiritual as well as rational facilities, while a proof of God's existence calls for an exercise of only the rational. . . . Therefore, it seems much more in accord with Biblical revelation to argue that human beings dwell in the person of God from the first moment of moral self-consciousness, but that they remain unaware of this enclosure until worldly pride yields to spiritual humility. God himself is the moral and spiritual environment of an upright man. (p. ix)

The main argument of Carnell is as follows. There are three types of truth, and thus three ways of knowing. There is *ontological* truth, the truth of what *is*. The proper method to gain knowledge of this kind of truth is *knowledge by acquaintance*, according to Carnell. Acquaintance is direct experience. What *is* can be known by experience. The second type of truth is *propositional* truth and the appropriate means of knowledge is *rational inference*. Valid inference can be simple or complex, but it always must follow the rules of logic.

---

[7] *Christian Commitment – An Apologetic* (Macmillan, New York, 1957)

(pp. 14–19) Thus far, Carnell presents a traditional rationalist epistemology, reflective of his early training.

What Carnell perceives as the fundamental problem is not that persons lack knowledge of truth gained through acquaintance and inference, but that there is a lack of the 'truth of personal rectitude,' or, to use another phrase, a lack of the 'imperative essence' of the free moral decision which 'closes the gap between what an individual is and what he ought to be.' (p. 19)

This leads him to posit a third type of truth with its corresponding, 'third way of knowing.' The truth of one's own 'moral and spiritual' existence as represented by 'free moral decision' is the missing link between abstract truth and personal truth. The appropriate method of knowing for this kind of truth is *moral self-acceptance.* (p. 22) The remainder of his book is devoted to a development of this 'third method of knowing' by exploring from several perspectives what is meant by moral self-acceptance as the imperative essence of faith.

Carnell's thesis is that every human being exists in a four-fold environment – physical, rational, aesthetic, and moral and spiritual. Each of these environments make claims upon the individual to live and think in such a way as to correspond to reality – that is to truth. Moral self-acceptance is the realization that we are already, by virtue of our very existence as **human** persons, bound morally and spiritually to the **person** of others. The degree of our moral and spiritual obligation is directly related to the 'circle of nearness' which occurs through ordinary human social contact. Even a stranger enters into this 'circle of nearness' when crossing an invisible boundary in approaching us so that we are compelled to give recognition and response. Failing to do so, constitutes an offence for which we will be judged by the other. Our acceptance of this reality constitutes, for Carnell, the core of existence which precedes both moral and religious law and behaviour.

> If we cannot approach one another without satisfying the claims of the moral and spiritual environment, how can we avoid these claims when approaching God? Is it easier to know God than a fellow citizen? We certainly dare not treat God as an object; he cannot be regarded as the conclusion to a rational argument. God must be spiritually experienced; he must be encountered in the dynamic of fellowship. (p. 127)

At this point, I feel that Carnell was excavating the same site as Donald Baillie. Digging in the ruins of faith Baillie thought that he had found a fundamental moral sense that answered to religious doubt. Digging in the ruins of morality, Carnell thought that he had found a fundamental core of faith as commitment that answered to moral impotence.

What links the endeavour of Baillie to that of Carnell is an attempt to establish a starting point **within** human experience for the reality of God. What both concluded was that faith in God requires an acknowledgement of the truth of one's own being as grounded in a sense of ultimate meaning and goodness which we are bound to recognize as issuing from a spiritual and moral claim upon our lives that we can neither create nor dismiss.

Faith in God, writes Carnell, is composed both of 'generic faith' – the resting of the mind in sufficient evidences – and 'saving faith,' a cordial trust in the person and work of Christ (p. 267). The 'sufficiency' of evidence is what is necessary for faith, says Carnell, not the kind of evidence. With respect to God as well as with other persons, the evidences of the moral and spiritual environment are what produce faith, not merely rational argument or empirical fact. We withhold commitment to another until the demands of the moral and spiritual environment are met. But at the same time, failure to make commitment when the evidences are present reveals a core of pride and sin that must be overcome.

Carnell also speaks of the 'moral paradox' (pp. 66f). The paradox is that an authentic moral response must issue freely out of the core of our being, in order to be accepted by the other. At the same time, we are not free to ignore the moral and spiritual demand of the other. The causal connections between free moral response and a life of duty and obligation are hidden from us, says Carnell. There are ultimately no rational grounds for this kind of faith, though failure to make commitment (faith) is not only immoral but irrational (p. 70).

While Baillie stresses the need for faith to overcome the doubt brought about by the pain and suffering of life, for which religious postulates provide no answer, Carnell probes more deeply in to the contradiction which sin poses for faith as moral commitment. Moral self-acceptance, says Carnell must also be prepared to accept the reality of our failure to live in the pure light of moral and spiritual truth. Faith must overcome guilt, not merely doubt. The 'moral predicament' is expressed by the fact that humility in the presence of the moral and spiritual presence of the other is a precondition for fellowship, but in reality, we all fail precisely at this point by giving preference to our own needs and desires over the other.

> Judged from within moral self-acceptance, an individual can satisfy rectitude in two different ways: either by spontaneously doing what is right or by spontaneously expressing sorrow for having failed. The gentle life is direct fulfilment, while the penitent life is indirect fulfilment. Both satisfy the claims of the moral and spiritual environment. . . . After every strategy of mind and will has been expended, we end with the admission that our affections are not naturally inclined toward humility. (p. 158)

The first step toward faith as moral rectitude, therefore, must be repentance. Rather than this being a religious disposition and action, Carnell argues that it is an 'imperative essence' grounded in the very structure of reality comprised by the moral and spiritual environment of every person. The 'anatomy of repentance,' suggests Carnell, is quite different from an apology. An apology deals only with specific incidents, while repentance 'throws a moral cover over the whole'. Whereas an apology places the other person under a kind of 'legal' obligation to respond with acceptance, repentance does not exist until one despairs of finding a legal way out (p. 168). When we reach despair over finding a means to extricate ourselves from the moral predicament, we experience grace and mercy (p. 168).

In somewhat the same way that Donald Baillie understood the dialectic between religious doubt and faith, Carnell sees the dialectic between moral despair and faith, with repentance the key that unlocks, or 'inspires' faith. Baillie has confidence that when faith is pressed to its limits by doubt, it will discover a positive affirmation of the ultimate moral goodness of life. Carnell has no such optimism, but uncovers the depths of the moral predicament in all such attempts – our knowledge of the moral and spiritual realities at the core of existence only serves to confirm our moral impotence. And there can be no authentic faith without release from that moral predicament.

The anatomy of repentance reveals the need for a sense of despair over one's own moral power to heal a relationship which has been broken. But despair has no generative power of its own. Thus, the anatomy of faith discloses the need for grace in the form of an intervention into our moral predicament sufficient to release repentance as a positive fulfilment of the moral and spiritual demand upon us. Carnell points then to the law of love as grounded in God and expressed through the image of God as the only source of the grace which releases repentance.

> [T]he real mystery of selfhood can only be taken in as one abandons all rational and legal hope that the self is capable of full revelation. A truly moral individual accepts our lives for what they are, both in the way they are revealed and in the way they are hidden. *This is only to say, in other words, that a moral individual is one who loves.* Love fulfils the law without consciously trying. . . . love is the only standard by which we judge those who enter the circle of nearness. The total effort of the third method of knowing has been directed to a clarification of this one truth. God and man share the same moral and spiritual environment, and the content of this environment is love. (p. 208)

Donald Baillie, we will remember came to much the same conclusion, through the route of contradiction and paradox.

> We do not know the method of this Divine Love in any detail. But we know whom we have trusted, and persuaded that He is able to keep what we have committed to Him . . . and it is only 'by Faith' . . . only by 'being rooted and grounded in love' that we can 'know that which passes knowledge' and 'be filled with all the fulness of God.' (p. 224)

It seems to me that Carnell has provided a clue as to how we might take the insightful contribution of Donald Baillie and extend it further so as to make it relevant to our contemporary concerns. Baillie rightly saw that religious, or Christian faith, is grounded in a commitment to life that had moral and spiritual implications as generic to human existence as personal existence. He was correct in suggesting that apprehension of the reality of God is intrinsic to apprehension of all reality. He was close to the truth when he insisted that as long as one continues to live one affirms some kind of meaning and ultimate value to life, even though that value is hidden and the meaning unrevealed.

Baillie grasped intuitively what Carnell called the 'moral and spiritual environment' and grounded faith in what Carnell called 'moral-self acceptance.' In the end, Baillie grasped at love as the transcendence which lies beyond paradox and which takes us beyond morality.

With Carnell, we are led one step further. The content of the moral and spiritual environment is defined as love. Love is the 'imperative essence' which provides the missing link between moral consciousness and moral existence as personal rectitude. 'An aroused judicial sentiment is but the negative sign of love. Even as acts of kindness show that one is in harmony with the moral and spiritual environment, so acts of injustice and inconsideration show that one is not. . . . Even as God blesses those who love, so he creates judicial unrest in those who hate. An offence against love is an offence against God.' (Carnell, p. 209)

In this way, Carnell shows that love is an intrinsic attribute of personal being, even when one is in moral and spiritual contradiction. Thus, the way out of the moral predicament is already provided in the reality of love to empower repentance, release positive moral actions, and thus indirectly to fulfil the moral imperative. This seems to be what lies behind my own tentative probing of doubt in the excerpt from my journal cited at the beginning of this essay.

> The logic is unassailable. Doubt brought realism and realism justified death. Not even love can conquer such wisdom . . . unless . . . love dares to include doubt as the first principle of faith. And then moves through its own logic, but now forced to move doubt into relationship finds that it is more important to doubt the one whom we have loved as the greater doubt. For how shall we be secure in doubt if someone yet accepts our love? . . . But love does not fear doubt, for love springs not from reason but from reality. (February, 1964)

The fact that this has biblical grounds did not escape the attention of either Baillie or Carnell.

> Owe no one anything, except to love one another; for the one who loves another has fulfilled the law. The commandments, 'You shall not commit adultery; You shall not murder; You shall not steal; You shall not covet'; and any other commandment, are summed up in this word, 'Love your neighbour as yourself.' Love does no wrong to a neighbour; therefore, love is the fulfilling of the law. . . . God is love, and those who abide in love abide in God, and God abides in them. (Romans. 13:8–10; 1 John 4:16. NRSV)

For Baillie this becomes a doxology; for Carnell it has epistemological significance and gives faith reasons to trust when contradictions to moral consciousness arise.

When both Baillie and Carnell put their thesis to the test, it is the problem of evil that each one sees as the primary challenge to faith.

The subject occupies the greater part of the last chapter of Baillie's book, *Faith in God.* Given his thesis that faith rests, in the final resort, on a commitment to the ultimate goodness of life, one wonders how he will respond when confronted by the presence of evil and personal suffering?

He recognizes that this is a particularly onerous problem for Christian faith which is informed by the story of Jesus and his manifestation of God's power over disease, demons, and death. The older, traditional view of the problem for Christian faith was to assure us that 'everything that happens in the universe happens by the will of an infinitely wise and powerful and loving God' (p. 268). Even the tragic consequences of sin as well as natural evil could be accounted for by appealing to the hidden wisdom of God who, though all powerful, nonetheless, for purposes hidden from us, allows evil to occur and will bring good out of it in the end.

Contrasted with this view, Baillie describes a 'newer' view which sees the 'moral absurdity' of saying that everything takes place according to the will of God, even sinful actions, which he does not will. According to this view, Christian faith does not acquiesce, but fights. Through faith and prayer, this kind of faith seeks healing for disease, and miracles to overcome natural laws, believing that God is not on the side of evil but promises to banish it. To have faith, in the New Testament, was not to believe that somehow all is well and in accordance with the will of God, but to believe that God both could and would *do* things for his people (p. 281). Thus, Baillie suggests that the 'newer' view is really the 'older' one!

At the same time, Baillie is not comfortable with a Christian faith which rests upon a *theory* of God's opposition to evil, and does not take seriously the reality that Christians must often live with suffering and fail to see God at work in banishing evil. He suspects that a theism which binds God to exercise power over evil will inevitably lead to an atheism created by the existence of evil over and against the reality of God! So what can he say?

Falling back on his thesis that faith is grounded in the ultimate meaning of moral goodness, Baillie offers the suggestion that 'suffering, nobly borne, has a peculiarly refining influence upon character. There is, indeed, produced in this way something spiritually finer than could be possible – as far as we can imagine – be produced in a universe where there was no suffering at all' (p. 284). Careful as he is to introduce a caveat against glorifying suffering, he concludes by affirming again that, 'suffering does become the occasion of great spiritual gain when faced in a Christian way.'

The 'Christian way' of facing suffering is 'faith in God.' Yes, he adds, but 'what God?' 'A God upon whom unfailing Providence faith can rest. . . . There must be an unfailing divine Purpose, to which faith can cling when the struggle seems hopeless and suffering refuses to depart; . . .' (p. 286). We should not be surprised at Baillie's conclusion. Having traced out the contours of faith in terms of a commitment to life's ultimate meaning and moral divine goodness, the presence of evil and suffering constitute a moral contradiction to a 'good world' but not ultimately to a 'good God.'

To Baillie's credit he warns against giving this as a prescription to others in a time of suffering. One can only discover this for oneself through suffering. What Baillie argues is that the testimony of many is that they have found a greater purpose and a greater meaning for their lives through suffering. He concludes that these persons have found the 'inspiration' of faith in their darkest hour, consequently, no power of evil can take it away from them. His argument is for the sufficiency of faith in God's moral goodness when confronted by the most extreme contradiction to faith possible – evil as a mortal enemy of moral reason.

Carnell likewise is sensitive to the fact that the problem of evil and human suffering poses a contradiction to faith which rests in the truth of the moral and spiritual environment. While the moral and spiritual environment provide criteria for coming under moral repentance sufficient to ground faith in God's moral reality, we cannot infer from that environment the totality of God's moral character and wisdom. There must be more to God than 'meets the eye'. At the same time, Carnell is not willing to stake all on that approach, for it can easily be abused; it can justify 'moral holidays' (p. 144). Those who see evil in nature but not in themselves, says Carnell, are asking the wrong question when they ask about God's moral purpose in creating a world where evil and suffering run rampant. For Carnell, the philosopher should 'put his hand over his mouth' when he questions God's moral character in the light of evil. 'Egoistically inflated by a contemplation of his own goodness, man thinks it is perfectly decorous to press moral demands on God. Only the blindness of personal sin could induce such arrogance, for a humble person will recognize that he is held in the relation of dependence from existence itself. God sustains human life from grace, not from necessity (p. 147).

This response, of course, will bring a howl of protest from those who accuse Carnell of defending the moral character of God by using human sin as a smokescreen to evade the issue. Carnell is well aware of this, and cites Paul in defense, 'Has the potter no right over the clay, . . .' (Romans. 9:20–1). In the end, Carnell says, the issue is can we *trust* God? (p. 148). Later in the book, he takes up the issue again when he has defined love as the content of the moral and spiritual environment. While God's sovereignty is the *metaphysical* foundation of a Christian world view, God's love is the *filial bond* which binds us to God's person and becomes the basis of trust (pp. 272f). Citing the case of Habakkuk who raised questions concerning God's apparent blindness and unconcern to the suffering of the righteous (Habakkuk 1–2), Carnell argues that Habakkuk's filial boldness is only surpassed by God's paternal love (p. 274). Carnell understands the context to be one in which the moral issue of the problem of evil is discussed within the filial bond of love, so that, if God and Habakkuk are not moral equals, they are bound together in covenant love. The appeal of God to Habakkuk is to trust this love and have patience, with no answer given as to the moral problem. There are then grounds for faith in God's justice manifested by covenant love – the righteous shall live by his faith (Hab. 2:4).

Carnell argues that Habakkuk found repose for his faith in this demonstration of love, so that trust replaced moral indignation and inquiry. He cites Habakkuk's praise of God as evidence of his faith: 'Though the fig tree do not blossom, nor fruit be on the vines, the produce of the olive fail and the fields yield no food, the flock be cut off from the fold and there be no herd in the stalls, yet I will rejoice in the Lord, I will joy in the God of my salvation' (3:17–19). To which Carnell responds, 'One may search the libraries of the world, but he will not find a more touching expression of man's faith in God' (p. 276).

In the end, both Baillie and Carnell fall back on the need for faith to **trust** the goodness and wisdom of God in the face of the contradiction of suffering and evil to the moral senses. Baillie argues that most persons **do** have a basic trust in an ultimate goodness which will prevail. God is the symbol of that ultimate goodness in the form of a love which transcends the moral paradox. This trust in ultimate goodness and a God that loves, is what he calls faith. Where it is found, it produces, paradoxically, a quality of life and character that would not be achieved if there were no evil.

For Carnell, the trust which empowers faith in the face of the moral contradiction of evil and suffering is engendered by a love of God which exposes our own moral contradiction as sinful pride and yet, sustains us in relationship through mercy and grace. This convicting and sustaining love is found in the divine covenant with Israel and demonstrated in the gospel of Jesus Christ who overcame the human moral predicament in his death and resurrection. There is no 'moral and spiritual gain' in suffering the contradiction of evil in Carnell's view, as there is with Baillie. Instead, the heart of the sinner finds repose in the gracious love of God where moral outrage at evil is permitted but produces no immediate answer.

It appears that Donald Baillie was indeed more concerned to answer the question of pain than that of sin. He sought to find some 'moral equivalence' between the longing for ultimate goodness on the part of the one who suffers and the transcendent goodness and love of God. This he called faith. Suffering the contradictions of evil and injustice in this world, one is challenged to discover this faith and trust in the ultimate vindication of the moral person. Attractive as this might be as an explanation for why most people do not simply give up, lose heart, and go into complete despair when confronted by injustice, evil and suffering, it fails to account for the deeper theological question – who is God that we should believe in him in light of moral outrages in the world which he created?

If there is finally no difference in practice between 'faith in God' and 'faith in ultimate goodness,' the religious doubter can simply become an agnostic, if not an atheist and still have a 'faith' which produces moral character. Baillie did not consider this an option for himself and consequently was not prepared to entertain it as a possibility for others. This is at least one reason why his thesis is no longer as compelling as it seemed at the time.

Carnell rightly saw that if the grounds for faith as knowledge of God are laid in the moral and spiritual environment, there is a moral predicament at the core of human existence which only God can resolve. This is the problem of sin. There can be no 'level playing field' when one engages God in moral discourse about the problem of evil, suggests Carnell. Furthermore, the 'generic' faith by which most humans manage to sustain a commitment to life despite its frustrations and failures is morally conditioned, but in such a way that repentance toward God is the **only** moral and spiritual act which is appropriate. Because the love of God has entered into this environment through Jesus Christ, the reality of love provides a basis for the sinner to trust the mercy and forgiveness of God, so that love for God and the neighbour becomes the moral equivalent of goodness.

Repentance toward God issues out of the same moral and spiritual environment in which repentance toward others is the condition for fellowship and trust. Human love presents the same moral demand as does divine love, and offers the same possibility of repentance and forgiveness. In this way, Carnell grounds faith in moral repentance rather than in moral ideals.

We might summarize the difference by saying that, for Baillie, moral faith is the intrinsic human reality which leads to repentance, forgiveness, and religious faith. For Carnell, moral repentance is the intrinsic condition which, when met, leads to faith and trust in God. For Baillie, divine love is the ideal which transcends the moral paradox and inspires faith in its trust of ultimate moral goodness. With Carnell, divine love embraces the moral predicament through Jesus Christ, releasing the sinner from moral despair and inspiring trust in the love of God which is merciful and faithful toward sinners.

In the end of the day, if we find Donald Baillie failing to satisfy us on the theological grounds that he failed to take into account the moral predicament that plagues every attempt to ground faith in God in moral idealism, we must also say that he took seriously the challenges to religious belief both from without and within. In the context of the theological and religious culture of his day, where the remedy of religion and the certitudes of the church's confessional theology were already failing to comfort and convince, he dug deeper into the dry well of an empty belief, hoping to find a flowing stream of faith. Theories and theologies come and go. The need to discover faith remains for every generation.

Like Abraham, of whom it was said, 'By faith he stayed for a time in the land he had been promised, as in a foreign land. . . . For he looked forward to the city that has foundations, whose architect and builder is God' (Hebrews. 11:9, 10, NRSV), so Donald Baillie, was a pioneer of faith. The legacy of Donald Baillie may well lie in the moral earnestness of his quest for faith. He dared to look for God where he was not easily found – amidst the ruins of religious belief.

> The human heart can go to the lengths of God . . .
> Thank God our time is now when wrong
> Comes up to face us everywhere,
> Never to leave us till we take
> The longest strike of soul men ever took.
> Affairs are now souls size.
> The enterprise
> Is exploration into God.'[8]

---

[8] Christopher Fry, *A Sleep of Prisoners* (Oxford University Press, 1961)

Chapter 3

D. M. BAILLIE:
A THEOLOGY OF PARADOX

George B. Hall

D. M. Baillie attached a very great importance to paradox not only in his highly regarded *God Was In Christ*[1] but also in his earlier and less well-known *Faith in God*.[2] Both works are luxuriant with paradoxes and it is clear that he was convinced that at every vital point the theologian was compelled to use paradoxical expressions of one kind or another. This is nowhere more evident than in his christology where the paradox of grace becomes the key to the meaning of the paradox of the Incarnation. Given the centrality of the concept of paradox in his theology it follows that an examination of his understanding of its nature and place in theology has its place in any retrospective assessment of his work. This essay will begin with a review of his treatment of paradox in his first book since there is evidence that the position he developed there remained dominant throughout his later work. This will be followed by a discussion and assessment of the central role played by paradox in the christology of *God Was In Christ*. The essay will conclude with a few general comments about paradox and theology.

I

Faith in God makes clear Baillie's conviction that paradox arises from the hazardous necessity of seeking to comprehend in human terms a mystery which eludes the reach of the human mind. The truths of religion 'can be apprehended only in the personal experience of

[1] *God Was In Christ* (Faber, London, 1948)
[2] *Faith in God and its Christian Consummation* (T&T Clark, Edinburgh, 1927)

religion, i.e. in personal religious faith'.[4] When we endeavour to think out our faith we find that it can never be fully conveyed by language since our 'ideas about God can be no more than symbolic of an ineffable Reality whose "ways are past finding out", but whose meaning we can trust as better than the best we can conceive.'[5]

This has some important implications for the place of paradox in theological discourse. Firstly, paradox not only arises from but is authenticated by personal religious faith. The compulsion or need to speak paradoxically arises not from logical considerations but from the attempt to articulate this faith. Here Baillie seems to stand with those who hold that paradoxes are descriptions of religious experience which by conjoining contradictory statements establish a tension from which there emerges a context or horizon of meaning that more adequately intimates the contents of religious experience than any alternative. If this represents his position, and here one is on uncertain ground, Baillie's use of contradiction may not need to be taken as outright contradiction. If his primary concern is with this 'horizon of meaning', it could as easily be evoked by apparent contradictions. This receives indirect support from his declaration that what cannot be comprehended in words is actualised and lived out in faith. There is, for Baillie, a very important sense in which faith includes a 'knowledge' that is more real than any knowledge obtained through the ordinary exercise of our powers of reasoning.[6] It receives further support when he quotes D. R. Inge's comment that 'Faith is the felt unity of unreduced opposites'[7] in order to indicate that in some sense faith is the locus of the unity of the contradictions contained in our crude and stumbling attempts to give voice to an apprehension which though it is not complete always outpaces our expressions of it in language. This connection between personal religious experience and the need to speak paradoxically is very suggestive but he does not develop it in relation to what he says elsewhere about contradiction, paradox and antinomy.

Secondly, his discussion of the nature of paradox is beset with ambiguity and at times one detects a degree of inconsistency. He tells

[4] *Faith in God,* p. 118
[5] ibid., p. 228
[6] ibid., pp. 234f.
[7] ibid., p. 298

us that our endeavours to articulate in human terms what we have apprehended are, even at their best, no more than rough approximations to what we mean and will inevitably involve us 'in hopeless contradictions'.[8] Baillie's basic point is clear, namely that there is a mystery which eludes the reach of our reason and imagination. His next point, namely that talk about God unavoidably involves us in 'hopeless contradictions' is not at all clear since this suggests that he has in mind outright logical contradictions and this simply does not cohere with what he says elsewhere. If we accept, as I think we must, that this strong claim is heavily qualified in his discussion of paradox, much remains unclear. How does he understand contradiction? Is it simply logical contradiction? How is paradox related to contradiction? These and other important questions come to mind if we follow the discussion of his key terms.

He speaks of our inability to express the realities of faith 'without contradiction'.[9] The idea that theology cannot escape from contradiction remains constant and is later associated with paradox when he says that in our endeavour to think out the knowledge of God ingredient in faith 'we lose ourselves in paradox'.[10] But he fails to give any account of his reasons for this shift of attention from contradiction to paradox and, on the whole, tends to treat them as interchangeable terms. The problem is not that paradox does not include an element of contradiction, rather it is a question of what distinguishes a contradictory expression from a paradoxical expression? And this will depend on how contradiction is understood in certain contexts. Is it outright contradiction, is it apparent contradiction, or is paradox better understood in other terms?

Baillie never explicitly adopts the commonly held view that paradoxes are not contradictions but only apparent contradictions, although it seems to be implicit in some of the things he says. For example, when describing the paradox of the Kingdom of God he speaks of the tensions between two polar strains of truth that must be held together even though they are 'apparent irreconcilables'.[11] The note of contradiction is clearly struck but

[8] ibid., p. 236
[9] ibid., p. 118
[10] ibid., p. 228
[11] ibid., pp. 293f.

the use of 'apparent' suggests that at least here he qualifies its stark presence elsewhere.

The situation is further complicated by his later characterisation of the element of contradiction as antinomy. At one point he says that 'we cannot get rid of antinomy without sacrificing depth and richness',[12] while, at another, he speaks of 'paradox and antinomy'.[13] It is not clear if this latter is intended to distinguish them as two distinct types or if it implies that they are interchangeable. Paradox and antinomy are similar in that each involves expressing or disclosing an inner contradiction. And while it is true that they are not always carefully distinguished, antinomy has a well-established philosophical use which clearly distinguishes it from expressions that are customarily identified as religious paradoxes. Baillie not only fails to take any account of this distinction or its discussion, he does not provide any account of the relationship between paradox and antinomy which might serve as an alternative.

It is difficult to avoid the conclusion that his use of contradiction, paradox, and antinomy to mark those points where theology seems to fall into some kind of contradiction is intended merely to indicate a general feature of theological discourse and that he does not think it necessary to provide a careful analysis of the terms by which it is variously characterised. There are numerous hints and suggestions relevant to such an analysis but no clear pattern of use or meaning emerges either from his general discussion or from the different contexts in which he applies these terms to specific issues such that would enable us either to distinguish contradiction, paradox, and antinomy or to equate them. About all one can conclude is that paradox is his preferred concept since he almost invariably discusses specific Christian doctrines in its terms. It also appears better suited to assimilate variations than either contradiction or antinomy. It appears that his primary concern was to draw attention to the ineliminability of the elements of contradiction or apparent contradiction from fully developed theological reflection and, then, to exhibit this feature of theological discourse through a careful consideration of a number of key Christian doctrines. One can

[12] ibid., p. 298
[13] ibid., p. 302

appreciate both the theological motive at work here and the way in which he applies this insight to concrete theological issues but, given the enormous weight he places upon paradox in his discussion of doctrine, his failure to analyse his key terms must be judged a deficiency. The ambiguity, even confusion, in his treatment and use of the concept of paradox is something to which we will need to return in a later section.

Baillie's discussion of Christian doctrines abounds with paradoxes. He identifies and discusses, among others, the paradox of suffering, the paradox of Providence, the paradox of forgiveness, the paradox of the Kingdom, the paradox of prayer, and, most importantly, the paradox of the Cross which is the supreme symbol of the overall paradox of faith. There is much of interest in his treatment of these paradoxes but they need not detain us since an examination of them merely tends to confirm the judgment that at certain crucial points his exposition is vague and lacking in focus. This does not mean that we cannot learn from what he has to say on fundamental matters of doctrine. His discussion contains some insights relevant to current theological discussion but what he says does little to advance our understanding of the unavoidable element of contradiction and its relation to paradox and antinomy. A close study of his treatment of one or more doctrines would have value but this can be deferred until we consider *God Was In Christ* since it represents his most fully developed use of paradox in relation to doctrine.

At the very end of *Faith in God,* Baillie issues some warnings that are worthy of notice. Firstly, he warns against the danger of being so impatient of antinomies that one settles for an undue simplification and a logical simplicity that sacrifices richness and depth. He acknowledges that in the past theologians may have accepted 'antinomy too complacently, as an asylum ignorantiae, with the result that faith became too complacent',[14] but he now considers the former danger as more immediate than the latter. This supports the earlier suggestion about his possible theological motives. Given his reading of the situation, his basic aim seems to have been simply to draw attention to the element of contradiction as forcefully and comprehensively as possible without worrying too

---

[14] ibid, p. 298

much about the details and implications of the various terms used to mark it.

Secondly, he warns against any easy acceptance of paradox. We are to acknowledge paradox and antinomy since, according to Baillie, the strength of Christianity 'lies in its willingness to sacrifice the requirements of logical consistency rather than those of moral faith.'[15] At the same time, we must also strive for 'a fuller light and a deeper experience in which the paradox will be less acute.'[16] This suggests that he did not think that paradoxes establish fixed boundaries beyond which we must not pass. If we heed his warning not to be too impatient or too tolerant of paradox we will 'not dare cease the effort to rise above half-truths and achieve a logical consistency, even if this ideal is, in the very nature of the case, impossible of attainment.'[17] His outlook is neatly summed up in a quotation he takes from Lily Dougall 'A paradox is not a cushion on which to rest our mental indolence; it is the pledge of further vision, the promise that by practising both sides of the truth we shall solve what we cannot solve if we content ourselves with one side.'[18] The transcendence of paradox demands more than hard thinking, it requires living it out in daily faith as well. Apparently paradoxes are flexible and not fixed barriers and this will assume greater importance later in this discussion. At the same time, his remark about the need to strive for logical consistency is very difficult to understand since it is far from clear how one's personal religious faith will resolve problems of logical consistency. This tends to confirm the judgment that his discussion of the nature of paradox is ambiguous and diffuse; a matter to which we will need to return after we have reviewed his later reflections on paradox.

This has been little more than a sketch of the principal features of Baillie's understanding of the nature of paradox and its place in theological discourse at the time of his writing *Faith in God*. A number of questions remains unanswered regarding his analysis of contradiction, paradox, and antinomy but we now have before us what he takes to be the source of paradox at the intersection of the apprehension of personal religious faith and the attempt to articulate

[15] ibid., p. 300
[16] ibid., p. 298
[17] ibid., p. 301
[18] ibid.

it through the inadequate medium of human language. It remains to be seen if this continues to provide the orientation and general framework for his later work and, if so, whether he carries forward the discussion and offers a more precise characterisation of the nature and implications of paradox.

II

It is over forty years since *God Was In Christ* was published and it is a tribute to the power of Baillie's theological imagination that his reflections upon christology continue to attract the attention of theologians. The first thing to be noticed about his christology is his determination to avoid what he takes to be two mistaken but well-travelled roads in christology. The first treats Jesus as merely a human figure, the other, which he terms 'logotheism', attempts to look behind the human figure to a divine Word which is the genuine revelation. The way forward, he was convinced, requires that we steer a middle course between these two extremes.

When he embarks upon this middle course he first has something to say about paradox since inescapably the Incarnation confronts us with the supreme paradox. However, and this is an essential part of his thesis, the Incarnation is not an isolated paradox but is the culmination of a paradox permeating every aspect of Christian life and thought. As Baillie says,

> The Incarnation presents us indeed with the supreme paradox, and I do not believe that we can ever eliminate from it the element of paradox without losing the Incarnation itself. But this is not the only point at which we are beset with paradox in our Christian belief: this is rather the point at which the constant and ubiquitous paradox reaches its peak. And if we try to isolate absolutely the mystery of the Incarnation, failing to connect it with the all-round paradox of our Christian faith and experience, we shall end by having on our hands a mystery which is not a *religious* mystery at all and has no bearing on our actual religious life. The mistake is not to assert paradox in the doctrine of the Incarnation, but to miss the paradox everywhere else.[19]

Paradox is an omnipresent and ineradicable element in Christian faith and the supreme paradox of the Incarnation must be seen as

---

[19] *God Was In Christ*, p. 107

continuous with all the paradoxes of faith if it is not to be 'too much a sheer mystery, whose meaning we do not know'.[20]

This is a refinement of ideas already put forward in *Faith in God* and its continuity with them is evident when we are told that as soon as we think or speak of God we inevitably run into paradox, dialectical contradiction, and antinomy. And in this connection he has no hesitation in appealing to Sergius Bulgakov's definition of antinomy to characterise what he means by paradox. 'An antinomy', writes Bulgakov, 'simultaneously admits the truth of two contradictory, logically incompatible, but ontologically equally necessary assertions. An antinomy testifies to the existence of a mystery beyond which the human reason cannot penetrate. This mystery nevertheless is actualized and lived in religious experience.'[21] In other words, what cannot be said without contradiction can nevertheless be actualised and lived out in our personal religious faith and it is this which authorises all our faltering attempts to form theological statements.

The quotation from Bulgakov is a very fine summary of the position adumbrated by Baillie in his earlier book and suggests that he is no more prepared now than he was then to expound in some detail what he takes to be the nature of paradox. What we find is largely a repetition of his earlier positions which has in certain important respects, been further developed and refined.

1. The paradoxical element is unavoidable in religious thought and discourse because we cannot comprehend God in word or in the categories of finite thought.

2. Once again there is the insistence that God can be known only in direct personal relationship, although he now relates the incapacity of thought to comprehend God to the fact that God, the supreme subject, cannot be comprehended as an object of which we can speak in terms of the spectator-attitude. He accepts and is heavily reliant on Martin Buber's representation of our relationship to God as an 'I-Thou' relationship. Baillie is also at pains to deny the charge that this leads to religious subjectivism.

3. We cannot objectify or conceptualise God, and, yet, theology cannot avoid objectifying God. We must have theology and we must

[20] ibid., p. 107
[21] quoted ibid., pp. 108f.

use human words in worship and in all our religious thought and expression, but we do so at a cost – 'it will always be a theology of paradox'.[22]

4. Baillie helpfully clarifies his position when he lays it down that we are not to make the mistake of thinking that because our statements about God are frequently self-contradictory, divine reality is self-contradictory. The contradictions arise inevitably since in objectifying divine reality we unavoidably distort it. Moreover, the self-contradictions we are compelled to utter are reconciled in a way that cannot be adequately expressed in words since 'it is experienced and lived in the "I-Thou" relationship of faith towards God'.[23] Paradoxes are justified in theology only if they meet this condition. 'There should always be a sense of tension between the two opposite sides of our paradoxes, driving us back to their source in our actually religious experience of faith.'[24] Without this direct connection we have a mere self-contradiction, not a religious paradox. This connection also provides the warrant and basis for refining and testing our paradoxes: no religious paradox is 'justified unless it can be shown to spring directly from what H. R. Mackintosh called "the immediate utterances of faith"; for since a paradox is a self-contradictory statement, we simply *do not know what we mean by it* unless it has that direct connection with faith which it attempts to express.'[25]

There is, with one exception, little need for extended comment on these items since, by and large, they are a rehearsal of points already covered. They support the thesis that Baillie's views on paradox remained basically those of *Faith in God,* although his later work clearly reflected his sensitivity and responsiveness to the movement of theological currents between 1927 and 1948.

The exception mentioned above is (4) where we find that Baillie, in making explicit what had been implicit in his earlier work, is led to attempt to clarify and develop his thinking in a very promising direction. What he says about divine reality not being self-contradictory is obvious and need not detain us but the way in which

[22] ibid., p. 108
[23] ibid., p. 109
[24] ibid., pp. 109f.
[25] ibid., pp. 110

he begins to grapple with the problem of distinguishing acceptable from unacceptable paradox is very welcome, though some of what he says is not entirely clear. He recognises that not just any old paradox is acceptable, that theologians are as capable of uttering unacceptable nonsense as anyone else. What he says about this matter can be usefully divided into two parts for the purposes of this discussion.

Paradoxes do not usually just leap at us out of the blue but arise from our experience and presuppose a framework of belief and interpretation. One does not need to endorse Baillie's description of this experience to appreciate the importance of examining what it is that leads or compels people to utter seeming contradictions when expressing thoughts and beliefs which are obviously of profound importance to them. He recognises the need to say something about the conditions and criteria of acceptability and non-acceptability. His discussion of the experience from which paradox springs and of the reconciling of the self-contradictions in lived faith may be as opaque here as in his earlier treatment but it is now set in a context in which it should be apparent that nothing in logic compels us to speak paradoxically. Whatever the constraint or need, it is not logical.

He also recognises that paradoxes, once formed, need to be examined critically even if we cannot give a general account of our procedures and criteria. The fact is that we do analyse particular paradoxes and this often leads to their refinement, dissolution or rejection. This is evident, for example, in Baillie's revision and refinement of some of his own formulations of doctrinal paradoxes and the critical responses of his readers is an integral part of this 'testing'. This process is a vital part of the whole discussion of paradox and it is often a rich source of fresh stimulation and creative innovation in theology. It would be inappropriate to break-off and develop these matters here, especially in view of Baillie's fleeting mention of them, but it is something to which we must return when the discussion can be set in a wider context.

There are a few other matters raised by Baillie in his preliminary remarks on the nature and use of paradox. Probably the most important of these is the greater prominence he accords dialectical contradiction, as he now calls it. We encountered it earlier where it was defined as the conjoining of two opposed propositions which must be held in tension in an attitude of mutual correction. It has now been refined and granted much wider scope in *God Was In Christ*.[26] It is embodied in the quotation from Bulgakov and, as we have seen, receives special emphasis in his discussion of the condition paradoxes must satisfy if they are to be justified. Precisely what is corrected by this 'corrective' is not easy to identify. From what has just been said it appears to relate to our personal religious faith where it serves to correct any complacent acceptance of the paradox and any temptation we might have to intellectualise faith.

The concept of dialectical contradiction has a worthy pedigree and it has an articulate exponent today in John Macquarrie who emphasises 'the need for a dialectical method which allows for the possibility that every statement made may need to be corrected by a statement of opposite tendency'.[27] Here the correction occurs on the plane of the paradox itself, in relation to its two terms and the dialectical relationship between them. If we consider what Baillie has said thus far, it appears that the corrective applies to the relationship between the paradox and the source from which it springs, personal religious faith. Macquarrie conceives of the paradox as the dialectical conjunction of opposites in order to avoid any possibility of irreconcilable contradiction. Baillie seeks to do the same but since he believes that these apparently irreconcilable propositions are reconciled in faith, he uses the dialectical contradiction, in the first instance, to guard against any tendency to fall back too easily on paradox. At the same time there is a very good example of it functioning in the way Macquarrie describes in Baillie's discussion of the difficulty in expressing the doctrine of the Incarnation without erring on the side either of Christ's humanity or his divinity.[28] Thus Baillie allows the 'corrective' to operate on the relationship between the two opposing propositions and on the relationship of the paradox to its source in religious faith. This is a very interesting position since it demonstrates that Baillie emphasised the necessity of maintaining that the opposed propositions are not irreconcilable while admitting that their reconciliation eluded any verbal formulation. Hence, his complementary emphasis upon the relationship between paradox and source.

[26] ibid., pp. 107ff.
[27] *Principles of Christian Theology* (SCM, revised edition, 1977) p. 306
[28] *God Was In Christ*, pp. 129f.

Baillie did find a vivid illustration of his point in the way in which cartographers represent a three-dimensional sphere on a two-dimensional surface. Such an exercise involves some 'falsification' which the cartographer seeks to compensate for by giving us two different maps, one of two circles representing two hemispheres and the other in an oblong. 'Each is a map of the whole world, and they contradict each other at every point. Yet they are both needed, and taken together they correct each other.'[29] This illustration does not do all the work Baillie asks of it. Strictly speaking maps do not contradict each other, and even if one allowed this usage, their 'reconciliation' is accomplished through languages thereby exhibiting, not the inadequacy of language, but its greater versatility over against maps. The illustration does have its uses but only in vague and impressionistic ways. Of course we should not attach too much importance to an illustration but it cannot simply be passed over since it represents one of the few amplifications of Baillie's understanding of paradox and its functions and perhaps illustrates why he is more comfortable working with concrete examples of paradox than with discussing them in the abstract.

Baillie also mentions two doctrines, *creatio ex nihilo* and Providence, which exemplify his contention that at every essential point Christian thought is bound to encounter paradox. He reminds us that Christian theology abounds with paradoxes all of which derive from and point to the supreme paradox of the Incarnation. These paradoxes arise only as a consequence of our attempts to think through the meaning and significance of the paradox of the Incarnation. This suggests that Baillie's insistence upon a direct connection between the paradox and religious experience or faith is perhaps more complicated than he realises. The processes which produced these doctrines are so complex that it is difficult to see how they spring directly from 'the immediate utterances of faith'. They arise as a result of thinking through the implications of the Incarnation – this is clear enough since if you begin with the incursion into time of eternity it is going to have implications for all doctrines. My puzzle concerns their direct contact with

[29] ibid., p. 109

religious experience. Baillie, of course, could point to their derivative character but this is not entirely satisfactory since different derivative doctrines seem to stand in different relations to religious experience, and, if in the case of at least some doctrines, one needs to trace them back to their source in religious experience it does not look as though they spring directly from it. Does this mean that in the case of some or all derivative paradoxes we should speak of indirect contact? This is not something requiring further attention here but given the importance he attaches to religious experience and, especially, the apprehension he associates with it, along with what he says about the source of paradox and the nature of the contact between them, it is something that cannot be ignored.

All of this has been a preparation for his introduction of the paradox that is to occupy a pivotal role in his christology, the paradox of grace. He writes of it:

> Its essence lies in the conviction which a Christian man possesses, that every good thing in him, every good thing he does, is somehow not wrought by himself but by God. This is a highly paradoxical conviction, for in ascribing all to God it does not abrogate human personality nor disclaim personal responsibility. Never is human action more truly and fully personal, never does the agent feel more perfectly free, than in those moments of which he can say as a Christian that whatever good was in them was not his but God's.[30]

This paradox lies at the heart of the Christian life and ample testimony to it is provided in the writings of those exemplars of the faith who, when confronted with some important task, realised that the choices they made and the effort they expended were their own responsibility, and yet any success they achieved was due to the prevenient grace of God. This is the deepest and most profound paradox of the Christian life and is more than any other 'a distinctive product of the Incarnation'.[31]

This comment alerts us to the use to which Baillie proposes to put the paradox of grace:

> What I wish to suggest is that the paradox of grace points the way more clearly and makes a better approach than anything else in our experience

[30] ibid., p. 114
[31] ibid., p. 117

to the mystery of the Incarnation itself; that this paradox in its fragmentary form in our own Christian lives is a reflection of that perfect union of God and man in the Incarnation on which our whole Christian life depends, and may therefore be our best clue to understanding it.[32]

The crucial step in Baillie's argument is taken when he decides that 'the deepest paradox of our whole Christian experience' may serve as the hermeneutical key to an understanding of Incarnation. What, then, are the opposed propositions which constitute the paradox? These are notoriously difficult to frame and part of that difficulty stems from the very elasticity of the theological notion of grace. Baillie, provides a number of formulations of the paradox drawn largely from devotional language. One of these commends itself by its very simplicity, though, as usual, simplicity may be misleading 'every good thing in him, every good thing he does, is somehow not wrought by himself but by God.'[33] A crude but workable propositional form of this might be:

1 Every good thing in her, every good thing she does, is wrought by herself.
2 Every good thing in her, every good thing she does, is wrought by God.

This form of words may not be entirely satisfactory but it does draw attention to a crucial feature of his argument for the paradox to be the sort Baillie requires it must include the word of 'every' or 'all' in both propositions. If either one of them is qualified the paradox is threatened with dissolution.

Baillie has been insisting that a paradox includes two contradictory propositions and everything he says in defining the paradox is consistent with this requirement. This, then, is the first step in my argument: Baillie's formulation of the paradox of grace takes the form of two contradictory propositions.

Secondly, Baillie almost immediately subverts his original statement of the paradox. This, I realise, is far from obvious but it follows from what he says about the paradox a little later. In speaking about what the word 'God' means he says:

[32] ibid.
[33] ibid., p. 114

It means the One who at the same time makes absolute demands upon us and offers freely to give us all that He demands. It means the One who requires unlimited obedience and then supplies the obedience Himself. It means the One who calls us to work out our own salvation on the ground that 'it is He Himself who works both the willing and the working' in our hearts and lives.[34]

He follows this with the assertion:

That it is God's very nature to give Himself in that way: to dwell in man in such a manner that man, by his own will choosing to do God's will (and in a sense it must depend upon man's own choice) nevertheless is constrained to confess that it was 'all of God'.[35]

How does this subvert the paradox? Baillie has established a context, the context of grace, in which all key concepts no longer mean the same as they did when we first encountered the paradox. Words like 'freedom', 'will', 'choice' and so on, mean something very different from what they mean when they are set outside that context. Genuine freedom and responsibility and choice are defined by and have their place within the context of grace. The conceptions of freedom, responsibility, etc., that do not define themselves in terms of the context of grace must be 'bogus', including the initial formulation of the paradox. If what Baillie says about God's grace is true, then he has dissolved the paradox by rendering its initial contradictory propositions self-consistent. For example, when he speaks of the 'paradox which combines the fullest possible freedom with the fullest possible divine indwelling, 'I, yet not I, but the grace of God',[36] I fail to see where there is any contradiction, at least not if things are as they have been described. Does this mean that the paradox of grace is not a paradox? Not necessarily, and for a number of reasons. I will discuss these reasons in ascending order of importance to my argument.

1. There are many different kinds of paradox and paradoxes can serve different functions. There are paradoxes which say things in a startling or shocking way in order to jolt us into a new way of looking at things. Here a paradox may serve as a gateway to a more insightful understanding of God, of reality, of our place in the world. By probing the suggestions contained within it we may enlarge our

[34] ibid., p. 121
[35] ibid., p. 122
[36] ibid., p. 123

vision of some aspect of our religious experience and there can be little doubt that this is precisely what Baillie sought to do. He takes the experience which leads a person to exclaim, 'I, yet not I, but the grace of God', and seeks to do justice both to the human element of choice and responsibility captured in the 'I' and to the sense that the person has that it was wrought by God. He rightly strives for the kind of consistency which is required if we are to understand this utterance, even in part. To accomplish this he places the apparent contradiction within the context of grace thus reorienting our understanding of the familiar ideas of freedom, choice and responsibility by suggesting that it is only in this context that our experience of being responsible moral agents can be properly understood. This account, perhaps unintentionally, suggests that there is no necessary inconsistency in the utterance. This does nothing to show that the propositions are consistent but it is important because it places the burden of proof on anyone who insists that the utterance is nothing but a self-contradiction and, therefore, unacceptable nonsense. Baillie sails so perilously close to equating paradox and mere logical contradiction and is so committed to a rigid, almost mechanical, notion of dialectical paradox that the problem of distinguishing a paradox from a mere contradiction never comes to the fore.

Baillie, however, would, I think, strenuously object to what I have clumsily called the context of grace. He would deny, and with some justice, that he has changed the ordinary meanings of freedom, choice, and responsibility. He looks upon the paradox of grace as a dialectical paradox and this means he is content to let the matter rest with two contradictory propositions each of which is true: 'I did it' and 'Not I, God did it'. He then operates the corrective with the result: 'I did it' and 'God actually did it'. This is unacceptable because the result is a straightforward contradiction of which we can make no sense. Baillie lets the matter rest but this has serious implications when one remembers that his principal purpose in writing the book was to unpack the meaning of the paradox of grace as the clue to the meaning of the paradox of the Incarnation. If the former is meaningless, that is to say, incoherent, it can hardly serve as the clue to the meaning of the latter. I have suggested that his account can be rendered coherent simply by significantly altering the sense of such terms as 'freedom', 'will' and 'responsibility'. Without some such adjustment, his account is untenable.

There is a long tradition, ably represented in theology today, which maintains that an action can be both free and determined by God. God simply wills the agents freely to perform the morally good act. In this way, 'I, not I, but the grace of God,' makes sense. Everything we have reviewed agrees with the succinct expression of Baillie's view when, referring to the, 'little fragments of good that are in our lives,' he goes on to say, 'if these must be described on the one hand as human achievements, and yet on the other hand, in a deeper and a prior sense, as *not* human achievements but things wrought by God'.[37] Add to this the constant note of prevenient grace as irresistible grace running throughout the book and you have a candidate for membership in the circle of theological compatibilists. Unfortunately, in Baillie's case, the membership subscription is expensive. There are two things which would have to be sacrificed and both lie very near the centre of his theological commitments. Firstly, he seems to hold a broadly libertarian view of human freedom and this, if it is his position, is incompatible with theological compatibilism. This might not be too high a price to pay in as much as he could continue to use the same language but with significantly altered meaning. Secondly, Baillie relies very heavily on the model of interpersonal relationship for his account of our relationship to God ('I-Thou') and this, too, is, as it stands, incompatible with theological compatibilism. The latter holds firmly to the view that God's relationship to human beings is so radically disanalogous to our relationships to one another that arguments by analogy with our interpersonal relations simply do not apply to God. This is not to say that everything would have to be jettisoned but it is likely that the overhaul would be fundamental.

The point of all this has been to indicate that it is possible to develop Baillie's account in a coherent direction. If successful, it does not resolve the contradiction, if it is one; it does not establish the truth of the paradox; it does not explain it; and it does not preclude the possibility of other coherent accounts. All it does is suggest that there are possible conditions under which the paradox is meaningful,

[37] ibid., p. 129

and makes coherent sense. And that is precisely what Baillie sets out to achieve.

2. The previous section dealt with only one side of the problem that has arisen in trying to render the paradox of grace coherent. Its achievement required the sacrifice of his broadly libertarian views on human freedom, choice, and responsibility as well as calling into question his interpersonal model of our relationship to God. Can a case be made for the retention of these sides of his theology without undermining the prevenience of God's grace? I think that this can be done and that it is a more promising line to pursue than the one outlined above. In many ways it would be more in keeping with the spirit of Baillie's theology but it is not something I intend to do in this essay. For one thing, it would require lengthy treatment. For another thing, it is necessary to say a brief word about possible objections to my handling of Baillie's material. It could be argued that my whole analysis misrepresents his positions. I recognise that my interpretation grates against the whole tenor and feel of his theology and I acknowledge that this may be so but then I always wonder why he did not take the opportunity to adopt a theological language that more reflects it.

There is a long passage that suggests a different view from the one I portrayed

> It is not as though we could divide the honours between God and ourselves, God doing His part, and we doing ours. It cannot even be expressed in terms of divine initiative and human co-operation. It is false to this paradox to think of the area of God's action and the area of God's action being delimited, each by the other, and distinguished from each other by a boundary, so that the more of God's grace there is in my action, the less there it is my own personal action.[38]

This is an important passage because it identifies and seeks to correct a widespread misunderstanding infecting much of what is said about the relationship between God and human beings. But does Baillie sense the full import of his own unexceptionable message? It is as though he is saying it is woefully wrong to think of our relationship to God by analogy with a chess game in which God makes a move, followed by a move by the human being, and so on and on. Rejecting this poor analogy, he proceeds to have God seize the whole board.

[38] ibid., p. 116

Nothing else seems to have changed. Of course, if Baillie was committed to the idea of irresistible grace, this would perhaps account for his not having sought the changes which I have indicated. What was called for was a total break with this model which would have been signalled by a change in vocabulary. But there is no clear sign that its spell has been finally broken, although there peers from beneath what Baillie says here and elsewhere a word or family of words straining to be released so it can be put into service, namely interpenetration and its near relatives. This notion carries dangers but so long as it is understood that it is God's grace, the Spirit of Christ, or the Holy Spirit which interpenetrates us, we can erect adequate safeguards.

If Baillie had moved in this direction it is likely that he would have seen the paradox in a different light and not given it such a stark formulation.

3. Paradox, for Baillie, was so central in religion that he could say that theology was inevitably a theology of paradox. And, yet, he never undertook a careful study of the nature of paradox and, as I have argued, this constituted a serious limitation in his understanding and use of the concept. This is nowhere more apparent than his tendency to teeter precariously on the brink of equating paradox and mere self-contradiction. He grappled fleetingly with the problem of distinguishing acceptable and unacceptable paradoxes but he never sought to analyse contradiction and its relationship to paradox. This was a serious shortcoming but his intuition that contradiction was bound up somehow with Christian paradox was, I believe, a sound one. The worrying thing for the theologian is that the interesting paradoxes appear to be contradictions.

Does this mean that paradoxes are just logical contradictions? Gordon Graham, in an important and illuminating article,[39] supplies us with a very helpful form of words by which to characterise a paradox when he describes it 'as the unavoidably objectionable in thought.'[40] This, he argues, enables us to avoid the mistake of thinking of paradox 'as a logical form akin to contradiction, conjunction or disjunction.'[41] He illustrates his argument by reference to the doctrine

[39] 'Mystery and Mumbo-Jumbo', *Philosophical Investigations,* 7.4, 1984
[40] ibid, p. 287
[41] ibid., p. 286

of the Incarnation where he underlines a point which I was trying to make within the context of Baillie's paradox of grace. The defenders of the orthodox doctrine of the Incarnation insist that it is true and in doing so they do not violate the law of non-contradiction. To say that Jesus is fully human and fully divine involves no contradiction until someone says that a man cannot be both fully human and fully divine. But this is just what the defender of the paradox will not allow and from this follow the disputes with which we are all acquainted. The first point to be emphasised here is that by observing the law of non-contradiction, and I do not see any circumstances in which we could acquiesce in its violation, we guard against falling into straight-forward contradiction or, as Graham calls it, 'mumbo-jumbo". The situation with Baillie's paradox of grace is obviously different from the paradox of the Incarnation but the same principle applies, hence my attempt to render his paradox in a form that was not merely a self-contradiction.

Graham proceeds to draw the lesson of his discussion of the paradox of the Incarnation and this, too, has a direct bearing on our discussion. The doctrine of the Incarnation is not a contradiction but there is little gain in pointing this out, 'because the sense in which it is a seeming contradiction is the sense in which it is impossible to show that it is not a contradiction, but equally impossible to show that it is . . . with the result that an unsatisfactory conclusion, the doctrine of the Incarnation, is unavoidable.'[42]

This leads to the second point that requires to be made about paradox in theology. We are unlikely to succeed in showing that the paradoxes that arise at the heart of Christianity are not contradictions but we must expend much effort in dealing with them if they are not to be revealed, through carelessness, to be nothing but contradictions. The prudent thing in theology is never to go looking for paradoxes but wait until you bump into one, as you inevitably will.

III

There are three matters which have not received the attention they deserve and they should at least be mentioned in rounding off this essay.

[42] ibid. p. 287

Firstly, there is the testing question of truth and paradox. There is widespread resistance to the idea that paradoxes assert anything. Any attempt to make a case for this is fraught with difficulty but it is something which, I believe, ought to be attempted, especially as many who use them in theology seem to assume that they are asserting something without seeming to realise just how problematic that assumption is.

Secondly, there is the matter of what it is that compels us to utter paradoxes. Here, again, I believe Baillie to have been profoundly right to locate them in our experience and reflection upon it, apart from any judgment on his own theory. I also made the point that there is nothing in logic which could compel a person to utter a paradox. But it is not enough merely to say that religious paradox springs out of the human situation of our difference from God. This is only a point of departure and while there has been some exploration of this terrain much remains to be done.

Thirdly, paradoxes allow us to affirm God even as we deny our comprehension of God. This is a deeper and more profound function of paradox than any we have considered in this paper. The way in which paradox, by pointing always to mystery, shades into negation is something which is too often overlooked. It is an antechamber full of hustle and bustle and much chattering but after long struggle with the incompleteness which it embodies, after the numbing bewilderment of wrestling with the intractable puzzles which is poses, and after the vertigo of staring into the unfathomableness of its deepest mystery, a gate may open and the chatter become a confused whisper only to give way, by the grace of God, to a silence of a higher order.

Chapter 4

THE CHRISTOLOGY OF DONALD BAILLIE IN PERSPECTIVE

John McIntyre

It is now well over forty years since Donald Baillie's book, *God Was In Christ,* was published (1948), and the decades between have witnessed an intensity of writing in the field of christology, which has not been surpassed, if even equalled, in the whole history of theology. These were the years which witnessed the spread of understanding of Barth's christology, through the translation into English of his *Kirchliche Dogmatik,* the intensification of the interest in Bultmann's christology through the monographs and the controversies which his existentialist approach generated; the considerable influence exerted by the process philosophy of Whitehead upon the christological writing of Pittenger; the emphasis upon the humanity of Christ in the christology of John Robinson; the new socio-political dimension given to christology by so-called 'liberation theologians' such as Sobrino and Boff; the new and imaginative directions given to christology by post-Vatican II Catholic theologians such as Rahner and Schillebeeckx; as well as the wide-ranging influence of Moltmann's relating of eschatology to christology, and of Pannenberg with his concerns about the historical elements in christology. The scale and volume of so much christological reflection leads naturally to three comments, when we relate it to Donald Baillie's christology. First it is, therefore, no longer possible to approach Baillie's work with the unencumbered immediacy which was the privilege of the reviewer of 1948. That problem is not just one of distance in time, or cultural change, or philosophical fashion. For these considerations are not in themselves obstacles to the interpretation of writers of another day or age. The problem, if such it be, is that not a few of the writers in these four decades have absorbed what Baillie wrote, and have given his book, *God Was In Christ,* the accolade of being one of the most distinguished works in this field in the years since World War II. Objectivity in this context and tradition is somewhat less easily attainable than in the case of some less well-known or less popular theologian.

Secondly, the other side of this volume of christological documentation is that it provides an immensely valuable vantage-point for the perusal of Baillie's work, with an almost unfair provision of the wisdom which comes from hindsight. One outstanding characteristic of Baillie's book is the way in which it combines a perceptive and concise review of the recent history of christology, which shows expert acquaintance with the classical themes, with an original and imaginative presentation of his own position. It was also a mark of H. R. Mackintosh's *The Person of Jesus Christ,*[1] with its division into 'history' and 'reconstructive statement' – a book with which Baillie's has often been compared for its contribution to the subject, and for its influence upon subsequent thought. It is predictable that John Macquarrie's *Jesus Christ in Modern Thought,*[2] which has the same structure as its two predecessors, will play a similar role for the rest of this century. It certainly gathers up in a comprehensive sweep the ways which christology followed in the years since Baillie wrote, offers a description of a christology set out in terms of 'modern thought', and in so doing provides a contemporary bench-mark for the analysis of Baillie's thought.

Thirdly, as we approach this latter subject with the hindsight aforementioned, we sense at once the presence of two dangers. On the one hand, it would not be difficult to draw attention to the many subjects now regarded as of prime importance in christology, which do not appear in Baillie's thought, for example, the liberation theme and its role in presenting the Christ of the poor, or the several ways in which classical Aristotelianism may be replaced by other metaphysical structures in christology for our time. On the other hand, in defensive reaction to such dismissive treatment of our subject, we might treat it as a fossil, an excellent example of the state of the art of

---

[1] *The Person of Jesus Christ* (T & T Clark, Edinburgh, 1912)
[2] *Jesus Christ in Modern Thought* (SCM, London, 1990)

christology in Scotland in the late 'forties, with little relation to, or significance for, the 'nineties. Aware of these twin dangers, I propose, nevertheless, to select several of Baillie's themes and some aspects of his method, which have persistent interest through the decades since he wrote, and are still with us today.

I

THE HUMANITY OF CHRIST
AND THE PROBLEMS OF HISTORICITY

The first of these themes, one on which Baillie pursues an independent line, is *the humanity of Jesus Christ*. Early in his theological education, he had learnt from H. R. Mackintosh to reject docetism, and that rejection, when overtly confessed, reverberates throughout most of twentieth-century christology, even though in some notable cases, it may be more honoured in the breach. Mackintosh could fairly be said to have based this rejection upon his acknowledgment of the success of the theologians and others who had pursued a christology of the 'historic Christ' or the 'historic Jesus'. Threatening the validity of the rejection of docetism was the classical dogmatic assertion of the deity of Christ and of his possession of all the recognised attributes of God. Mackintosh met this threat, as is now said by some, heretically, with his theory of kenoticism. Although Baillie could echo with approval the remark of Principal A. M. Fairbairn that 'the recovery of the historical Christ [is] the most distinctive and determinative element in modern theology' which resulted in 'the rejuvenescence of theology',[3] he does not follow his mentor Mackintosh along the way of kenoticism. Quite the contrary: he is categorical in his objections to it as a christological theory.[4]

Baillie's own position on the humanity of Christ develops out of his criticism of what he designated 'the new historical radicalism', which he found to be operative in two areas of theological scholarship. The first of these occurred in biblical studies, and was associated with the *Formgeschichte* or Form criticism school. Departing from the methods

---

[3] A. M. Fairbairn, *Christ in Modern Theology* (Hodder and Stoughton, London, 1894) p. 3, quoted in *God Was In Christ* (Faber, London, 1948), p. 1

[4] *God Was In Christ*, ibid. pp. 94–98

of the source critics, who seek to trace the origins of the texts of the New Testament, the Form critics distinguish within the Gospels the different literary forms in the texts – narrative, anecdote, parable, thaumatargy, apophthegm, hymn, homily – which together make up the content of the preaching, the *kerygma,* in the early Church concerning Jesus Christ. In other words, the New Testament tells us about the early Church and what it thought about Jesus, but, in the words of Bultmann, from such fragmentary documentation, 'we can know almost nothing concerning the life and personality of Jesus'.[5] At once we notice how complete a reversal such a conviction is of the confident claim of the 'Jesus of history' movement to present a fairly accurate description of Jesus as he was known to his contemporaries. In passing, we may make an observation to which we shall later return, that there is an undeclared theory about the nature and validity of historical knowledge, which amounts to near-total agnosticism, 'radicalism' being perhaps an unduly kind characterisation of it.

This agnosticism adopts a much more explicit form in the theologians to whom Baillie next turns, in pursuit of his theme of historical radicalism, notably Brunner and Barth. In a vein similar to Bultmann, Brunner, for whom the essential centre of Christianity is the belief that the Word was made flesh, accepts an old antithesis and affirms that 'the Jesus of history is not the same as the Christ of faith',[6] and he re-affirms the conviction that 'the Christian faith does not arise out of the picture of the historical Jesus'.[7] Barth shares this form of radicalism, expressing it in the same cavalier way as does Brunner, affirming that it is historically difficult to get information about Jesus and when it is obtained, it contains little that is distinctive or impressive. His personality was in no sense convincing or attractive. In Barth's case, the problem is compounded by his adding, in effect, that even if it did prove possible to obtain much more comprehensive information about the historical Jesus, it would be to no avail, for that is not the way to faith in Jesus the Word. The human life is a concealment not a revelation of God, and Barth goes on to make a great deal of the notion that, in the human life of Jesus, God was present as a 'divine incognito'.

[5] *Jesus and the Word* (Scribners, London, 1934) p. 8
[6] *The Mediator* (Lutterworth, London, 1934) p. 184
[7] ibid. p. 172

Before proceeding to the full scale of the problems raised by this radicalism and the significance of the responses which Baillie makes, let me mention first an *ad homines* objection he makes to Barth and Brunner. Both of them accept as the centre of their theology, as it is the centre of the Christian faith, the biblical statement that the Word was made flesh and dwelt among us, and the consequent primacy of the fact of the revelation of God in Jesus Christ. Now, as Baillie indicates, 'the eye of faith', in Barth's view, may discern revelation in the resurrection of Jesus, and in those miracles and the transfiguration of Jesus which anticipate the resurrection, but it is unclear what it is that 'the eye of faith' perceives in the other areas of the earthly life of Jesus which do not fall within these limits, and not least the teaching of our Lord. It would not be altogether unkind, or inaccurate, to suggest that here we are encountering what amounts to a rather sophisticated form of latter-day docetism, insofar as it fails to affirm the total relevance of the humanity of Christ to God's revelation; and, on the contrary, the humanity is virtually the bearer of the revelation, without participating in it. That agnosticism may be traced in part, to the biblical critics, whom Baillie identifies as the Form critical school, though radical presuppositions were not peculiar to them; and, in part, to the almost universal influence of Kierkegaard upon twentieth-century theology – an influence delayed by half a century, through the lateness of translations.

It was maintained earlier that Baillie's views of the humanity of Christ developed out of his dialectic with the representatives of 'the new historical radicalism'. It falls now to pursue his responses, keeping one eye always on 'the years between' with their story of subsequent christology, pondering how far his responses are still adequate, and how far the lessons he taught us have been learnt. We shall look firstly at his responses to the Form critics. Somewhat astutely, Baillie uses one who is versed in the ways of the Form critics, namely, C. H. Dodd[8] to counter the radicalism of the movement, citing the persuasiveness with which he quotes passages to demonstrate that they 'do set Jesus before us as a clearcut Figure in word and action. And although the points of view differ, we cannot avoid the impression that it is the same picture that we are seeing

---

[8] *History and the Gospel* (Nisbet, London, 1938), pp. 90–101

from them all.' Indeed, Dodd can argue that, if several such groups are taken together, 'a remarkable fact emerges. Each group taken by itself gives a picture *of* the ministry of Jesus from a particular point.'[9] But, taken together, this great variety of strands of tradition converges, to exhibit 'Jesus as an historical personality distinguished from other religious personalities'.[10] Now since Baillie adopts, one might even feel uncritically, this response to the Form critics, what the response actually involves may be worth considering. At one level, it could be said that all that Dodd has done has been to manoeuvre the texts, which the Form critics employed, in order to obtain answers that they either would not or could not recognise as being 'in the cards'. It could be objected that Dodd's method leaves us with a logical gap between propositions in texts, diagnosed to be of considerable heterogeneity, and the conclusion which Baillie formulates precisely for us, that 'the historical personality of Jesus comes to stand out unmistakably'[11] from the convergent sets of texts. The method and the conclusion of this argument, employed by Dodd and followed to the letter by Baillie, call for comment, as regards both its method and its conclusion. As to its method: *prima facie*, it would appear that the argument proceeds from a series of literary groupings to a statement of historical fact, concerning a person called Jesus. The impropriety of such logic would be apparent if, from the perusal of Palgrave's *Golden Treasury*, we attempted to make factual-historical statements about daffodils, mice, clouds, summer, and so on – all of which subjects, and many, many others, appear in a variety of literary forms in that volume. Is this objection unanswerable? Not quite, for this reason. While it is true that the biblical material which refers to Jesus is heterogeneous in character, and may perfectly validly be collected into the categories so favoured by the Form critics, that circumstance does not in itself deprive the passages concerned from having reference beyond themselves or in any way imply that they refer only to one another. Putting the case positively, we may say that in one way or another, most of the different types of Gospel materials, classified by the Form critics, already contain the reference beyond themselves to Jesus, and it does

[9] ibid. p. 92
[10] ibid. p. 94
[11] *God Was In Christ*, op. cit. p. 58

not have to be injected into them as some element alien to their nature. The greater the convergence of traditions and themes noted by Dodd, the more is that reference in the individual cases reinforced. Bluntly, Jesus is the person whom they are 'about'. If there were ever any doubt on that score, it would be answered by considering the examples to which reference has already been made, in C. H. Dodd's *History and the Gospel* in which, despite their variety of 'forms', the different passages and shorter texts bear an ostensive reference to Jesus, to his teaching, his ministry, to his actions or the events that befall him.

We have been considering at length the nature of the argument followed by both Dodd and Baillie, to answer the Form critical school, which regards the New Testament documents as evidence, not of the person of Christ, but of the faith and life of the early church, an argument from individual documents of differing literary type to a single person, Jesus Christ, upon whom they all converge. It now falls to consider the conclusion of that argument, namely, 'that the historical personality of Jesus stands out unmistakably'.[12] As we saw above, Dodd did not hesitate to use the word 'personality,' either, in the sharpest distinction to Barth and Brunner who totally eschewed the idea, partly, because it savoured too much of the nineteenth-century concepts of the 'hero' and the 'genius', and partly, because it looked like a denial of the *anhypostasia,* the so-called 'impersonality' of Jesus' human nature. If, however, we find ourselves unencumbered by such suspicions, we are free to explore both its possibility and usefulness. Allowing that a case has been made for the illumination which the converging lines of text shed upon Jesus, is it right to say that they reveal his personality, primarily to the eye of faith, but conceivably also to some extent to bystanders, as the Scriptures themselves suggest? Clearly, the New Testament documentation is not likely to provide a comprehensive description of Jesus, but what it does provide is, as far as it goes, or more accurately as far as we are able to appropriate it, a totally veridical and authentically reliable clue to the nature of his being, his attitude to God, his love for ourselves, and its self-sacrificial range, his concern for his brothers and sisters and ours, and so on. Somewhat later when Baillie returns to this

[12] ibid. p. 58

subject, he speaks not so much about the personality of Jesus but 'Jesus as he really was in his life on earth'.[13] Nonetheless, the two descriptions are, I think, coincidental in meaning for him. Nor need we be deterred from using the word 'personality' or the phrase 'as he really was on earth', because we do not have total awareness of Jesus. Our knowledge of other selves never approximates to that level of comprehension. It works rather by clues and indicators, as we so often discover when we get it wrong, and are surprised or disappointed, even by our best friends. That uncertainty derives from the unclarity of the signals we receive from our friends, or our own obtuseness, or both. In Jesus' case, the signals are unequivocal and inviting. For my own part, I find it hard to deny that on such occasions we have to do with personality, and if not, it is even more difficult to see what the word can mean in any other reference.

There are two terms that are normally rejected when a discussion such as this takes place concerning the humanity of Christ and the records of his life told in the words and images of his contemporaries, or of those to whom they told their story. The first of these words is 'biography'. The word is misapplied to the Gospels, if it is ever intended that they keep to a definitive time-line, that they iron out internal consistencies and integrate the narrative, that they cover the formative years and structure with fine precision, the years that matter – all of which is true, but rather obvious. On the other hand, what we are looking for in a biography is some description of motivation, attitudes, ambitions, hopes, fears, and, if he is a religious person, his relationship to God. We forgive a few wrong timings, or mis-locations, for these are easily corrigible, if indeed they always matter; but the others are all-important if we are to know who it is with whom we have to deal. At some point the phrase 'the self-consciousness of Jesus' obtrudes upon such a discussion, and its very mention is designed to sist proceedings, giving warning of an invasion of privacy, or perpetrating the old cliché, which is also quite false, for not only are we constantly aware, however at times inaccurately, of what is in other people's minds, with no sense of invading their privacy; but it would also defeat the eternal purposes of God if what he intends for us should be locked away for ever from us,

[13] ibid. p. 47

because it was in the mind of that Other whom he has sent, even Jesus Christ our Lord. But we must not be frightened off by a phrase. The fact that the term 'consciousness' occurs most often now in controversy in its appearance within the phrase 'the messianic consciousness of Jesus', and the reluctance of many scholars to agree that Jesus was self-consciously aware of his messianic purpose under God's will, has somehow generated a suspicion over the general use of the term. Yet, unless we are prepared to eliminate agnosticism at one point, the textual, only to introduce it at another, the psychological, then we do well to retain the term 'consciousness' as a comprehensive term to cover talk about the mind, the will, the attitudes, the purposes of Jesus, and to recognise that knowing what was in the mind, or the consciousness of Jesus is part of the revelation that God has given us in him.

The second term which often is introduced into discussions of the role of the New Testament as a record of the historical Jesus, or of Jesus in his humanity, for purposes principally of rejection (as was the fortune of the term 'biography' as we have just observed) is the term 'photograph'. The theological interest in photography, as it might be called, originates in a major way in Brunner's *The Mediator*.[14] There Brunner is arguing that St. John in his Gospel 'does not draw a picture of the Christ which the historian would recognise . . . but as He can be recognised only by faith, as the historic, and yet at the same time as the glorified Christ. His picture is not a "photograph"; it is a "portrait" painted by an artist.' By using the illustration of St. John's Gospel, Brunner does not intend to exclude the Synoptics from his category of 'portrait', but would place them somewhat lower on his scale, which has now become one also of ascending 'humanity' and 'historicity'. So, in answer to the question, 'Which is the historical "photograph" of the life of Jesus?', he answers, 'The historical picture is possibly even still more "human" than the picture given us by the Synoptics'. Baillie finds these views wholly unsatisfactory, partly because of the assumption that a camera could provide a better historical picture than could a good portrait, partly also because of its depreciation of both humanity and historicity, and their central importance to any adequate account of the incarnation. We shall

[14] op. cit, pp.185f.

return soon to this nexus of humanity and historicity hitherto implicit in our discussion, but not so far overtly explored, but for the moment I should like to plead the case of photography, in the theological connection. Maybe, forty, fifty years ago, photography was, except in a few cases, a somewhat under-developed technology – it would not be accurate to call it an art. But circumstances have changed beyond recognition, and photography, particularly as a result of television camera techniques, and partly through the rapid expansion of technical sophistication, has evolved its own art-forms, its own access to heightened truth, and its own perception and comprehension, united in all cases with a remarkable ability to communicate its discoveries. In fact, when applying such models to the Gospels, I find myself thinking more in terms of the photograph model than of the portrait model, though I would never attempt to grade or evaluate either above the other – they perform different tasks, and they perform them with equal excellence, when each is operating at its best. But the portrait is a 'one-off' whereas, photography, as now practised, opts for whole runs of photographs, with angles, light, and lens being modified, corrected and adjusted, in order to catch every possible nuance. When run in sequence we have, of course, the cinema picture, which we should not forget is simply a very long series of single photographs following one another at amazing speed. It is not surprising that the comment, 'The camera never lies', has acquired a new degree of truth in our day. Indeed, it would not be fanciful to suggest that the several texts, anecdotes, parables and so on, favoured by the Form critics, and used so adeptly, as we saw, by both Dodd and Baillie, could be regarded as so many photographs, very large in number, and taken from different perspectives and with an eye to constantly changing circumstances, but usually with one subject in mind. Probably the time has come to depart from one of our most cherished theological models, the portrait, and give space to the rising photograph, so long despised and maligned by many theologians.

In the introductory paragraph to this essay, attention was drawn to the very impressive volume of writing on christology since Baillie's time, and most recently, by Canon John Macquarrie. There is one point where his method, albeit unintentionally, approximates very closely to that followed by Baillie where, in line with Dodd, he seeks to refute the Form critics' insistence that the Gospels yield little knowledge of the historical Jesus. Some of the texts which the Form critics had used for this purpose, Dodd and Baillie turn against them, to argue that the Gospels here provide lines that converge upon 'an assured knowledge of the historical personality of Jesus'. Macquarrie records a short piece of autobiography, reminding us that, when writing *The Scope of Demythologising* (1960) he was tackling the question, raised acutely by his interpretative study of Bultmann's theology, of the measure of historical knowledge concerning Jesus which was available or even necessary, given the existentialist approach to the Gospels and their subject-matter.[15] In his 1960 publication, Macquarrie had used the phrase, 'a minimal core of factuality', to describe the limit beyond which the existentialist method should not go. At the time, he had not defined it, but his more recent suggestion is that it was understood in much too concise terms. Citing E. P. Sanders,[16] Macquarrie presents a list of 'basic facts' about Jesus recorded in the Gospels. These supplement the details of a 'bare outline of the life of Jesus' extracted from St. Paul's letter. Macquarrie then goes on to draw an interesting comparison with the 'personal characteristics' of Jesus derived from our knowledge of his activities as listed by Bultmann himself.[17] These three lists – and we note that they do not include the sayings of Jesus, which could surely be considered a valid source of further incontrovertible material – yield some ten or twelve items, historical data, about which Macquarrie holds 'we can have reasonable certainty'.[18] But he goes farther, and adds that 'from these strands [of tradition] a tolerably reliable picture can be constructed'[19] concluding that 'the one who confronts us in the Gospels is no mythological demigod but a genuine human being in the fullest sense'.[20] For me the parallels with Baillie are all the more interesting for being entirely unintentional on Macquarrie's part – his concern to deal with the historical scepticism

---

[15] *Jesus Christ in Modern Thought,* op. cit. pp. 352ff.

[16] *Jesus and Judaism* (SCM, London, 1985). Cited by Macquarrie, op. cit., pp. 53f.

[17] 'The Primitive Kerygma and the Historical Jesus' in C. Braaten and R. Harrisville (eds.), *The Historical Jesus and the Kerygmatic Christ,* (Abingdon Press 1964 p. 20).

[18] Op. cit., p. 351

[19] ibid. p. 353

[20] ibid. p. 358

of which he had been so conscious in the 'sixties, as Baillie had been in the 'forties; his use of the textual work of Sanders (comparable to Baillie's appropriation of Dodd's research) to reinforce his own convictions about the basic historical facts concerning Jesus; and, finally, his conclusion from these facts to the construction of a reliable picture of Jesus and the recognition of the 'genuine human being' who meets us in the Gospels, which echoes Baillie's conclusion to the unmistakable historical personality of Jesus.

Earlier in our discussion of Baillie's consideration of the influence of historical radicalism upon the Form critical movement, and through it upon christology, as well as upon Barth and Brunner, briefest mention was made in passing of the part played by Kierkegaard in introducing such radicalism into theology and biblical studies. Baillie quoted from the passage which made Kierkegaard notorious:

> If the fact spoken of were a simple historical fact, the accuracy of the historical sources would be of great importance. Here this is not the case, for faith cannot be distilled from even the nicest accuracy of detail. . . . If the contemporary generation had left nothing behind them but these words, 'We have believed that in such and such a year God has appeared among us in the humble figure of a servant, that he lived and taught in our community and finally died', that would be more than enough.[21]

Or more sharply still,

> Can one learn from history anything about Christ? No . . . not about Christ, for about him nothing can be known, he can only be believed.[22]

This agnosticism as regards history, influenced not only Barth, Brunner and Bultmann, but, through the teaching of Kähler, also Tillich; and it is remarkable that, despite their disagreements and antagonisms over so many other theological issues, they should not find the imposition of such an alien and damaging restriction wholly intolerable. Not one of these theologians, or of the dozen and more who mould their style to the pattern of these masters, would countenance for a minute a challenge to the autonomy of theology, still less, to the theonomy of the discipline; yet they feel no need to protest against the heteronomy of a certain philosophy and

[21] *Philosophical Fragments* (Princeton University Press, 1936) p. 35
[22] *Training in Christianity* (Princeton University Press, 1941), p. 28

epistemology of history. Both Baillie and Macquarrie, as we have seen, resisted the pressures of historical radicalism, through the assistance of biblical scholars, reinforced with their own meticulous attention to textual critical points, and were both able to express confidence in the 'picture' or the 'personality' of Jesus as he encounters us in the Gospels and through the Epistles.

But there is another possible way of tackling this problem, and it, in some respects, represents a lost opportunity in the years since Baillie wrote. He considers the suggestion that the phrase 'Jesus of history' is doubtless being 'used with a false preconception of what "history" is', namely, a figure described and authenticated by a cold and detached criticism'.[23] For his part, Baillie objects to setting 'faith' and 'history' too sharply against one another, implying that if we are to describe Jesus as he really was while upon earth, we have to allow faith a say in the description. But there he rather leaves the matter, and there, in a sense, it has remained ever since. He quotes Hoskyns and Davey's *The Riddle of the New Testament* where they claim that the emergence of the modern method of historical investigation across the past two hundred years is to be ascribed primarily to biblical and theological studies,[24] though such a judgment would have to be modified, but not basically altered in the light of Herbert Butterfield's study of the history of historical scholarship.[25] It was left to another historian, this time turned philosopher, to advance the study of the nature of historical thinking and historical criticism beyond the point where Hoskyns and Davey left it. R. G. Collingwood's *The Idea of History* (1946), with its themes of history as the re-enactment of the past, of the *a priori* imagination as constituting the nature of historical thinking, to mention only two, set the stage for a sustained investigation into the nature of history, of historical thought and of historical knowledge. Bultmann was a rarity among theologians to turn to Collingwood for guidance on the nature of history and historical thinking, though his subjectivism would not be acceptable to Collingwood. It was, however, the philosophers and not the theologians with the exception of Van A.

---

[23] *God Was In Christ*, op. cit., pp. 46f.

[24] *The Riddle of the New Testament*, pp. 101f. Cited in *God Was In Christ*, op. cit., p. 46

[25] *Man on His Past* (Cambridge University Press, 1955)

Harvey, who carried forward discussion of the topics raised by Collingwood, even when disagreeing with him, notably, W. H. Walsh, Christopher Blake, Patrick Gardiner, Rex Martin, J. L. Gorman, W. H. Dray and Leon Pompa. Over a period of about thirty years, 1951 to 1981, there were essays and books in the field of what has come to be called 'the analytic philosophy of history', the implications of which for the theologian's problem of 'faith and history' have not so far been explored. Nothing less than such an exploration will bring to light just how false the preconception of what 'history' is in the phrase 'the Jesus of history', of which Baillie warned us over forty years ago.

II
THE DEITY OF CHRIST

We may begin by allowing Baillie to fix his position for us on a christological map.[26] He helps us to do so by clearing the ground of a few mis-placements. First, when we speak of the incarnation, and so of the deity of Christ, we do not mean that Jesus was not a man but 'a God', for the clear reason that the word 'God' being a proper name or noun, can not be used with the indefinite article. Secondly, he distances himself from any possibility of Arian interpretation. Jesus was not some kind of intermediate being between God and man; he was both God and man. Thirdly, he rejects the heresy associated with the name of Apollinaris, that Jesus, as the Son of God, inhabited a human body (*soma*) which had its human vital principle, (*psyche*), the human mind or spirit, (*nous, pneuma*) being replaced by the Logos. This heresy violated the principle of the integrity and the completeness of Christ's human experience, and reduced the incarnation somewhat to a form of divine theophany. Christ was fully human, and his humanity was not reduced by his deity. Fourthly, the deity of Christ was not something to which he graduated through the quality of his life. He will not have the word 'divine' as an adjective to describe Jesus, adding that 'divine' hardly ever occurs in the New Testament. He prefers to say outright that Jesus is God, provided that statement does not stand by itself but is read in the context of the

---

[26] *God Was In Christ*, op. cit., pp. 79ff.

doctrine of the Trinity. Fifthly, he disallows any proposal that at a certain point in the process of incarnation, the eternal Word of God was transformed into a human being, and then at his death transformed back again into the eternal Word. This consideration is to be used later by Baillie, in his refutation of the Kenotic theory, to bring to an end the immense influence of H. R. Mackintosh, whose promotion of that theory had dominated Scottish christological thought from 1912, through its prescription for the B. D. degree in each of the Scottish Faculties of Theology.[27] Baillie confesses that this run-down of misinterpretations may seem unduly negative and elementary, but as we shall see they are to prove of importance in subsequent attempts to expound and explain his position. Moreover, they are, when examined, much more affirmative than Baillie seems to realise, not least of all because, as we learned from the logicians, it is impossible to make a negative statement without at the same time either making, or certainly implying, an affirmative one.

Having staked out Baillie's position as regards the 'that' of the deity of Christ, we have to indicate what he considers to be the substance of the 'what'. Against the background of the biblical teaching about God, he concentrates upon the nature of the God whom we find in the teaching of Jesus, 'a God who takes the initiative, a God who is always beforehand with men, a prevenient God who seeks His creatures before they seek Him'; and finding them in their prodigality, brings to them the forgiveness which only he can give and which their hearts and lives so sorely need. But this is not just 'teaching' about the nature of God; rather the nature of God is incarnated in the One who has come the whole way for our salvation. This is certainly a dynamic christology, concentrating not upon a static nature, but upon the activity of the 'God in Christ'. Baillie does not, however, leave the matter there, for he wonders whether justice has sufficiently been done to the *distinctively* Christian conception of God as Trinity.[28] His reply to this implicit query is that the doctrine of the God who is three in one and one in three derives from the Gospel history and from the Christian's experience of God in Christ. This God is the one whose nature it is freely to create and to love human persons who are

[27] ibid., pp. 79ff.
[28] ibid., p. 122

themselves free, to love them even to the point of imparting himself to them in the incarnation of his eternal Word, and to go on loving them still by indwelling them so that, through his Holy Spirit, they are enabled to do that which God requires of them and which they cannot achieve of themselves. 'All of this . . . is of the eternal nature and essence of God's outgoing love. . . . And this outgoing love of God, His self-giving, is not new nor occasional nor transient, but '"as it was in the beginning, is now, and ever shall be, world without end."'[29]

Before passing to the next section of the essay, perhaps a word ought to be said about the brevity of this section. Two reasons offer themselves. The first is that in fact Baillie himself does not expatiate upon the content of the doctrine of God, remaining within the limits indicated above, that is, the teaching of Jesus concerning God and an elaboration of the doctrine of the Trinity, which is fairly fully taken up with a discussion of different interpretations of the doctrine, both orthodox and heretical. In this respect, his method is considerably different from that of a writer like Mackintosh, whose kenoticism obliges him to give full attention to the content of the divine nature of Jesus Christ.

A second reason for the scarcity of statements by Baillie concerning the content of the deity of Christ is much more complex in nature, and it would amount to saying that Baillie's account of the deity of Christ concentrates more upon the form, which the deity takes, or alternatively, the manner of the incarnation, than upon content. The forum for this account is his use of the paradox of grace as the pattern or model for the understanding of the compresence of the human and the divine in Jesus. Consequently, we must move on immediately to our next section on the human and the divine in Jesus.

III
JESUS, HUMAN AND DIVINE

Having discussed the 'that' and the 'what' of the deity of Christ, we have found that to complete the latter theme, we are obliged to consider the 'how' of the co-existence of the deity and the humanity

[29] ibid., p. 123

of Christ in one being. In exploring this part of Baillie's christology, we must re-affirm what Baillie himself had made clear: namely, that while the incarnation truly remains the *mysterium Christi,* 'it is not sheer meaningless mystery'.[30] Rather, because there occurs in the Christian's own experience of the paradox of grace of God something of the God who was incarnate in Christ, the possibility has been created of bringing out what is meant and what is not meant by the paradox of the incarnation. The distinguishing mark of Baillie's christology consists, therefore, in 'the connection and analogy between . . . the paradox of grace and the paradox of the Incarnation'[31] which he describes, develops and defends.

The key text for Baillie's thesis is to be found in the well-known words of St Paul in 1 Cor. 15:10: 'By the grace of God I am what I am: and his grace which was bestowed upon me was not found in vain; but I laboured more abundantly than they all: yet not I, but the grace of God which was with me'. The essence of the paradox of grace enshrined in these words is the recognition by all Christian people that every good thing that they do, all virtue in them, is not achieved of themselves, but wrought in them by the grace of God. This recognition which ascribes all to God entails no diminution of human freedom or abrogation of human responsibility. 'Never is human action more truly and fully personal, never does the agent feel more perfectly free, than in those moments of which he can say as a Christian that whatever good was in them was not his but God's.'[32] It is a theme which can be illustrated from across the entire history of Christian devotion – St. Augustine, St. Anselm, St. Thomas à Kempis, the Westminster Confession, down to Harriet Auber. In this paradox, Baillie is careful to point out, the human and the divine are not coordinate; rather, because the human is totally dependent upon God, and he lives and acts in us, it has to be emphasised that 'the divine side is somehow prior to the human'[33] God takes 'our poor human nature into union with his own divine life', without robbing us of our humanity, even when we are most willing to say that all is of God.

[30] ibid., p. 124
[31] ibid., p. 125
[32] ibid., p. 114
[33] ibid., p. 117

This paradox of grace, which is but one of several which Baillie indicates are characteristic of the Christian faith, he proposes to use as the 'clue' to the understanding of the greater paradox of the perfect union of God and man in Jesus Christ. The presence of the paradox in the incarnate Lord is evidenced, Baillie holds, in Jesus' 'deep and humble and continuous consciousness of God'. When he healed the sick and the suffering, it was to his heavenly Father that he turned for strength, and when they were cured he directed them to give thanks and the glory to God and not to himself. Even when a man once called him 'good', he declined the designation, claiming that it was God only that was good, (Matt. 10:17f.) At John 5:30, Jesus says, 'I can of myself do nothing: as I hear, I judge . . . I seek not my own will, but the will of him that sent me'. Baillie's own comment is, 'Though it is a real man that is speaking, they are not human claims at all: they do not claim anything for the human achievement but ascribe it all to God . . . The God-man is the only man who claims nothing for Himself, but all for God'[34] Baillie recognises that because the experience of the *grace* of God belongs to sinful men, for some theologians, it cannot be part of the mystery of the incarnation. It is not an argument that carries any weight with Baillie. He wishes to go farther and to say that the New Testament speaks not only of the grace of God being given to Christ, but more often of the grace of Christ being given to us. Our experience of God depends on Christ's. 'If God in some measure lives and acts in us, it is because first, and without measure, He lived and acted in Christ'.[35]

Baillie's relating of the paradox of grace to the paradox of the incarnation proved such a subject of controversy that it is important to take account of the different terms which he actually uses to describe it. 'Clue' we have noted, but he also speaks of the former being a 'reflection' or 'a fragmentary form' of the latter,[36] and a pointer to the latter,[37] while most definitively, in my judgment, and most frequently, the terms 'analogy' and 'analogue' appear.[38] There is yet another description, which has been the prime cause of

---

[34] ibid., p. 127
[35] ibid., p. 128
[36] ibid., p. 154
[37] ibid., p. 128
[38] ibid., e.g. pp. 125, 127, 128, 129

controversy: he refers to the paradox of the incarnation as the 'prototype' of the paradox of grace and as being the same type of paradox as the paradox of grace, 'taken at the absolute degree'.[39]

One of the major commentators upon, and critics of, Baillie's christology is John Hick, who, writing some ten years after the publication of *God Was In Christ*, addressed himself to what he called 'the rather central inadequacy in D. M. Baillie's theory'.[40] Hick recalls the well-known distinction between deity and divinity, the former properly used in the phrase 'the deity of Christ' to designate the consubstantiality of Christ with the Father, and the latter improperly (that is, in the classical Chalcedonian tradition) attributed to Jesus Christ for it implies membership of a class and shared qualities. One is grammatically a proper noun or name, and the other an adjective. Hick acknowledges that Baillie is fully conscious of this distinction, and that his loyalty is to the full Chalcedonian position in the matter of the deity of Christ, even quoting Baillie's own commitment on the subject: 'while the life lived by Jesus was wholly human, that which was incarnate in him was the essence of God, the very Son of the Father, very God of very God'. But the burden of Hick's criticism of Baillie is that he does not abide by this commitment or honour the distinction between deity and divinity. On the one hand, he points to the references mentioned above, where Baillie seems to be saying that the paradox of grace as it exists in humans is the same *type* of paradox as that found in the incarnation, taken to an absolute degree, and concludes that all that Baillie is offering is a clarification of the adjectival concept of divinity. On the other hand, Hick argues that if Baillie still wishes to adhere to the Chalcedonian position of the uniqueness of the incarnation he can only do so by adopting what Hick calls a predestinarian interpretation of the paradox of grace. Such an interpretation gives priority to the divine element in the paradox, irresistible divine grace jeopardising human freedom, as might be deduced from Baillie's view of Jesus' continual obedience to the will of the Father, that such human choices are 'never prevenient or cooperative, but wholly dependent upon divine prevenience.[41] Hick does not accept that Baillie would subscribe to such a

---

[39] ibid., p. 129
[40] 'The Christology of D. M. Baillie', *Scottish Journal of Theology*, 11.1, 1958, p. 8
[41] *God Was In Christ*, op. cit., p. 131

predestinarian view of the paradox of grace, because it jeopardises the whole notion of God's affirmation of human freedom and autonomy.

So, Hick sets out to construct a more sophisticated account of Baillie's position which, he is convinced, places Baillie firmly in the 'divinity of Jesus' camp. He refers to a quotation from p.116 of *God Was In Christ*, where in one of several accounts of the paradox of grace, Baillie acknowledges that when we make wrong choices, our consciences condemn us for we are responsible; whereas when we make right choices, we do not expect our consciences to applaud and congratulate us. In the latter case, in saying, 'I, yet not I', we allow that, in this human free choice, somehow the divine element has logical priority. It is this latter statement that is the nub of the controversy. What Hick takes it to mean is that 'when, in the mystery of personal freedom, a Man does choose rightly, what he has done is to allow the divine grace to operate through him'.[42] In other words, on this 'more moderate interpretation of the paradox of grace', God is not able to cause a Christian to choose rightly; should he do so, 'his choice is at once taken up into and inextricably interpenetrated by the prevenient divine grace'.[43] With this interpretation in position, Hick carries his case forward, to argue that though God had sought throughout human history to inspire men with his enabling grace, it was not until Jesus Christ that there emerged one, whose total obedience to God's will embodied both human freedom of choice and total receptivity to prevenient divine grace. Hick wishes to distinguish this view from traditional adoptionism, on the ground that according to the latter Jesus was adopted as the medium of the incarnation of the Logos on the basis of a perfect life to the age of thirty, while on the so-called 'continuous adoption' attributed by Hick to Baillie, the adoption was co-terminous with Jesus' earthly existence. Hick could at this point have repeated his previous rather epigrammatic summary of Baillie's view, namely, that 'what in other men is inspiration, in Christ amounted to incarnation'.[44] Hick is, therefore, in no doubt that on this showing Baillie's christology has to be regarded as abandoning the traditional belief in the deity of Christ, in favour of that in the divinity of Christ.

[42] Hick, op. cit., p. 9
[43] ibid.
[44] ibid., p. 6

This interpretation of Baillie's christology by Hick was destined to be very influential in Hick's later work on the relation of Christianity to other faiths, where he repeats it in one form or another. For example, in an essay on 'Trinity, Incarnation and Religious Pluralism', after rehearsing Baillie's account of the paradox of grace in relation to the paradox of the incarnation, in terms with which we are now fully familiar, he writes that 'in making the idea of incarnation intelligible in this way Baillie has to discard the traditional Chalcedonian language of Jesus having two natures, and of his being in his divine nature of one substance with the Father'.[45] In view, therefore of the importance for Hick of Baillie's christology, as interpreted, it is necessary to consider the validity of Hick's case. Donald's brother John moved to the defence of Donald within months of the publication of Hick's criticisms.[46] That response will be considered in the comments now to be made on Hick's account of Baillie's christology.

John Baillie's first point is to insist that when the paradox of grace is taken 'at the perfect and absolute pitch' at which it occurs in the mystery of the incarnation, then that difference in degree becomes a difference in kind, and God may validly be said to be in Christ in a unique way. If we pursue that path, we can scarcely avoid saying that Jesus was fully man and fully God, in line with the words of Col. 2:9 (RSV): 'For in him dwells the fulness of deity bodily'. That, I should have thought, was exactly what the Chalcedonian formula was affirming with its statement about Christ being 'of one substance with the Father'. However, it has to be admitted that, given that that affirmation was Donald Baillie's intention, he does trail his coat somewhat in his view of the paradox of grace and the paradox of the incarnation being 'of the same type' – a matter to which we shall have to return.

The other important point in John's defence of Donald is his claim that Donald would have accepted the so-called predestinarian position, which Hick thinks Donald would have rejected. Hick's rewriting of Donald's position, which suggests that the person who

[45] 'Trinity, Incarnation and Religious Pluralism', *Three Faiths-One God*, eds. John Hick & Edmund S. Meltzer, (Macmillan, London, 1989), pp. 206f.
[46] 'Some Comments on Professor Hick's Article on "The Christology of D. M. Baillie"', *Scottish Journal of Theology*, 11.3, 1958, pp. 264–70

acts rightly has allowed the divine grace to operate within him, interprets God's prevenience as God's prior offer of grace to the person to exercise it; and it falls short, according to John, of what Donald means by prevenient grace. In fact, says John Baillie, there is no paradox at all in the familiar notion of someone being made an offer of some good thing and subsequently deciding to accept it. The problem for anyone wishing to escape from the predestination controversy is how to avoid recognising that not only does God make the offer of salvation to us; he also gives us the grace to accept that offer. It is that consideration which is at the heart of the paradox of grace, and it is the problem which it causes which has led Hick to provide a way out, with his notion of God's prevenient grace interpenetrating human right decisions. But not only is there no justification in Donald Baillie's text for Hick's account of how prevenient grace works, but it involves a most strange understanding of the term 'prevenient', one which effectively destroys the element of paradox. Moreover, it is Donald's commitment to, and full awareness of the nature of predestination, which is the ground for his affirmation of the paradox of grace, and his choice of it as the clue to the understanding of the mystery of the incarnation.

There is another matter in John's defence of Donald which he does not treat with the importance assigned to the two which we have just been discussing, that is, Donald's affirmation of the pre-existence of Christ, and which must surely be one of the strongest arguments for the rebuttal both of the charge of adoptionism and of that of the denial, by implication, of the deity of Christ. John introduces the subject when rejecting an argument of Hick's which was designed to show, rather unconvincingly, that, since the paradox of grace is not a peculiarly Christian phenomenon, and so cannot be related causally to the incarnation, Christ's uniqueness must be one of 'degree of divinely enabled moral achievements.[47] But in the original, consideration is given to the doctrine of the pre-existence of Christ in a rather different context. There, in the original, Donald is declaring very emphatically that consideration of Christ's strong sense of vocation, of always doing the things that are pleasing to the Father, leads back to his origin and eternal source within the Godhead. In

[47] Hick, op. cit., p. 8

fact, drawing on the very notion of prevenience, which Hick had used to justify his attribution to Donald Baillie of commitment to the divinity as opposed to the deity of Christ, Donald affirms that justice is only done to the true character of the Incarnation, when it is seen as the coming into human history of the eternally preexistent Son of God. This element in Donald's thought is so forcefully expressed that it is hard to see how it could be ignored without grave distortion.[48]

There is another comment to be made on Hick's criticism of Donald Baillie's christology, which seems to me to be more important even than those we have examined. It relates to the term which Donald himself actually used to describe the relation between the paradox of grace and the paradox of the incarnation, namely, analogy. We noted earlier the various words that he had used for the relationship – clue, pointer, reflection, prototype and analogy or analogue. The last is the logically firm or hard one. Now it may appear to some that to take up the notion of analogy from the collection is to court trouble, but, nothing daunted, we may find the risk worth taking. We need not embark upon the application to our subject of the complicated theories of analogy. Suffice it to say that the theory of analogy will help us at a number of points. For example, it allows us to draw the distinction between the positive analogy and the negative analogy, roughly between the elements in which the two entities compared resemble one another and those in which they differ. I find, when I consider Donald Baillie's statement, that in some of them he is assimilating the paradox of grace in Christ to the form of its existence in ourselves, and there are enough of these statements to enable me to see why Hick wants to concentrate on these to the exclusion of others.[49] These would form the positive analogy. But then again, there are other statements, such as that which refers to the absolute degree of the paradox in Christ, or that which openly holds to the difference between Christ and ourselves in that he is the pre-existent Son of God, which do not fail to indicate the difference between the paradox as it is in ourselves, and as it is in Jesus Christ. Here we have the negative analogy. The compresence of the positive analogy and the negative analogy is the explanation of the two lines of

[48] *God Was In Christ*, op. cit., pp. 149–51
[49] ibid., p. 129

thought in Baillie's presentation of the relation of the paradox of grace to the paradox of the incarnation.

The application of the notion of analogy to our discussion enables us to see that, even if Hick had noticed Baillie's references to 'analogy' in the text, he would be interpreting them as instances of what the traditional logicians called 'analogy of inequality or generic predication'. In this form of analogy, entities or attributes participate to differing extents (hence the 'inequality') in the same generic or specific concept. While this form appears to have the marks of analogy, the analogates combining unity in difference, it is really only a form of predication, an instance of univocity, a pseudo-analogy. Hick, therefore, would regard the relation of the paradox of grace to the paradox of the incarnation as analogical only in this sense.

I do not think that, having negatived the possibility of analogy of inequality, we would find it fruitful to try to fix positively where Baillie's understanding of analogy lies along the spectrum of the defined forms of analogy, analogy of proportion or attribution, and analogy of proportionality. That we cannot do so with precision accounts for the attraction of Hick's widely promoted view that the paradox of the incarnation is of the same type as the paradox of grace, and perhaps explains why Hick should have disregarded Baillie's use of the term. It does mean trouble for those who try to use it.

There is, however, one element in the doctrine of analogy which he has not considered, the element which came to the fore in the controversies over half a century ago about the *imago Dei*. There was a distinction, much canvassed then, between the *analogia fidei* and the *analogia entis,* one party holding that in virtue of the *imago Dei,* and by reason of his very nature, man shares in the divine Being (*Ens*), while on the other view, it is only through faith (*fides*) and in faith, that redeemed man comes to share in God's Being, through the restoration of the *imago* lost at the fall. I can find two passages in which Baillie seems to be stating the relation of the paradox of grace to the paradox of the incarnation in terms which come very close to the intention of the concept of the *analogia fidei*. On p. 117, he speaks of 'the man in whom God was incarnate . . . desiring to take up other men into His own close union with God, that they might be as He is'. Such men will experience the paradox of grace in fragmentary ways, and understand somewhat 'the perfect life, in which that paradox is absolute and complete'. Again, at p. 128, Baillie this time quotes scripture, to make the point that as 'God dwells in Christ, so Christ dwells in us'. Thus St Paul, 'I live; yet no longer I, but Christ liveth in me' (Gal. 2:20), and, it is God's purpose that Christians should be 'conformed to the image of His Son, that he might be the first-born among many brethren', (Rom. 8:29). The relevance of such passages to Baillie's view of the relation of the paradox of grace to the paradox of the incarnation, interpreted in terms of the *analogia fidei*, is as follows: the relation is only set up when Christians are taken up by Christ into relationship with God; then, even in their inadequate understanding of the union of God and Man, the complete and absolute paradox of grace in the incarnate Christ, they are enabled to experience and to interpret the paradox of grace in themselves. The analogy, thus described and discerned between the paradox of grace as it exists in the incarnate Christ and as it exists in human experience is an *analogia* only of *fides,* and for *fides.* To try to press it beyond that point is to distort the subject-matter in favour of a logic not designed for this purpose.

My conviction, therefore, is that the christology of Donald Baillie remains firmly within the parameters of the Chalcedonian formula of the two natures, human and divine, co-existing in one person, Jesus Christ, and that this consideration controls the interpretations which we put upon his statements which at times, it has to be confessed, seem almost to violate the conditions which he sets. One such statement puzzled me both at a first reading,[50] and even at a careful revision some three years ago. Its validity has only now become clear, through the emergence of similar views in contemporary writers, notably John Macquarrie. Let me quote the passage.

> Therefore when at last God broke through into human life with full revelation and became incarnate, must we not say that in a sense it was because here at last a man was perfectly receptive? If the life of our Lord is to be conceived as a truly human life, subject to the hazards of all human life on earth, we must indeed say that the Incarnation of the Divine Word in Him was conditioned by his continual response.[51]

[50] Cf. The present writer's review of *God Was In Christ, Reformed Theological Review,* 7.2, 1949, pp. 11–19, and 'A Tale of Two Christologies', *In Diverse Manners,* ed. D. W. D. Shaw, (St. Andrews, 1990)

[51] *God Was In Christ,* op. cit., p. 149

Baillie in these terms was seeking to do full justice to the humanity of Christ, by recognising the genuine freedom and humanness of Jesus' every choice. But it is obvious that this remark is a hostage to fortune, in that it appears almost to secure the integrity of Christ's humanity at the dangerous price of adoptionism. Now I can see that it has to be understood in the context of the *analogia fidei*, which allows full recognition of both the humanity and the deity of Christ, neither reducing, jeopardising or stultifying the other.

It is, however, in a passage in John Macquarrie's *Jesus Christ In Modern Thought*, that I have found both a modern echo of this view which we have just considered in Baillie, and a more complete statement of what Baillie had in mind. Macquarrie, after a very comprehensive review of most known christologies, offers a view of Christ, as human and divine, which he believes interprets him for us today. On the one hand, he construes the human being as a being-in-transcendence, with the capacity for growing towards God and manifesting the divine life',[52] and says that in Christ this possibility has become an actuality.

This form of 'christology from below', present according to Macquarrie in some passages of St. Paul, in Irenaeus, Schleiermacher, Pittenger, Pannenberg, Rahner and others, is only half of the story, the other half recognising God's self-revelation and self-realisation in Jesus Christ. Therefore, 'in Jesus Christ we are confronted with both the deification of a man and the inhumanisation (incarnation) of God'. On the one hand, in Christ the process of 'deification' (*theopoiesis*), a term which early Christian theologians had applied to the effect of salvation upon the redeemed, is carried to perfection in the human life of Christ, a life wholly open and receptive to God. On the other hand, that movement may be thought to happen in the reverse direction, with the inhumanisation' (*enanthropesis*) of the divine Logos. Macquarrie describes this process of 'inhumanisation' also as a kind of self-transcendence on God's part, as he surpasses himself, reaching out to the world and mankind, in creation and redemption, and, it has to be added, in the indwelling of the Holy Spirit. That self-transcendence on God's part, present throughout creation and history, focusses supremely and uniquely on Jesus Christ.

---

[52] *Jesus Christ in Modern Thought*, op. cit., p. 372

For Baillie, there is that same coincidence of the appearance of 'a Man that was perfectly receptive' to God, and the incarnation of the Divine Word in him, and the same insistence that the incarnation is the necessary condition of that continuous and open receptivity to God (Baillie), which Macquarrie calls 'deification'. So while Macquarrie dubs Baillie an exponent of christology 'from below' similar in intent to that which he outlines in his book, neither Baillie nor Macquarrie is in any doubt about whether the whole of christology can be written from that stand-point or about where priority lies. Chronological priority may lie with the approach to christology from the human life of Jesus upon earth ('from below'), but logical priority must lie with the approach which moves in the opposite direction of the incarnation of the Divine Logos, with the descent of the Logos 'from above', as Macquarrie points out[53] It is clear that equally for Baillie and Macquarrie there is full commitment to both approaches to christology and that these approaches answer to what older christologies called 'the two natures of Jesus Christ', though Macquarrie certainly raises questions about the propriety of the term 'nature',[54] and Baillie betrays uneasiness about it also.[55] Yet both theologians affirm general support for the Chalcedonian position, while declaring dissatisfaction about the way it is formulated, and, further, are convinced that the interpretations of it which they offer 'make sense of Chalcedon in the modern age'.[56] This alignment of Baillie with Macquarrie's final summing-up of his own position illustrates the prophetic quality of Baillie's christology and is evidence for the judgment that *God Was In Christ* has come to be regarded as one of the most outstanding works in this field in modern times.

[53] ibid., p. 373
[54] ibid., pp. 384f.
[55] *God Was In Christ*, p. 152
[56] Macquarrie, op. cit., p. 385

Chapter 5

REFLECTIONS ON DONALD BAILLIE'S TREATMENT OF THE ATONEMENT

Donald M. MacKinnon

It was Professor John McIntyre's judgment that Professor Donald Baillie had in his greatly esteemed work – *God Was In Christ* (1948) – delivered a virtual coup de grace to Kenotic Christology, at least in the form it had assumed in Professor H. R. Mackintosh's deeply influential work – *The Person of Jesus Christ*. Yet a study of Baillie's lectures on the atoning work of Christ makes the reader wonder whether if Baillie had attended more closely to other presentations of Kenosis, he might not have seen in that very complex tradition, a continuing plea for the reconstruction of the whole understanding of God's relation to the world implicit in Anselm's answer to the question: *Cur Deus homo*. Baillie rightly acclaimed the magnitude of Anselm's achievement, still powerfully authoritative on the eve of the 21st century. But what are we to say of a God that could thus become man?

If I may put the question in language almost dangerously mythological, do we not have to reckon here with a creator whose transcendence remains somehow inviolate, when he puts himself at the mercy of his creation? In Christ God is revealed as submitting himself to the very substance of human life, in its inexorable finitude, in its precarious ambiguity, in its movement to despair: (despair of the kind marvellously expressed in his 'terrible Sonnets' by Gerard Manley Hopkins, who himself as a disciple of Duns Scotus, saw the circumstances of the Incarnation as a *pis aller*.)[1] If we are to make

[1] In a letter to his friend Canon R. W. Dixon on the latter's failure to be elected to the professorship of poetry at Oxford.

anything of this submission, the languages of myth and of ontology must jostle each other in the effort to portray a particular human career as paradigmatically indicative of the divine as it is in itself. And that not in aversion from concrete historical detail, but in acknowledgment of its deep significance. Anselm's treatise – *Cur Deus homo* – tempts the serious student to define the task of its sequel as *Quomodo Deus homo* – even though he knows himself lacking the gifts at once spiritual and intellectual to essay even the prolegomena. Aristotle in the *Poetics* insisted that the poet was the superior of the historian in that he was concerned with that which is universal: whereas the historian was concerned only with that which is individual, the detail of Alcibiades' doing and suffering. But the evangelists, and not simply, though supremely, the fourth evangelist, were concerned with individual human detail (for instance, the position of the Samaritans, and the *publicani,* the politics of Caiaphas, and Pilate), yet compelled to write as poets in as much as the events which they recorded, helped to constitute that which humanly was ultimately interpretative.

Καὶ ἤρξατο ἐκθαμβεῖσθαι καὶ ἀδημονεῖν

(Mark 14:33)

This statement of a bewilderment akin to that of a total stranger in an alien land suggests a crossing over into a world where all signposts are gone, and is surely crucial where the question of the limitations of Christ's human knowledge is concerned. Already Mark has shown him insistent that 'the hour' of the apocalyptists is the Father's secret.[2] His disciples are bidden for that very reason to watch, a command repeated urgently in Gethsemane, where their failure to respond deepens their master's growing isolation as 'the hour' of his supreme crisis approaches and the last stability of his human life begins to disintegrate, while the secret of the burden laid upon him becomes more and more opaque. His relation to the Father, the Sonship that is his eternal substance, is now found transcribed into a murky, human obscurity. And through this transcription, the divine puts itself at the mercy of the human as if only so could the limitations of human existence (finitude infected by sin) be converted into an instrument

---

[2] Mark 13:32

of confession: as if there were depths of the human condition that only the divine could penetrate. *Quomodo Deus homo*. It is creation and the work of the creator that must be reinterpreted through this experience of the cost and way of redemption.

To begin thus by the defence of a position that Donald Baillie rejected may seem an unfitting tribute to the work of so considerable a theologian. Yet when a critical reader sets Baillie's unpublished lectures at St Andrews on the Atonement alongside his acknowledged masterpiece *God Was In Christ*, it is in this direction that he is drawn. Baillie rightly emphasised the importance of the (first) 'quest for the historical Jesus'. Although by the time he wrote, the development of 'form-criticism' and its successor, 'redaction-criticism' had compelled a revision of judgment in respect of the Gospels' value as biographical sources, he rightly saw that the first effort to set the man Jesus of Nazareth in the context of his society and his age, and to experience the innovative boldness of his teaching as it was received by his contemporaries, had made an indelible impression on the theological world. As his lectures on the Atonement well bring out, he discerned here the resonance in a world that had known Enlightenment and Romantic Movement, that had achieved a deep self-consciousness concerning historical relativity, of the same impulse that he had discerned in Anselm's masterpiece.

Professor Denis Nineham, in his contribution to the symposium – *The Myth of God Incarnate* (1977) has asked: 'Is it any longer worthwhile to attempt to trace the Christian's ever-changing understanding of his relationship with God directly back to some identifiable element in the life, character and activity of Jesus of Nazareth?'[3] It would seem to be an implication of the negative answer that Professor Nineham anticipates will be given to his question that any attempt to construct, however tentatively, a doctrine of the Atonement is a sheer waste of time: we must leave the Cross as a bare *Dass*, defiant of any essay in interpretation, however qualified, and therefore detached from any conceivable historical location. In *God Was In Christ* Donald Baillie expressed admiration for Professor A. B. Macaulay's book: *The Death of Christ*, mentioning with approval its author's attempt to provide an intelligible account of the grounds

[3] *The Myth of God Incarnate*, ed. J. Hick, (SCM, London, 1977), p. 202

of Jesus' condemnation and execution. It is important to remember that alongside the development of 'redaction-criticism', recent years have witnessed a deepening interest in precisely these issues, stimulated in part by 'Liberation' theology, but also by memory of the Holocaust, compelling Christians to look very closely at the roles to be assigned to Romans and Jews in the decision to bring Jesus to judgment and death. If the Cross is the site of an atoning act, it was also a place to which Roman power and Jewish ecclesiastical statesmanship combined to bring the preacher of Matthew's 'Sermon on the Mount'. And again here one must not forget the contribution of Roman historians to the quest for the 'historical Pilate'.[4]

Baillie could never have endorsed Nineham's facile depreciation of the extent to which for the Christian: *Im Anfang war die Tat*. To recognize the complementarity within the New Testament itself of various interpretative schemata, employed to illuminate the work of Christ, to acknowledge the ultimate inadequacy of all alike, should not issue in a blandly comfortable shrug of the intellectual shoulders. There are degrees of penetration, and an attitude totally dismissive of the ultimate significance of the historically concrete is in the last resort inacceptable. And it is inacceptable because however remote the world of Jesus of Nazareth from that of the contemporary believer (and his ancestors) that remoteness does not issue in a total estrangement. The world of Pharisee and Jewish temple-priesthead, of Zealot, and Roman provincial administrator is not wholly unintelligible to the modern student. It is surely also significant, as Professor C. H. Dodd pointed out, that the theologically sophisticated author of the fourth Gospel excelled in characterization. His vignettes of Nicodemus, of the woman of Samaria, of Caiaphas, of Pilate stay in the memory, as if by the skill with which he conveyed their character, the writer emphasized that the word had been made flesh in a world at once of his own time, and of those of generations unborn. And it is perhaps not irrelevant here to recall the impact of a great performance of Sophocles' *Electra* on Londonderry in 1992. The Athens of Pericles and his one-time colleague in the stratēgia saw the birth of a tragic masterpiece that speaks to the condition of those

---

[4] See for instance Barbara Levick, *Tiberius the Politician* (Thames and Hudson, London, 1976), pp. 136–7

caught up in the horrific violence born of sectarian intransigence. It would be strange to deny a comparable power to the tragic history of Jesus, of whose inexpungably tragic character contemporary study makes us more and more aware.

Where the doctrine of the Atonement itself was concerned, Baillie rightly saw that the path had to be threaded between the crudities of a penal substitution and the moral naiveté that would deprive the suffering of Christ of anything more than an exemplary or declarative significance.[5] His lectures show the range and extent of his theological culture, including a very careful and sympathetic treatment of the closely related contributions of John McLeod Campbell and R. C. Moberly. He is sensitive to the depth of spiritual perception contained in the suggestion that Christ achieved on behalf of sinners, a level of penitential grief from which they were debarred in consequence of the very guilt for which they must feel sorrow. He recognizes that it is not enough to dismiss the notion of vicarious penitence as a self-contradiction, but that we rather recognize the need so to enlarge one's concept of penitence as to find in it something that can be undertaken by the sinless on others' behalf as the only one fully to plumb the depths of their every iniquity. It is a pity that Baillie did not go on to consider Peter Taylor Forsyth's emphasis on reparation to the outraged holiness of God. For in Forsyth as much as in Campbell and Moberly there is material requiring the kind of deeply appreciative, yet critical, modernization which Baillie saw to be needed.

How shall the universals of morality be mediated through the particularity of an individual human existence? How shall that fragmentary biography speak not simply to the near contemporaries of its subject but to all men and women everywhere? Yet how else shall atonement be made except in the irreducibly particular? Baillie in his work – *God Was In Christ* – sustained a serious polemic against the alleged impersonality of Christ's human nature: and whatever one's final judgment on that part of his work, it shows him strongly

---

[5] Baillie is too inclined to accept Hastings Rashdall's view of Abelard, much too much that of a *simplificateur*. One finds a valuable corrective in the wide-ranging work of Professor David Luscombe (one of the greatest living authorities on Abelard), but also in the late Dr. Richard E. Weingard's excellent book – *The Logic of Divine Love* (Oxford University Press, 1970)

aware of the significance of the particular. Again his indebtedness to the quest for the historical Jesus protects him from the temptation to escape attention to circumstantial detail as if such minutiae were only peripheral to the central case of the gospel-message. If it is in flesh and blood that the work of redemption is done, then that work must be datable and locatable, its particularity yet patient of universal significance.

Although in his lectures on the Atonement Baillie writes illuminatingly on the treatment of Christ's high priesthood by the writer to the Hebrews, it is a strange defect in his Christological work that he seems to avert from sustained treatment of the Resurrection. Yet as Professor Christopher Evans has pointed out, the Gospel-writers in different ways present Jesus as *capax Resurrectionis,* as if the significance of his life, his teaching and his actions must always be sought in their term, namely his passage through death to a mysterious life of seemingly universal authority to which his Father brings him. I say: a mysterious life; for the self-revelation of the risen Lord defies any sort of categorization. In one sense limitation is gone; yet in another his comings and goings are restricted to an élite, often hardly capable of recognizing him. The sign of the empty tomb remains; but it is a sign, pointing ambiguously – to what? Again we have to reckon with limitations.

And so we return to the point of departure: Kenosis. In an article contributed to the Scotsman by Professor Donald MacLeod of the Free Church College in Edinburgh,[6] the author pleaded with those on both sides of the present bitter conflict in Northern Ireland, who professed and called themselves Christians, to ponder the mystery of the divine Kenosis. Here a voice sounded across the divide from the same Highland evangelical tradition, in which the young Donald Baillie was schooled, and the notion invoked was precisely that of the divine self-emptying that he has so gravely criticized as a key to the understanding of the Incarnation. 'The things that had grown old are being made new.' But in their renovation it is clear that if the notion of Kenosis is to have a central place in Christology, that will only be achieved when it is seen as demanding that we extrapolate such concepts as limitation, vulnerability and their like into the framing of

[6] *Scotsman,* 22 January, 1992

our doctrine of God. We must find his sovereignty as made perfect in weakness, in the weakness of the Cross, as that is certified and interpreted for us by the the mystery of the Resurrection. If we seem to have come full circle, we have done so because the intense seriousness with which Baillie confronts the doctrine of Christ's atoning work, both in the St Andrews lectures, and in the posthumously published *Theology of the Sacraments,* where he treats with great perception of the Eucharistic sacrifice, demands that we do so. For if the ratio of the Son's coming in the flesh is found in that work, the very ground of its possibility is only approached if we dare to ask: *Quomodo Deus homo.* And asking that question, we are made to see that the seeking after that ground thrusts us towards the very arcana of the deity itself, revising we know not fully how our anthropomorphic models of God's knowledge and God's power.

It is indeed only when the notion of divine self-limitation is explored in depth (and I emphasize again the need here never to forget the New Testament polarity of crucifixion-resurrection) that the ontological setting is secure which Baillie's searchingly interrogative soteriology demands.

Chapter 6

JOHN BAILLIE:
ORTHODOX LIBERAL

David A. S. Fergusson

Any attempt to assess the development of John Baillie's theology from his abortive 1915 doctoral thesis to the posthumously published Gifford Lectures in 1962 must reckon with two problems. The considerable change in theological fashions during Baillie's lifetime, particularly between the two World Wars, entailed that his theology was in large measure reactive, being determined by issues imposed upon his theological agenda. In addition, the occasional nature of much of his theological writings indicates that, unlike several of his contemporaries, he never aspired to the writing of a comprehensive systematic theology. Books such as *And the Life Everlasting* and *The Belief in Progress* are addressed to specific problems, and are not presented as components within a single theological program. Nonetheless, I believe it is possible to detect in Baillie's work a preoccupation with some fundamental problems in theology to which he periodically returned with proposals that reveal a gradual shift of emphasis.

I
THEOLOGICAL INFLUENCES

From the outset, Baillie's theology was determined by the influence of Kantian philosophy, but as mediated by the work of two of his teachers, the Edinburgh philosopher, A. S. Pringle-Pattison, and the great Marburg theologian, Wilhelm Herrmann.[1] Baillie studied

---

[1] For Baillie's own account of the influence of Pringle-Pattison and Herrmann see 'Confessions of a Transplanted Scot' in *Contemporary American Theology: Theological Autobiographies*, (Round Table Press, New York, 1933) ed. Vermiglius Ferm, pp. 33–59

under Pringle-Pattison from 1904–8 after which he served as his assistant, and he attended Herrmann's lectures while in Marburg during the summer semester of 1911. Two years earlier a young Swiss student, Karl Barth, whose work would later fascinate and infuriate Baillie, had also sat in Herrmann's classes.

(a) The Kantian Approach to Religion

In the philosophy of Kant we meet all the classical objections to the proofs of natural theology with the consequent claim that the existence of God cannot be established by the use of pure reason. The ontological, cosmological and teleological arguments for the existence of God are shown to be invalid and the prospect of a metaphysical proof of God is thus dismissed. Kant, however, insists that the noumenal world of things in themselves, while largely unknowable, nonetheless presents itself in our consciousness of duty, albeit in a purely formal manner. In our rational apprehension of the laws of morality we are aware of obligations which are not prescribed by our desires but which bind us unconditionally. These laws although not created by God are of theological significance. The three postulates of practical reason – God, freedom and the immortality of the soul – are justified by their necessity for the successful conduct of the moral life.

While Kant's arguments for the postulates of practical reason are notoriously contrived, there was something in this approach which appealed profoundly to the young Baillie. The rejection of the classical proofs for the existence of God was philosophically incontrovertible and this had to be recognized by the theologian. Yet Kant had made something of a virtue out of this necessity by locating the source of religious knowledge in the practical life of the moral agent. Kant's emphasis upon the categorical demands of duty which were intuitively known by the human being must have had strong resonances with a student who had been nurtured in the Westminster Calvinism of the Scottish Highlands. It provided him with a means of reconciling the moral seriousness of his upbringing with his education in the traditions of the Enlightenment. Baillie followed Kant in tracing the roots of religion to an experience of moral obligation in which the person is confronted by the ultimate. Yet instead of perceiving God as auxiliary and subservient to the moral law, as Kant had done, Baillie identifies God as the source and ground of morality.[2] Religious knowledge derives from the inescapable consciousness of value, and our knowledge of God is therefore inseparable from our awareness of moral obligation. We can see how this move was suggested to Baillie by the manner in which his teachers revised Kant's thinking.

(b) A. S. Pringle-Pattison (1856–1931)

Andrew Seth Pringle-Pattison[3] was perhaps the leading Scottish philosopher at the turn of the century. His work was distinguished not so much by originality as by an ability to accommodate some of the best insights of Kant and Hegel within the more moderate Scottish tradition. His philosophical criticism of these two great philosophers was to provide Baillie with an epistemological framework for his early theology. According to Pringle-Pattison, Kant's greatest ethical insight was to recognize the categorical form of the imperatives of duty. What had further to be recognized was that in these demands imposed upon us we have our best clue as to the ultimate nature of things. The nature of reality had to be interpreted according to our deepest insights. Here Pringle-Pattison went beyond Kant in arguing that God is the source and author of the moral law, and that there is thus an organic connection between morality and religion.[4] Our religious knowledge is not gained from the invalid arguments of natural theology but instead from an encounter with God through the deliverances of practical reason.

At the same time, Pringle-Pattison followed Hegel in arguing that the categories of thought do not separate us from the world as it is in itself but rather disclose to us something of the nature of that world. The historical process, moreover, must be seen as embodying a moral purpose in which individuals and nations participate, even if Hegel's

[2] For Baillie's criticism of Kant see *The Interpretation of Religion* (T & T Clark, Edinburgh, 1929), pp. 236–46. The material for this book was prepared from 1922–5

[3] The double-barrelled surname was adopted in 1898 as a condition of inheriting the Pringle-Pattison estate near Selkirk in the Scottish borders

[4] For a brief statement of Pringle-Pattison's ethical theism in relation to Kant and Hegel see his *Two Lectures on Theism* (Blackwood, Edinburgh, 1897). 'The moral law is not first imposed by the individual self (in the theory of ethics), and then ratified or re-imposed by an external lawgiver (in the theory of religion). Rather the two are one from the beginning. God is the source and author of the law, but only in the sense that He is the higher self within the self which inwardly illuminates all our lives.' (p. 28)

philosophy had made too close an identification between the being of God and the processes of nature and history. It was necessary to affirm both the identity, worth and immortality of the individual whose being could not be swallowed up by cosmic processes, and also the transcendence of the God who was both the source and moving spirit of all nature and history. The identity and distinctness of both human and divine personality are threatened by Hegel's philosophical system.[5]

In his critical appropriation of Kant and Hegel, Pringle-Pattison provided Baillie with a possible approach to theology at a time when the traditional proofs for the existence of God had broken down and the doctrine of the plenary inspiration of Scripture had become discredited by historical criticism.

(c) Wilhelm Herrmann (1846–1922)

Herrmann was the leading theologian of the Ritschlian school in Germany at the beginning of the twentieth century. His theology was marked by an emphasis upon the practical and personal character of faith. While the task of science and philosophy is to explain the public, empirical world, the task of religion is the practical transformation of the inner life. Faith arises not through scientific or metaphysical explanation, but through the religious experience of personal life. Theology thus has its own peculiar subject-matter which can only be grasped from within the life of faith.[6]

For Herrmann, faith is connected with the moral life insofar as it is discovered at a point of crisis in the latter. The attempt to fulfil the imperatives of the moral law leads inevitably to guilt and failure, and it is the realisation that ultimate goodness confronts us and redeems us in Christ which brings us into an experience of authentic religion. Faith arises through the impulse that the person of Jesus makes upon one's inner life. This has significant practical implications in that it enables us to realize the moral life as life under the fatherly rule and

---

[5] 'The radical error both of Hegelianism and of the allied English doctrine I take to be the identification of the human and the divine self-consciousness, or, to put it more broadly, the unification of consciousness in a single Self.' *Hegelianism and Personality* (Blackwood, Edinburgh, 1893), p. 226

[6] 'Knowledge of God is not generally valid or proveable knowledge, but is the defenceless expression of individual experience.' 'Der Begriff der Religion nach Hermann Cohen', *Schriften zur Grundlegung der Theologie* II, (München, 1967), p. 322

care of God. Baillie was clearly impressed not only by the piety of Herrmann's teaching but by his resolute claim that religion is *sui generis* and can only be understood from the inside. Alongside the philosophy of Pringle-Pattison, it showed him the manner in which a moral approach to Christian faith can yield a doctrine of the grace of God, and can also be integrated with the doctrines of the person and work of Christ. At the same time, Baillie found himself taking issue with Herrmann (particularly the later Herrmann) on two counts. The consciousness of moral obligation should not only be seen as the gateway to religion; in itself it provides us with an awareness of the reality of God. And Herrmann's Christocentrism, as Baillie saw it, failed to allow sufficient scope for an awareness of God outwith the revelation given in the person and work of Christ. While Barth reinvigorated Herrmann's Christocentrism Baillie resisted it.[7]

Baillie's D. Phil. thesis was abandoned incomplete in 1915 but the unpublished manuscript shows the depth of his immersion in Kant's philosophy.[8] Although he does not discuss in detail the extent to which the moral consciousness affords religious knowledge it is clear that this was the direction in which his thought was moving. Chapter X, Section 14 was never written, but Baillie's stated intention was to show that in Kant's 'Doctrine of the Highest Good we have already made the *Schritt zum Religion*'. We find a fully developed theology built upon this foundation in his early writings.

II
EARLY THEOLOGY

The moral theism expounded by Baillie throughout the 1920s is best analysed through a study of his longest and most scholarly work, *The*

---

[7] 'Professor Barth listened to Herrmann's lectures at Marburg very nearly at the same time as I was listening to them, but we must have been attracted and repelled by very different sides of our teacher's thought.' 'Confessions of a Transplanted Scot'. op.cit., p. 52. For Baillie's criticisms of Herrmann see *The Interpretation of Religion*, op.cit. pp. 291–8

[8] The unpublished manuscript, 'A Study of the Kantian Ethic' is amongst the Baillie papers in the New College Library, Edinburgh. Some material from the thesis was published as 'The Meaning of Duty: A Plea for the Reconsideration of the Kantian Ethic', Hibbert Journal, 24, 1926, pp. 718–30

Interpretation of Religion.[9] Here we discover something like a phenomenological approach to the theological study of religion. The traditional proofs are criticised not merely for being fallacious but for being misguided attempts to buttress religious belief with external support. Such arguments are entirely otiose due to their failure to relate the justification of religion to its actual origin and practice. To justify religious belief by the rehearsal of the design argument (as Chalmers, Tulloch and Flint had all done in nineteenth-century Scotland) is to replace a vital insight with a speculative hypothesis which makes the authenticity of faith subject to the latest pronouncements of the professors of metaphysics.[10] In such a situation, 'the religious man finds himself in the doubtful position of a schoolboy who is fortunate enough to get the answer to his sum right, though his working-out was wrong'.[11]

A more satisfactory theological method will deal with the actual processes by which religion arises in individuals and communities. This approach, according to Baillie, is suggested by the philosophy of Kant and is elaborated in the theology of Schleiermacher and the Ritschlian school in their different ways. Religion has its own subject matter which is reducible neither to the sciences nor to metaphysics. The task of the theologian is to locate the source of the religious impulse and to examine its structure and effects; as such, it is a task which can only be undertaken by one who has personal acquaintance with the reality of religion. Here Baillie echoes Herrmann's claim that religion is *sui generis* and does not require to be anchored in or supported by considerations from outwith its own domain. The object of faith must be seen as its epistemological ground.

The enduring insight of Kant is that religion is in some sense an outgrowth from our experience of moral value. This position implies an absolutist and transcendent notion of moral value, and Baillie considers the moral realism of Kant's philosophy to be unassailable.

---

[9] *The Roots of Religion in the Human Soul* (Hodder and Stoughton, London, 1926) is a more popular and apologetic rehearsal of the argument of the later book. The basic strategy is already presented in 'The True Ground of Theistic Belief', *Hibbert Journal,* 21, 1922, pp. 44–52

[10] *The Interpretation of Religion,* op. cit. pp. 93–106

[11] ibid. p. 94

Loyalty and love and honour, truthfulness and purity and unselfishness – there is no knowledge of which I am surer than that these things are infinitely well worth seeking and that there is laid upon me an absolute obligation to seek them. No doubt there is room for uncertainty enough about the detail of duty. No doubt it is often painfully difficult to know, in an individual case, what we ought to do. And we need not even deny that there may be occasion for *some* honest perplexity even with regard to the broad outline of dutiful conduct. But we do claim that, in respect of this broad outline of it, the path of duty is as clear as any knowledge we possess, and that in our awareness of the call wherewith it summons us to follow it, we come as near to absolute certainty as it is ever given to the race of man to do.[12]

Morality concerns what is ultimately required of us, and in moral obligation we are conscious of an inescapable demand being placed upon us. This unconditional claim cannot be explained by its utility value or by our social conditioning. We do not invent what is right; we discover it and we cannot escape it however much we try. Moral realism constrains us to believe that we experience in the dictates of conscience some insight into the nature of ultimate reality. This is to be seen not so much as an inference made by the believer as a deepening apprehension of moral reality.

A further point of departure from Herrmann, as has already been noted, is the claim that the moral awareness of God is integral to all genuine religion and cannot be restricted to Christian faith. The status of other world religions was a subject that exercised Baillie throughout his writings, even at a time when it was largely eclipsed in European theology. Against the Ritschlian school (and later Barth) he claims that in the philosophy of Socrates and Plato and in the other religions of the world there is a knowledge of God present in the ultimate demands that confront all people. The religious striving of the human race is generated by the presence of God everywhere and this is confirmed by the tendency in the world religions to conceive of the ultimate ground of reality as personal, moral and spiritual.[13] Not surprisingly, Baillie has some difficulty in accommodating Buddhism within this hypothesis.[14]

[12] ibid. pp. 342–3
[13] ibid. p. 381
[14] ibid. pp. 386ff.

Religion, however, is not to be reduced to morality. The contents of religious faith (belief, worship, fellowship, private devotion, etc.) extend and enrich our understanding of moral value. Baillie speaks about the relation of religious faith to moral experience as a double one in which faith emerges from the moral consciousness but at the same time quickens and fulfils that consciousness.[15] He is clearly confident that a sensitive scrutiny of our moral apprehension will issue in a set of beliefs regarding the personal and transcendent nature of moral reality. We cannot believe in the sanctity of personal life without believing that the source of that sanctity is itself personal (a point repeatedly argued by Pringle-Pattison). Moreover, we must conceive of this same reality as transcendent (not of our creaturely realm) and yet immanent (present in the claims made upon us by fellow human beings). This generates a belief in creation and providence, insofar as the purpose and *raison d'être* of the physical universe is to be understood as moral and religious. There is almost a sense in which through the closing stages of *The Interpretation of Religion* the central doctrines of the Christian faith are deduced from a phenomenology of moral experience. In Hegelian fashion, Baillie argues that the Christian witness to the incarnation of God is the summit of all religion. The cross of Christ is the crowning example of the redeeming love which is the meaning and source of creation.[16]

From this analysis we can see the extent to which Baillie's theology can be described as both liberal and orthodox. The setting of his work conforms to the typical liberal strategy of locating the sense of God in patterns of experience which are common to almost all human beings. Theological knowledge is here the articulation of what is given in experience, and this experience is, in principle, universally accessible. The grounding of religious knowledge in a phenomenology of experience is what separates the liberal approach from the rationalism which establishes theological truth by metaphysical argument and from the conservative orthodoxy which appeals to the revealed propositions of Scripture.[17] Baillie's epistemology is based

[15] ibid. p. 332

[16] ibid. pp. 431–47

[17] This characterisation of liberalism is akin to George Lindbeck's 'symbolic-expressivist' conception of religion in the typology advanced in *The Nature of Doctrine* (SPCK, London, 1984) pp. 31ff.

firmly upon moral and religious experience, and the particular deliverances of the Christian faith are derivative from this base. But before offering further assessment of this we should consider the ways in which Baillie is committed to an orthodox formulation of Christian doctrine.

In the closing stages of *The Interpretation of Religion,* and in *The Place of Jesus Christ in Modern Christianity* (1929) we find Baillie attempting to do justice to the formulations of classical Christian doctrine while wrestling with the difficulties of Chalcedonian metaphysics and the problems raised by historical criticism.[18] Baillie's dissatisfaction with the traditional two-natures doctrine and his interest in the quest of the historical Jesus are typical liberal concerns, but the positions he adopts on the person and work of Christ and the doctrine of the Trinity place him within the orthodox Christian tradition. In this respect, he may be seen as something of a traditionalist attempting to challenge the modernism he encountered in North America during the 1920s.[19]

In dealing with the person of Christ, Baillie eschews the traditional Chalcedonian formula of two natures in one person,[20] arguing that its assertion of a conjunction between two heterogeneous and complete natures fails to make sense of the unity of Christ's person. The historical life of Jesus is one in which God is made fully manifest in and through a human being; the Chalcedonian doctrine obscures this by dividing the person of Christ into two discrete natures. At the same time, Baillie is careful to avoid adoptionism. The grace and condescension of God in Christ cannot be made sense of by an adoptionist Christology which speaks of a human becoming divine

[18] There are early indications of his desire to combine liberalism with a recast orthodoxy in 'The Idea of Orthodoxy', *The Hibbert Journal,* 424, 1926, pp. 232–49

[19] '[W]hen I first went to America immediately after World War I. I then found myself in an atmosphere of conflict between 'modernism' and 'fundamentalism'; and if the latter was quite strange to me as something not represented among either the teachers or the students whom I had so far known, I often enough felt myself ill at ease with the former. Certainly in my own teaching I was more at pains to convince the students of the truth and profundity of traditional doctrine than to combat a too rigid and literalist attachment to it, though there were frequent enough occasions when I found myself, as it were, having to fight the battle on both fronts at once.' 'Looking Before and After', *Christian Century,* LXXV, 1958, p. 400

[20] *The Place of Jesus Christ in Modern Christianity* (T & T Clark, Edinburgh, 1929), pp. 123ff.

rather than God becoming human. In the person of Jesus we see the supreme instance both of God's downward movement towards humanity and also of the perfect human response to that divine grace.[21] It is in this sense that Baillie seeks to do justice to the orthodox idea of incarnation.

In the same context, the Anselmian theory of the atonement is rejected for its setting of divine justice over against love.[22] In its place, Baillie offers an account of the redeeming love of Christ which not only opposes evil but actually overcomes it. In the gospels we read of the love of Jesus suffering for the sins of others and bringing about a redemption from sin. This love continues to redeem human beings through the proclamation and service of the Christian community, and it signifies for us the eternal, redeeming love of God. This, for Baillie, is the key insight in all traditional theories of the atonement.

On the doctrine of the Trinity, we find Baillie affirming the threefold distinction between the Father, the Son and the Spirit but without embracing the Patristic conceptuality of three persons or hypostases in one substance.[23] God is to be regarded from three different perspectives as the transcendent Father, as revealed in the life and death of Christ, and as present in our hearts, but we should not and cannot advance beyond this to the confused categories of traditional trinitarian theology.

We shall have to ask how far these interpretations of traditional dogmas are to be considered 'orthodox' but it is important to note that Baillie's intention throughout his theology is to do justice to the traditional language of Christian doctrine, particularly with respect to the person and work of Christ. While his theological method is typically liberal, his doctrinal orientation is generally orthodox. (This attempt to mediate between distinct theological positions is characteristic of Baillie's entire theological enterprise.) The orthodox setting of Baillie's liberalism is confirmed in the concluding section of *The Place of Jesus Christ in Modern Christianity* where he considers the question of whether there is revelation and salvation outside of Christ. His response is the

[21] It is interesting that almost all the positions taken up in *The Place of Jesus Christ in Modern Christianity* foreshadow those later developed in Donald's *God Was In Christ*.
[22] *The Place of Jesus Christ in Modern Christianity*, op. cit. pp. 156ff.
[23] ibid. pp. 185–95

ancient one of Justin Martyr. Where there is knowledge of God beyond the Church's proclamation of Jesus we must regard this as a glimpse of the Logos which is present throughout all creation but which is fully and uniquely disclosed in its incarnation in Jesus Christ. The uniqueness and finality of Christ is thus affirmed throughout Baillie's theology. Quoting Alice Meynell, he concludes with the bold thought that Christ will be the Lord of spiritual beings even on other planets.

> But in the eternities
> Doubtless we shall compare together, hear
> A million alien Gospels, in what guise
> He trod the Pleiades, the Lyre, the Bear.
>
> O, be prepared, my soul!
> To read the inconceivable, to scan
> The million forms of God the stars unroll
> When, in our turn, we show to them a Man.[24]

Baillie's theology until around 1930 may be summarised in the following four propositions.

1 The awareness of God in the human soul arises initially from a consciousness of moral values not of our own making to which we are ineluctably obligated.

2 The beliefs, worship, fellowship and practice of authentic religion enrich and extend our understanding of what is given in the experience of moral obligation.

3 The evolution of religion can be traced in terms of an increasing human perception of the nature of the ultimate moral reality. The crowning point of this evolution is the Christian witness to the incarnate love of God in Jesus of Nazareth. This represents both the gracious activity of the personal God and the highest human response to that activity.

4 The traditional doctrines of the Christian faith – incarnation, atonement, Trinity – are to be affirmed in terms of the genuine and unique insights that they embody, but their classical formulations are no longer intelligible.

[24] ibid. p. 211

By assessing each of these propositions in sequence we can gain a critical perspective upon Baillie's early work.

1 The appeal to human awareness of ultimate moral realities was made by Baillie at a time of gradual dissociation from the beliefs and practices of the institutional church. If the traditional language and activities of organised Christianity seemed remote to the post-war generation it remained possible to appeal to a common awareness of the values of honesty, friendship, honour and love. These contained within them the seeds of true religion insofar as they were known as authoritative, binding and worthy of the highest self-sacrifice. Here at least was an implicit religious commitment which Christian preaching and apologetics could legitimately exploit.

The principal difficulty with this theological strategy is that its perception of moral phenomena is back to front. This interpretation of morality reflects the prior and formative influence of Christian culture and upbringing. Its understanding of the form and content of values tends to presuppose a Christian world-view and, thus, it cannot function as the basis upon which such a world-view is erected. Systems of morality do not precede and suggest metaphysical visions. On the contrary, most moral codes make sense only in terms of perceptions of the way the world is, of human nature, and of the ideal life. A shift in *Weltanschauung* will inevitably be accompanied by a corresponding shift in moral perception since value judgments tend to track beliefs. Hence, any attempt to generate a system of belief from our deepest moral intuitions is fundamentally misguided.

In an important essay, the philosopher, Elizabeth Anscombe, has suggested that the Kantian description of the categorical imperative can only be understood with reference to the historical situation in which it was written.[25] Kant's analysis of the categorical moral 'ought' can only be rendered intelligible by reference to a Christian world-view which backed human duties with divine authorisation and sanctions. Yet the purely formal nature of the moral law in Kant's philosophy is symptomatic of the gradual breakdown of traditional metaphysics and the increasingly problematic attempt to provide a

[25] G. E. M. Anscombe, 'Modern Moral Philosophy', *Philosophy*, 33, 1958, esp. pp. 2–6. Reprinted in *Ethics, Religion and Politics: Collected Philosophical Papers*, Vol. 3 (Blackwell, Oxford, 1981), pp. 26–42

content for morality which does not presuppose a specific world-view.

Anscombe's thesis has been developed in Alasdair MacIntyre's seminal work, *After Virtue*. MacIntyre's analysis of the crisis in moral philosophy since the Enlightenment suggests a connection between morality and metaphysical perception which is deeply problematic for Baillie's apologetic strategy. The differences between the characteristic virtues of the Aristotelian philosopher, the mediaeval monk, and the Japanese warrior can only be explained in terms of their contrasting perceptions of human nature, the ends of human life, and the nature of the cosmos. The attempt by Enlightenment thinkers to establish a universal code of morality, which was valid independently of culturally specific beliefs, was therefore doomed to failure. What human beings consider worthwhile and desirable in both private and public life cannot be detached from the way in which they seek to understand the world, society and human nature. The ultimate end of human life is an object of the mind and not merely the will, and, consequently, our deepest intellectual assumptions will necessarily condition our moral commitments.

Kant's moral theory owes to its 'predecessor culture' both a teleological perception of the proper ends of human life and a theological framework which provides an ultimate and eternal basis for the legitimacy of these ends. Yet the impossibility of appealing either to teleology or to theology creates deep problems for Kant's ethical theory. His notion of universal and categorically binding moral laws seems to require the support of both teleology and theology, but in the philosophical climate of the Enlightenment this is no longer possible.[26]

One implication of this analysis is that a description of the form and content of morality must be embedded within an intellectual world-view. It cannot be possible, therefore, to deduce both a teleology and a theology from a phenomenological description of morality. Baillie's program in *The Interpretation of Religion* must inevitably founder on this rock. Our moral judgments are not so much the causes of our religious beliefs as their effects.

[26] *After Virtue* (Duckworth, London, 1981), p. 60

Yet despite this criticism, there may still be something to be said in support of Baillie's observations, even from the more pluralist perspective of the late twentieth century. There are definite limits to the moral diversity within our society and it is clear that many persons continue to hold to strong moral convictions even in the absence of any commitment to a particular world-view. Appeals to fundamental human rights, while not unproblematic, continue to have force across societies and nations, and these indicate that there are some moral commitments which most people would regard as authoritative and unconditionally binding. While any attempt to deduce a full-blown theology from these moral intuitions is implausible, the question still remains as to how we are to make sense of this moral consensus. In particular, the principle of the sanctity of human life is one which continues to inform much of our moral discourse and this is a principle that meta-ethics requires to explain. If Christian theology can sustain and integrate this moral insight more adequately than competing ideologies and world-views then this is one way in which the rationality of faith can be evinced.[27] While we may not derive a knowledge of God from moral experience, this may nonetheless be one way in which the Christian faith can demonstrate its ability to make sense of the world in which we live. Our moral intuitions may not supply the basis for theological epistemology but the knowledge of God may integrate and illuminate these same moral intuitions. In this respect, it might be argued that Baillie failed to distinguish a valid apologetic argument for Christian faith from an implausible epistemological strategy. Once this distinction is clearly drawn Baillie's argument may yet be harnessed to more modest but not insignificant theological ends.

2 Criticism of the second proposition is already implicit in the foregoing. The doctrines of God, creation and providence cannot be read out of our moral experience. On the contrary, these doctrines are themselves constitutive of moral experience. They provide an intellectual framework in which perceptions of the nature and end of human life are determined, and they prescribe, in some measure, the form and content of our value judgments.

[27] This is developed by Basil Mitchell, *Morality: Religious and Secular* (Clarendon Press, Oxford, 1980), Chapter 9, pp. 122–37

Similarly, in the light of the above criticism, it is harder to view the incarnation as simply a striking instance of general human apprehension of ultimate reality. Yet this appears to have been Baillie's early position.

> Regarded in this light, and as the culmination of the long history of divination, the doctrine of our Lord's divinity is surely expressive of the profoundest religious truth. It alienates us only when it is interpreted in such a manner as to obscure its organic connection with the history of revelation as a whole. The true Christian teaching has never been that God is incarnate in Jesus alone, but that in Him He was incarnate supremely. Revelation and incarnation are not unique historical prodigies but are, by God's grace, of the very warp and woof of our human experience.[28]

Here Baillie's claim is that belief in the incarnation extends the religious insight that has already been derived from moral experience. The special revelation peculiar to the Christian tradition is to be understood in similar terms to the general revelation imparted through the deliverances of conscience. If, however, we emphasise the distinctiveness of the Christian world-view and its determination of moral values, then greater weight is likely to be placed upon the uniqueness, discontinuity and givenness of special revelation. As I shall argue shortly, Baillie's later theology is marked by a much greater preoccupation with the notion of special revelation, although the linkage with general revelation is never abandoned.

3 The third proposition is also vulnerable to the first criticism registered above. If there are no independent moral criteria which can be used to assess the relative merits of cultures and religions it is difficult, if not impossible, to grade religions in terms of an ascending order of insight in the manner of Hegel's *Phenomenology of Spirit*. This confident assessment of religions through empirical study belongs to the scholarship of the late nineteenth and early twentieth centuries and now seems strangely antiquated. It tends to produce a Procrustean analysis in which important differences are concealed and continuities exaggeratedly stressed. In his later work, Baillie is more inclined to underline the extent to which the world religions are

[28] *The Interpretation of Religion*, op. cit. p. 469 In an unpublished paper 'John Baillie and Emil Brunner in Conflict' David Cairns reports that Baillie in later years repudiated the latter part of *The Interpretation of Religion*, warning his students against reading it

self-contained systems which do not translate into a theological Esperanto.[29]

4 Baillie's critical affirmation of the classical Christian tradition is a clear sign of a theological instinct which was at once liberal and orthodox. While wishing to affirm 'the faith which was once for all delivered to the saints', he is nonetheless at pains to stress the essential continuity between the tenets of Christian orthodoxy and the data of universal moral experience. This orients his thought towards something like an inspirational view of the person of Christ, a subjective theory of the atonement, and a modalist doctrine of the Trinity. The statement, cited above, that 'the true Christian teaching has never been that God is incarnate in Jesus alone, but that in Him he was incarnate supremely' is clear evidence of this. While it would be unfair to his fundamental intentions to present him as doctrinally reductionist, there is clearly some connection between his theological epistemology and his criticisms of classical dogma.

This is also apparent in Baillie's only treatment of the theology of the resurrection.[30] Alert to the problems raised by historical criticism and anxious not to reduce the resurrection to a 'proof miracle', Baillie follows Herrmann in claiming that belief in Christ's resurrection is not so much the cause of Christian faith as its expression. Although his discussion is extremely cautious, Baillie seems anxious to stress the continuity between the apostolic vision of the resurrection and other visions which characterise human religion.

> There is every reason to class the appearances of the Risen Jesus with many other 'visions and revelations' as St. Paul calls them, which play so important a part throughout Biblical history, and not there alone.[31]

Stress is laid upon the resurrection appearances thus interpreted while less weight is given to the empty tomb narratives. Consequently, Baillie is able to perceive again a continuity between general and special revelation, and thus to combine orthodox belief with his brand of liberalism. We may wish to question the adequacy of this theology of the resurrection and of his related treatment of the

---

[29] *The Sense of the Presence of God* (Oxford University Press, London, 1962), p. 203
[30] *And the Life Everlasting* (Scribner's, London, 1934), pp. 144ff.
[31] ibid. pp. 153–4

presence of Christ,[32] but this should not obscure the care with which he sought to do justice to the particularity of the central doctrines of the Christian faith.

After *The Place of Jesus Christ in Modern Christianity* Baillie never returned to a detailed exploration of issues in Christian doctrine. However, the increasing attention devoted to the subject of revelation in his later thought and his insistence on the uniqueness and finality of Christ suggest that, had he returned to these issues, he would have emphasised with equal vigour his oneness with the classical Christian tradition.[33] We shall observe in the subsequent discussion the manner in which his later theology is increasingly Christocentric.

III
OUR KNOWLEDGE OF GOD

After about 1930, Baillie's theological position entered a process of development which can still be detected in the posthumous Gifford Lectures. His later theology did not seek to establish an alternative theological system. Rather, it represented a series of attempts to revise and to refine positions advanced earlier but perceived to be deficient in certain respects. The effect of this is that his later theology, although more creative and original, lacks the overall coherence of his earlier position.

While he later confessed to being vaguely haunted by the feeling that the path of his early theology had reached a dead end, it is clear that the arrival of Karl Barth on the theological scene was the principal catalyst for the ensuing change.[34] It appears that Baillie met Barth for the first time while visiting Bonn around 1930, and from then onwards the writings of Barth, and others associated with the movement known as 'dialectical theology', featured with increasing prominence in his lectures and published works. During his time at

---

[32] *The Place of Jesus Christ in Modern Christianity,* op. cit. pp. 195–202

[33] This is confirmed by his defence of the orthodox interpretation of Donald Baillie's *God Was In Christ.* 'Some Comments on Professor Hick's article on "The Christology of D. M. Baillie"', *Scottish Journal of Theology,* 11, 1958, pp. 265–70

[34] 'Looking Before and After', op. cit. pp. 400–2. Baillie's inaugural lecture at Union Seminary in 1930 is largely a repetition of previous themes and suggests that his early theology had reached its terminal point. 'The Logic of Religion', *Alumni Bulletin of Union Theological Seminary,* 3, 1930, pp. 6–16

Union, Baillie, in typical mediating fashion, drew the attention of sceptical colleagues to the significance of Barth's theology as part of a legitimate protest against the naive optimism and smugness of post-Enlightenment theology.

> It so happened that I think in the year 1933, it was my turn to read a paper at a social meeting of the Faculty of Union Seminary, and I called my paper 'A Preface to Barthianism'. I was not indeed anything that could be called a Barthian myself, but there were those among my colleagues who could see no significance at all in the movement, and I was bold enough to think that I understood something of what it portended. My thesis was that what was here happening in theology must be taken very seriously, because it was closely parallel to what was at the same time happening in many other fields, and especially in poetry and *belles lettres,* in painting, sculpture, architecture and music. I remember saying, that if we understood just how and why Victorian poetry had given way to such poetry as Mr. Eliot's *The Wasteland,* Victorian fiction to such novels as James Joyce's *Ulysees* and Proust's *A La Recherche du temps perdu,* the painting of Landseer and Sir John Millar's to that of Picasso and Paul Klee, and so forth, we should better understand how and why Dr. Barth and so many others of his generation were in revolt against the teaching to which he and I were together subjected in the German universities in our student days.[35]

The publication of Baillie's best-known theological work, *Our Knowledge of God* (1939), revealed some striking changes in his thought.[36] We see here the influence of new movements of thought not only in theology but also in philosophy. Despite the disjointedness of the argument this may be Baillie's most creative work, and it is one which continues to repay study. Its

[35] 'Some Reflections on the Changing Theological Scene', *Union Seminary Quarterly Review,* 12, 1957, pp. 4–5

[36] *And the Life Everlasting* (1933) shows evidence of the work of Barth, Brunner and other dialectical thinkers but the central argument of the book is consistent with Baillie's early theology, i.e. our belief in everlasting life is grounded not upon the authority of special revelation (important though this is to Baillie) but upon a conviction regarding the supreme value of human personality as created by God. In this respect, I depart from the analysis of Baillie's theological development offered by Donald Clinefelter in 'The Theology of John Baillie: A Biographical Introduction', *Scottish Journal of Theology,* 22, 1969, pp. 419–36. Klinefelter asserts that Baillie's thought moved into a neo-orthodox phase in the 1930s and then reverted to a post-Barthian liberalism. Both these classifications seem to me too imprecise and lacking in sufficient evidence. I can find no evidence that Baillie was at any time in the 1930s a subscriber to 'neo-orthodoxy', while a later writing, *The Idea of Revelation in Recent Thought* (1956), is surely the most 'Barthian' of all his books

argument displays both continuity and discontinuity with his earlier work.[37]

Underlying the argument of the book there is a significant shift in Baillie's approach to epistemology. In his earlier work we see the influence of the post-Kantian philosophy of Pringle-Pattison in which all knowledge is dependent upon the primary data of experience. An epistemology in which the conscious subject reflects upon and interprets the primary deliverances of moral experience is implicit in his theological strategy. We now find this being replaced by a critical realism in which experience and self-consciousness are firmly set within the social and physical environment inhabited by the human subject. Baillie's argumentation reflects the influence of writers such as the American philosopher W. E. Hocking, and the early Martin Heidegger, whose work has since become a landmark in twentieth-century protests against Cartesian epistemologies.

Our knowledge of other persons and of the tridimensional spatial world are described by Baillie as 'primary modes of knowledge'.[38] While this knowledge comes through the sensory media of sight, sound and touch, we must not think that the existence of other minds and the public world is inferred from the deliverances of raw experience. Consciousness of self and the contents of experience is only possible by a prior awareness of the world of objects and other persons with which we interact. 'Alles Dasein is Mitsein.' (Heidegger)[39] While the knowledge of self, others and the world are primary modes of knowledge, each of these is always mediated through the other two. This gives rise to Baillie's renowned concept of 'mediated immediacy' which has important theological implications.[40]

In line with this shift in epistemological outlook, Baillie now places greater emphasis upon what might be called the 'contextuality' of religious knowledge. Our awareness of God is not simply the result of

[37] Baillie himself was ready to acknowledge this. '[T]hough my present findings may seem to myself to be for the most part a not unnatural development of my findings of twelve or fifteen years ago, I am well aware that the agreement between the two is far from complete.' Our Knowledge of God (Oxford University Press, London, 1939), p. vii

[38] ibid. p. 217

[39] Quoted ibid., p. 217

[40] Cf. Donald Klinefelter, '"Our Knowledge of God" in the Theology of John Baillie', Scottish Journal of Theology, 30, 1977, pp. 401–27

an interpretation of religious experience. It is profoundly conditioned by the history and tradition to which the human subject belongs.

> Our modern Western conscience, and again such diffused religious ideas as seem now to be almost part of the Western mind, are in no small measure deposits left by the Christian religion itself in the course of its long progress through the generations of European history.[41]

Our knowledge of God, while not inferred from some more primary awareness, is nonetheless mediated by history and tradition. This insight paves the way for a stronger theology of revelation than has hitherto been apparent in Baillie's theology.

Following the lead of the thirteenth-century theologian, Bonaventure, Baillie argues that our knowledge of God in this life is neither direct nor inferred. It is given 'in, with and under' other presences and hence conforms to the pattern of 'mediated immediacy'. Four media of our knowledge of God are outlined.[42] (i) The natural world in its beauty and order communicates something of the presence of God to us. Again, we are not dealing with an inference in the manner of Aquinas' five ways. Borrowing George Adam Smith's expression, Baillie comments that, 'Nature is not an argument for God, but is a sacrament of Him'.[43] (ii) Our fellowship with and service of other people also disclose to us something of the mystery of God. 'If we love one another, God dwelleth in us.' This appears to be similar to the earlier moral approach to belief in God; as we are aware of the claim made upon us by the other and as we commune with our neighbour, so we discover something of the One who is the ground and source of all love. (iii) It is within a specific history and tradition that the knowledge of God is given. Our awareness of the divine presence is mediated by the witness of the historical religion to which we belong. This is true, *a fortiori*, of the Christian religion which experiences God only through the history of a particular people. (iv) This last medium bring us to the story of one person, Jesus Christ, and to the disclosure of God once for all in a human life. All history has its centre and meaning in Christ, and Baillie appears to make the further claim that the knowledge of God

---

[41] ibid. p. 41
[42] ibid. pp. 178ff.
[43] ibid. p. 178

which is mediated here controls and shapes what we know of God from elsewhere.[44] His use of Luther's dialectic of the *deus revelatus* and the *deus absconditus* illustrates the way in which the incarnation and the cross mediate the glory of God.

> When Luther affirms that Christ is the Mediator of the knowledge of God, he does not mean that we argue from Christ to God; he means that it is in Christ that we see God. We see Him veiled and humiliated, but it is nevertheless God that we see. The kind of directness for which we have contended in our knowledge of God is thus not at all interfered with, but is rather implemented, by the fact of Christ's mediatorship. This is what I have tried to express in the conception of a mediate immediacy. In Christ we know God not by argument but by personal acquaintance.[45]

It is clear that we have here an important development in Baillie's thinking which brings with it a greater emphasis upon special revelation and the contextuality of all human knowledge. At the same time, there are points of continuity with his earlier theology in which we find his argument being directed against Barth.

The Kantian derivation of a knowledge of God from the universal awareness of the categorical imperative is still advanced by Baillie.[46] The Christian apologist is charged with the task of bringing to the top of the mind what is already present in the bottom of the heart.[47] By identifying an implicit knowledge of the absolute in the moral demands that are imposed upon each person Baillie seems to be reiterating his earlier theological epistemology.[48] It follows from this that there is a knowledge of God already present in the hearts of those who have not yet responded to the call of the Christian gospel. Here Baillie tends to side with Brunner against Barth in the famous dispute over the validity of a natural knowledge of God. Although he believes that Brunner has conceded too much to Barth's position, he argues that the communication of the Christian message must in some sense make contact with what is already there in the heart of the 'unregenerate

---

[44] ibid. p. 180

[45] ibid. pp. 196–197

[46] ibid. pp. 240ff.

[47] Baillie's claim that all people are, in some sense, unconscious believers is criticised by H. D. Lewis, *Philosophy of Religion* (English Universities Press, London, 1965), pp. 113–22 and John Macquarrie, *In Search of Deity* (SCM, London, 1984), p. 44

[48] Baillie explicitly recommits himself to the substance of the argument from *The Interpretation of Religion, Our Knowledge of God*, op. cit., p. 245

sinner'. The *imago dei* has not been wholly obliterated insofar as every person is aware of the conflict and shortcomings within her nature.

> The Christian preacher knows full well that his task in endeavouring to lead men to a saving knowledge of God in Christ would be a very different one were he called upon to preach to stocks and stones or to beings not already endowed with reason and some sense of awe before the holy thing. He is indeed calling upon God to perform a miracle, but not that miracle.[49]

The distinction between special and general revelation is deployed in order to point to the ways in which adherents of other religions may possess a fragmentary but genuine knowledge of God. The expression 'general revelation' is misleading insofar as Baillie wishes to see all revelation as mediated through specific historical traditions, but it is useful in providing him with the conceptual means to challenge the Barthian thesis that there is no knowledge of God outwith the divine self-revelation in Jesus Christ.[50] The problem of the relationship between Christianity and other faiths thus remains on Baillie's theological agenda and sets him apart from much dialectical theology.

It is clear from the foregoing that there is both change and continuity in the theology of *Our Knowledge of God*. The main difficulty with the argument is its disjointedness. We have seen how the strategy of the 1920s reappears, yet it sits alongside fresh emphases regarding the contextuality of religious knowledge and the constitutive nature of the incarnation and the cross within the Christian faith. No attempt is made within the book to resolve this tension and it is to Baillie's later work that we must turn for clues to the ongoing development of his theology.

---

[49] ibid. p. 25

[50] ibid. pp. 89ff. Baillie's principal objections to Barth are that he ignored the need for theology to be subject to human reason and conscience, and that he denied a knowledge of God outwith the revelation given in Christ. These are already apparent from *Confessions of a Transplanted Scot*, op. cit. pp. 52–3 and in his review of G. S. Hendry's *God the Creator*. British Weekly, March 25, 1937 p. 287. David Cairns recalls the following exchange between Barth and Baillie in St. Andrews in 1930. 'John Baillie . . . asked Barth if he regarded the goodness of God as having any resemblance to the goodness of man, and Barth answered, "None whatever", to which Baillie looking grim replied: "That is a statement to which I can ascribe no meaning whatsover". Not unnaturally, an uncomfortable silence ensued.' 'Another View of the Kirk and the Hitler Regime', *Life and Work*, July, 1983, p. 22. It is not clear how well Baillie actually knew Barth but in 1951 at the WCC advisory commission Barth was to describe 'the devastating Baillie from Edinburgh' as the most remarkable of the British representatives. Eberhard Busch, *Karl Barth*, (London, 1976) p. 395

IV
LATER THEOLOGY

In several writings during the years of the Second World War, Baillie's thought shows an increasing awareness of the extent to which Christian values are sustained by particular beliefs.[51] In view of the gradual secularisation of society, he sees approaching a situation in which moral values alter their complexion and even become pathologically distorted under the influence of pagan ideologies. There is little doubt that the sombre overtones of these writings were due to the circumstances in Europe at that time, and Baillie himself was involved in the evacuation from France in 1940. The subsequent war years were a period of increased political and ecclesiastical activity for Baillie, and this leaves its marks in his writings.[52] At the same time, however, we have also to reckon with a further development in his theology. The relationship between belief and value is recast as it is claimed that the distinctive beliefs of the Christian faith are accompanied by value judgments which express a unique and precious ethic. The moral teaching of the Church is integral to the world-view that is embedded in Christian revelation.

> It is from Christianity far more than from any other source that we have learned to value the individual human personality – a fact which is all the more significant because Christianity values the individual personality only in relation to the beloved community of the Kingdom of God. Yet it seems clear that we cannot hold to the Christian ethical teaching about personality while rejecting the Christian view about its status in reality. You cannot be a Christian in your moral principles and a Buddhist or a Nazi or any other kind of pagan in your religion. If you try your Christian moral principles or your pagan religion will soon come to grief; and though I hope for the latter result, I fear the former.[53]

Baillie speaks with respect for those who would uphold Christian values even after abandoning the belief system in which these once

---

[51] *Invitation to Pilgrimage* (Oxford University Press, London, 1942); *Prospects of Spiritual Renewal* (Blackwood, Edinburgh, 1943); *What is Christian Civilization?* (Oxford University Press, London, 1945); ed. *God's Will in Our Time* (SCM, London, 1946)

[52] Cf. 'Does God Defend The Right?', Christian News-Letter, 53, 30 October, 1940. Cf. Isobel Forrester, 'A Cousin's Memories' in John Baillie, *Christian Devotion* (Oxford University Press, London, 1962), p. xviii. At the outset of the war Baillie travelled to the US at the behest of the British government to plead its cause amongst influential American contacts.

[53] *Invitation to Pilgrimage*, op. cit. pp. 102–103 It is noticeable that Baillie's sermons from 1940 onwards display a much more robust Christocentrism. This is especially true of the great sermon on 'bringing into captivity every thought to the obedience of Christ' (2 Cor. 10:5) preached in Cambridge in 1944. *The Cambridge Review*, 2 December, 1944, pp. 134–5. I am indebted to Professor Cheyne for drawing my attention to this

belonged. Yet he fears that they may be 'men of the Afterglow' whose lives reflect the last rays of light from a source that has been extinguished.[54] Unless the light is rekindled the prospect for succeeding generations is one of spiritual and moral darkness. There are signs here that Baillie's response to the increasing secularisation of society is one of combative dogmatic assertion. The gospel is to be proclaimed vehemently and not apologised for.[55] At the same time, he is clearly nervous of a theological totalitarianism which refuses to stand at the bar of human reason. This may explain his continuing appeal to our sense of living under a transcendent moral authority which is the root of all human awareness of God.[56] But this reassertion of his earlier moral theism sits very uneasily with his claims about the manner in which values tend to track beliefs. There still remains an unresolved tension in Baillie's theology which suggests a failure to think through a theological epistemology consistent with the positions he holds. Is our knowledge of God derived primarily from the revelation attested to in Scripture and proclaimed by the Church or is it derived primarily from the moral sense which is common to all religions and traditions? If both are to admitted as sources of theological knowledge how are they to be related and integrated? Although we can discern hints of a possible resolution in his last work, these questions are not adequately dealt with at any point in Baillie's corpus, and this may be the outstanding weakness in his theology.

[54] ibid. p. 126 This pessimism is in stark contrast to his earlier optimism. 'Instead of the denial of God acting as a corrosive upon our directly-intuited loyalties, rather will these loyalties stand firm and lead us in the end back to God.' 'The Predicament of Humanism', *Canadian Journal of Religious Thought*, 22, 1931, pp. 109–18

[55] ibid. p. 35. At the same time, Baillie was aware of the complexity and moral ambivalence of the secular society. It was neither pagan nor un-Christian but in the process of becoming post-Christian. Thus he cites with approval T. S. Eliot's remark that 'A society has not ceased to be Christian until it has become positively something else.' There is both continuity and discontinuity between the mores of those inside and those outside the visible Christian community, and this requires to be recognized by the preacher and the theologian. Cf. 'The Theology of the Frontier', *The Frontier*, 6, 1952, pp. 212–26

[56] *Invitation to Pilgrimage*, op. cit. pp. 37ff.

His later writings also display a keener awareness of the communitarian dimension of Christian life and witness. The ground for this is prepared by the move towards a more realist epistemology in *Our Knowledge of God*, but an interest in the social and political nature of faith is only a distinctive feature of Baillie's theology after 1940. An important influence in this respect may have been Reinhold Niebuhr's Gifford Lectures delivered in Edinburgh in 1939 during the outbreak of war. Niebuhr and Baillie had been colleagues at Union Seminary in the early 1930s and Baillie was largely instrumental in bringing his friend to Edinburgh as Gifford lecturer.[57]

The Belief in Progress (1950) was based on lectures delivered shortly after the end of the war, and it is perhaps Baillie's most underrated work. After examining classical cyclical theories of history and post-Enlightenment progressivist theories, he argues that the Christian view is ranged equally against utopianism and a pure other-worldliness.[58] The utopian neglects the tragic dimension of human life and underestimates the powers of evil. An eschatology which looks to the discontinuous gift of the kingdom is necessary in the light of the cross and resurrection of Christ. At the same, neither nihilism nor other-worldliness are permitted. This world remains God's creation and the Church is given the time and place to preach the gospel in the power of the Spirit. We may hope and pray that the same Spirit will work in the lives of individuals, communities and nations. Both the apocalyptic and prophetic modes of utterance are contained in Scripture and cannot be neglected in Christian preaching.

> Christianity must always maintain a realized and a futurist eschatology in balance, if never in equipoise. In neglecting the latter it either shuts its eyes to the tragic realities of our continuing warfare or, alternatively, harbours utopian illusions of the possibility of their disappearance from the earthly scene. But in neglecting the former it is failing to understand the specific character, the promise and opportunities, of the years of grace.[59]

[57] Published as *The Nature and Destiny of Man* Vols 1–2 (Nisbet, London, 1941 & 43). For an indication of Baillie's close relationship with Niebuhr see Ursula Niebuhr, *Remembering Reinhold Niebuhr* (Harper Collins, San Francisco, 1991), pp. 17–22, 161–86

[58] Here the influence of Niebuhr is openly acknowledged. *The Belief in Progress* (Oxford University Press, London, 1950), p. 215

[59] ibid. p. 207

Baillie's final works *The Idea of Revelation in Recent Thought* and *The Sense of the Presence of God* display his continuing interest in the concept of revelation, and they reveal an increasing Christocentrism in his thinking towards the end of his life. His analysis of the concept of revelation reflects the influence of the first part volume of Barth's *Church Dogmatics*. The content of revelation is to be understood not as a deposit of information about God but as the self-revealing of God in Jesus Christ.[60] This leads to a Lutheran and Reformed emphasis upon the personal, relational character of faith. As the disposition of mind in which revelation is received, faith reflects the personal and dynamic nature of God's self-revelation. A further implication of this is that the authority of Scripture is to be derived from its content as witness to Jesus Christ.[61] This offers a critical perspective upon the doctrine of the plenary inspiration of Scripture. If the character of Scripture is to be understood in terms of its evangelical subject-matter we cannot ascribe an equal weight to every sentence within the canon. Neither are we justified in attributing a formal infallibility to all that is in Scripture. The writers were fallible human beings working within the context of a particular time and place. There is no miraculous suspension of their humanity, and the reader is required to interpret the Scriptures both critically and piously in order to hear their message.

> [T]he intelligent reading of the Bible – 'in the Spirit but with the mind also,' and the reading of it so as to understand how it *Christum treibt*, depends entirely on our ability to distinguish what is central from what is peripheral; to distinguish its unchanging truth from its clothing in the particular cultural and cosmological preconceptions of the times and places in which it was written; to distinguish also between its essential message and its numerous imperfections.[62]

This attitude of 'believing criticism' is a constant feature of Baillie's theology. The Scriptures are authoritative and are to be interpreted in the light of the unique message they impart. But, at the same time, we must bring to the task of interpretation all the critical tools that modern scholarship can supply. Theories of inerrancy are

---

[60] *The Idea of Revelation in Recent Thought* (Oxford University Press, London, 1956), p. 28
[61] ibid. p. 117
[62] ibid. p. 120

now untenable in the light of historical criticism, and in any case these tend to distort the essential theological character of the Bible.

In the same context, Baillie is unwilling to limit God's revelation to the medium of the Scriptural canon. The revelation of God is imparted to peoples outwith the covenant community; this is itself part of the witness of Scripture.[63] Wherever goodness is found in human persons and communities we must perceive this as due to the revelatory action of God. This 'general revelation' is not to be seen in terms of the Stoic notion of an innate idea but rather as the ongoing, dynamic involvement of God with creatures everywhere.

Although Baillie never lived to deliver his Gifford Lectures the manuscript was found to be complete and was later published as *The Sense of the Presence of God*. The lectures return to the dominant themes of his thought: the interaction with contemporary philosophy; the uneasy conversation with Barth; theological epistemology; and the relationship between Christianity and other faiths. Much of his argument is essentially a reiteration of positions already adopted in *Our Knowledge of God* but now set within a different philosophical climate. The realist interpretation of moral judgments continues to be advanced as well as the claim that knowledge of the public and social world is given rather than inferred from more primary data. However, the discussion of the notion of a 'frame of reference' marks a further development in Baillie's theology.

All religious perception takes place within a particular frame of reference which conditions and shapes both thought and practice.

> The conscience of each great culture was formed within the matrix of religious ideas apart from which its deliverances could not be easily justified.[64]

The Christian faith provides its participants with a specific frame of reference which enable them 'to make the appropriate response to every circumstance of life'.[65] This framework is not exclusively for the ordering of one's thoughts and beliefs; it informs an entire 'way of living, which includes a way of thinking, a way of feeling and a way

[63] ibid. pp. 125–33
[64] *The Sense of the Presence of God*, op. cit. p. 131
[65] ibid. p. 132

of behaving.'[66] The gospel of Christ generates a Christian perspective and it provides the believer with an appropriate way of perceiving the world and of relating to others. It is rightly grasped only within the context of Christian worship and fellowship.

The Gifford Lectures also indicate the extent to which Baillie's view of the office of Christian doctrine remained constant over many years. As in *The Place of Jesus Christ in Modern Christianity*, he distinguishes between the formulations of orthodox dogma and the primary perceptions of faith that they seek to articulate. These primary perceptions are vital to Christian faith but they should not be so closely identified with any one metaphysical approach as to obscure this distinction.[67] The doctrines of the Trinity and the person of Christ have the negative function of guarding against improper expressions of the essential insights of faith, but they also have their limitations as finite and imperfect attempts to express the inexpressible. Baillie proposes that the proper method in dogmatics is to return to these primary perceptions of faith which lie behind the orthodox formulations of classical dogma. Although his remarks are somewhat elusive, the earlier description of his position as both orthodox and liberal remains warranted. In this respect, there is again an apparent disjointedness in his argument. His understanding of the office of doctrine suggests an epistemological distinction between primary experience and the language in which that experience is articulated. Yet the fresh emphasis upon the role of a frame of reference suggests an alternative epistemology in which the primary apprehensions of faith do not precede but are mediated by the language and thought patterns of Christian discourse. It appears that the development in Baillie's epistemology was never accompanied by a corresponding development in his understanding of the nature of doctrine.

One consequence of the notion of a 'frame of reference' is its provision of a possible means of integrating the two sources of religious knowledge in Baillie's theology; special revelation and general revelation. This possibility is realised by the claim that the Word which became incarnate in Christ is at work not only in the

---

[66] ibid. p. 137
[67] ibid. pp. 163–4

Old Testament but also in other cultures and religions.[68] Baillie had made this claim many years earlier but, in the context of this discussion of the Christian frame of reference and the centrality of the person and work of Christ, it enables him to outline a Christian theology of religions. The uniqueness and finality of Christ is not offset or compromised by the (unavoidable) recognition that there is revelation outwith the Christian community. We may trust that a greater insight into the piety and beliefs of other faiths will disclose to us 'serious shortcomings both in our traditional understanding of the revelation of God in Christ and in our obedience to it.'[69] Thus, for Baillie, the revelation of God 'in sundry ways and diverse manners' is to be understood christologically as further disclosure of and witness to the one Word of God.

On reading this one is left with the impression that a rapprochement between the later Baillie and the later Barth is possible for a succeeding generation. In the final portions of the (uncompleted) *Church Dogmatics,* Barth, unknown to Baillie,[70] spoke of the ways in which the Word of God is active outwith the visible Christian community. The sphere and dominion of the Word of God is the entire creation and in the light of the Biblical witness we cannot exclude the possibility that this Word will be attested to by people and events not directly engaged in Christian proclamation.[71] Barth goes on to speak of the little lights of creation which are not extinguished by sin but which have their own speech and language. These can only be understood in terms of their relation to the one great light in virtue of which they exist and are given their proper place.[72] This cosmic dimension of Barth's theology answers the charge

---

[68] ibid. p. 193

[69] ibid. p. 201

[70] It is not clear that Baillie had ever read much beyond *Church Dogmatics* I/2

[71] Barth sets out four criteria for the distinguishing of such witness to God's Word. a) agreement with Scripture; b) agreement with the dogmas and confessions of the Church; c) fruits which such witness bring forth in the world; d) its significance for the life of the Christian community under the Lordship of Christ. *Church Dogmatics* IV/3 (T & T Clark, Edinburgh, 1961), pp. 126ff. While Barth did not apply this notion to the other religions of the world this line of interpretation has recently been developed by David Lochhead, *The Dialogical Imperative* (SCM, London, 1988)

[72] Barth's constant drive to integrate the doctrines of revelation, reconciliation and creation is what is lacking in Baillie's later theology.

that he retreated into a narrow positivism of revelation.[73] It may thus be possible to reconcile the Barthian insight that there is a unique, irreducible and final knowledge of God given through Jesus Christ upon which the being of the Church depends, with the Baillian insistence that God is at work and is disclosed in diverse ways throughout the entire creation.

V
CONCLUSION

It is invidious in a short commentary to attempt to do full justice to the range and richness of Baillie's theology but several concluding comments are called for. While we have noted development, change and incompleteness in much of what he said, Baillie's theological virtues nonetheless stand out.

John Baillie lived through one of the most important phases in the history of modern theology, and he was acquainted with many of the leading thinkers of the twentieth century. He sought to combine the deep faith that had grown in him from his childhood with the intellectual insights of modernity. If he remained both orthodox and liberal throughout his life, it is also true that neither his orthodoxy nor his liberalism were unaffected by the other. The creative blend of Christian piety and intellectual honesty is a worthy desideratum for any theologian.

It has sometimes been remarked that Baillie was a 'mediating theologian'.[74] He sought to reconcile the methods of philosophy and theology, liberalism and orthodoxy, Christianity and contemporary culture, and hope for this world with faith in the life to come.

> My purpose has been the irenic one of endeavouring to distinguish the true insight within each alternative from that blindness in it which renders it insensitive to the insight of the other.[75]

[73] This criticism made by Bonhoeffer of Barth is quoted with approval by Baillie. 'The Theology of the Frontier', op. cit. p. 224

[74] John MacKay, 'John Baillie, A Lyrical Tribute and Appraisal', *Scottish Journal of Theology*, IX, 1956, pp. 225–35; William Power, 'John Baillie: A Mediating Theologian', *Union Seminary Quarterly Review*, XXIV, 1968, pp. 47–68; Donald Klinefelter, 'The Theology of John Baillie: A Biographical Introduction', op. cit.

[75] *Our Knowledge of God*, op. cit. p. vii

Yet Baillie's strategy of mediation was not an easy and comfortable compromise between opposites. It involved the defence of positions which were under attack from several fronts, and, while his style was unfailingly irenic, he never sought a false peace with rival opinions.[76]

Baillie's perpetual search for an understanding of the way in which Christian witness to the uniqueness of the person and work of Christ can be set alongside a recognition of the disclosure and activity of God amongst other religions and traditions was one of his life's preoccupations. (Here we must include his lifelong appreciation of the philosophy of Plato.)[77] This problem is at least as pressing today as it was during Baillie's lifetime, and his discussion of it is always illuminating and instructive.

Finally, we cannot end without commenting on the harmony and style of his work. A spirituality pervades Baillie's philosophical, dogmatic, apologetic, and devotional writings and this is reflected in his calm and elegant prose style.[78] His most abstract philosophizing at times is suffused by a sense of the presence of God, while his sermons and prayers always reflect a penetrating, intellectual acuteness. Through all his work John Baillie was at once a student of culture, a servant of the church, an academic scholar and, above all, a lover of Jesus.

> I shall conclude by saying this – and it is something of which I have continually to keep reminding myself: every man who calls himself a Christian should go to sleep thinking about the love of God as it has visited us in the Person of His Son, Jesus Christ our Lord.[79]

If the appropriation of his work must always be critical, it must also be grateful for its highest achievements.

[76] Lesslie Newbigin has described Baillie's similar *modus operandi* at heated WCC discussions. 'He was a member of the famous committee of 25 theologians, which included Barth, Brunner, Niebuhr, Vogel, Wingren, Schlink and others on the theme of the Evanston Assembly – 'Christ, the Hope of the World' – generally known as the 25 hopeless theologians. Unlike Niebuhr, who was so incensed by Barth that he threatened to walk out, Baillie always kept his cool but made his points'

[77] 'I think that in our school-days most of us found the proofs of Phaedo strangely unconvincing. Something in the dialogue impressed us tremulously. I am myself not ashamed to remember how more than one evening I wept over the preparation of that Greek lesson' *And The Life Everlasting*, op. cit. p. 93

[78] Cf. T. F. Torrance, 'A Living Sacrifice: In Memoriam John Baillie', *Religion in Life*, 30, 1960–61, p. 331

[79] *Christian Devotion*, op. cit., p. 77

Chapter 7

THE SENSE OF THE PRESENCE OF GOD

George M. Newlands

I

If God is to be affirmed as the ultimate reality, and the source, sustainer and goal of human existence, then there should be grounds for this affirmation. Beyond this, the reality of God is said in Christian tradition to be experience of a personal presence. Claims to experience of that reality are hard to substantiate. Are there other grounds for the affirmation? But even if there are, how relevant to human existence is the reality of a God to people for whom he is who is rarely if ever experienced as a personal presence? These are issues which have pressed upon modern European society, and never more so than in a century which has experienced two world wars. They are issues with which John Baillie was concerned throughout his life, and to which he returned with renewed concentration in his final work, the posthumously published Gifford Lectures, *The Sense of the Presence of God*.

On first re-reading *The Sense of the Presence of God* seems dated enough. The debates of the sixties, seventies and eighties are still to come, with all their claims to seminal breakthrough in theological scholarship. Worse still, one is aware that Baillie is working out the mature fruits of his thoughts of the thirties, now even more distant. It would be wrong to assert that there has been no progress in theology in the last sixty years. What I do suggest in this essay, however, is that a reading of Baillie in the light of what has happened in the interval considerably strengthens his claim to be considered one of the most perceptive and judicious of twentieth-century theologians.

II

I come now to Baillie's text.(Ch. 1), 'Knowledge and Certitude', deals with some of the most basic problems in the philosophy of religion, introduced in more familiar form to generations of Edinburgh theological students through Baillie's 1939 volume, *Our Knowledge of God*. Knowledge seems to imply certitude but often does not go beyond probabilities. The concept of faith always contains both the idea of knowing and the idea of not knowing fully. 'No Christian, then, can say that he knows nothing.'(5) But equally, 'all human thinking is defectible'.(6)

There are indeed certainties, in the natural sciences, in moral and especially in our religious convictions. A distinction is drawn between knowledge of truth and knowledge of reality. Our knowledge of the realities is primary, and our knowledge of truths concerning them secondary. This is a neat way of affirming a position which I have described elsewhere as a combination of ontological realism and epistemological scepticism.

But does it work? Turn to Chapter Two, 'The Really Real'. Many have doubted our knowledge of any reality, certainly any beyond what can be verified by the methods of natural science. But what about the conviction that honesty and loyalty are required of us all? Moral convictions are central. Here reality presents itself to us, requiring concern for others. This phenomenon is described further in a chapter on 'The Range of Our Experience.'

Early man felt himself to be at one with nature, not alien from it. 'Our total experience of reality presents itself to us as a single experience.'(50) Analysis of individual elements comes later. This is especially true of moral convictions. The point of this train of argument becomes clear by the time we reach chapter four, 'The Epistemological Status of Faith.' How do we 'reason things out?' Procedures for verification and falsification are discussed. 'A faith that is consistent with everything possible is not a faith in anything actual.'(71) Complete agnosticism is less frequent than we often imagine. For Baillie, the ultimate refutation of doubts is theological and incarnational. The claim made upon me by the presence of my neighbour is made by unconditioned being, by God. It now becomes possible to consider 'The Nature and Office of Theological Statements'.(Ch. 5)

Faith is 'an awareness of the divine presence itself, however hidden behind the veils of sense.' God reveals himself within a tradition and a community. The indirectness of faith's apprehension of God is explored through the Bible, Aquinas and Kant. Kant was clearly of decisive significance for Baillie. But Hegel, Bradley, Mansell and Sabatier in the nineteenth century are now invoked, and then in the twentieth, 'four schools – the Thomists, the Barthians, the existentialists and the linguistic analysts.' Baillie notes affinities between the last three schools, placing Barth in his cultural context. The last witness is Tillich. The result is a division of characterisation of theological language as analogical or symbolic.

Chapter Six is then entitled 'Analogy and Symbol.' Analogy and symbol, 'in the widest sense of the term all language may be said to be symbolic.'(113) But not all theological statements are analogical. Despite being known in, with and under other realities, yet there is a certain directness in apprehension of God. However this two-way communication is in the nature of the case internal to the mind of the believer, and is always open to doubt on the part of the non-believer.

Chapter Seven, 'The Framework of Reference' seeks to relate theory to practice. Christianity is a way of living. Love of God is always related to love of neighbour, and beyond this to a new humanity. This leads on to 'meaning and reference.' The gospel needs to be translated into the language of the present. Otherwise it is inevitably dismissed as irrelevant to contemporary life. In particular, it is important not to confuse dogmas with the primary perceptions of faith. Chapter Nine raises the wider issue of 'Faith and the Faiths.' The Greeks and the Romans developed philosophies of religion. Did they have a true knowledge of God? What does it mean to speak of Salvation in a name (Ch. 10)? For Baillie, there is some awareness of God in 'the pagan religions', but the Way of Christ is decisive.' 'It is Christ himself that has created the world's desire for him.'(209)

Chapter Eleven deals with Providence. Scientific and religious accounts of the world complement one another. Through modern physics, 'contradiction has been turned into complementarity.' What others may see as coincidence, Christians will read as providential. This naturally brings Baillie to a chapter (12) on Grace and Gratitude. 'He lov'd us from the first of time, He loves us to the last.'

'Gratitude is not only the dominant note of Christian piety but equally the dominant motive of Christian action in the world.'(236) This is *imitatio Christi*. We should also recognise vestigial forms of gratitude in those who are not explicitly Christian. The last chapter 'Retrospect', reconsiders the argument. Analysis and clarity in linguistic analysis is not sufficient. But neither is Barthian exclusivism. Faith is trust. Propositions are necessary but not sufficient. We have to do with 'a God whose living and active presence among us can be perceived by faith in a large variety of human contexts and situations'. Baillie ends characteristically with Vaughan's prayer, 'Abide with us, O most blessed and merciful saviour, for it is towards evening and the day is far spent. . . .'

It is not hard to see why Baillie's classic soon appeared dated. His scepticism concerning the modern philosophy of language appeared to be the incomprehension of the older man in the face of recent scholarship. Much was still to be promised from this tradition. His argument for moral theism had the same air of déjà vu. He spoke of a sense of God at the bottom of men's hearts. The 'sixties were the age of secular Christianity, in the confidence of entering a completely new era. New Testament scholarship was now to be dominated by the heirs of Bultmann and the Barthians were to reach new heights of professional self-confidence. The collapse of some of these certainties in the 'seventies produced more new directions, in the search for transcendence in eastern religions, in new Roman Catholic thought beyond the Thomism which Baillie considered, in Wittgensteinian turns in the philosophy of religion. In the 'eighties narrative theology blossomed, and post-modernism became a new magic wand which could be waved over the tradition to justify any theological position from extreme conservatism to extreme liberalism. As the influence of the Christian community declined, at least in Britain, a radical pluralism in theology, with an increasingly conservative majority, became increasingly apparent. In Scotland the continuation of an creative theological tradition has become increasingly problematic, and therefore increasingly urgent, in recent years.

It is always in some respects a dubious procedure to seek to find guidelines for coping with present predicaments in past examples. For of course we are all children of our time, writing for a particular situation. On the other hand, it is precisely reflection on past thought in the light of present issues that characterises the human being as a reflective creature. It has been through reflection on its past in the light of the present that modern scholarship in the human sciences has developed. All depends, for better or for worse, on the particular use made of the past in the present. I intend to explore and defend the view that Baillie may be a remarkably useful guide to some of our contemporary dilemmas.

III

I return to the text. Hundreds of volumes have been written on knowledge and certitude since Baillie's essay. All sorts of subtle distinctions have been recalled. But the balance which Baillie strikes in his first chapter on knowledge and certitude, speaking of the need for confidence in faith without arrogance, remains as apposite now as it was then. The next section on 'The Really Real' is perhaps less immediately cogent. Reality is referred, quite appropriately, to relationships. But the underlying questions concerning the grounds of these relationships remain on the agenda. However, Baillie is right to stress next the communal context of individual experience. I want to look more closely at the next two sections of the argument, in Chapters Four and Five.

Chapter Four deals with the challenge of verifiability. Essentially Baillie's answer to the problem is close to that of some versions of the 'forms of life' approach. He says of different sorts of experience, 'Each is verifiable only by an appeal to the experience out of which it arose.' As far as religious experience is concerned, 'It is by faith that we apprehend the things of God'.(64) Faith is not founded on religious experience, because the experience already contains faith. But faith remains a mode of primary apprehension of God, and it is unnecessary to be afraid of speaking of religious experience at all. Doctrine has to be related to faith. How far is faith itself justified?

'Faith would be lost only if this primary apprehension should itself utterly fail, if we were no longer able to discover any such meaning in any events but came to regard the whole of our experience and everything that has ever happened as a meaningless jumble.' Faith is sustained by what Mannheim called paradigmatic experiences, which are not verifiable by ordinary sense perception. In fact, complete agnosticism is not common.

The comments of Santayana and others 'betray some residual presence "in the bottom of their hearts" of that primary mode of apprehension that is faith'.(81) Further 'there is some ground for believing that failure of faith is frequently associated with some failure or other of the more delicate modes of primary apprehension'. This comment is very close indeed to the main theme of George Steiner's 1990 Gifford Lectures, *Grammars of Creation*. As for doubts about the reality of the external world and of other selves, 'I shall have to confess that for me their ultimate refutation is theological and incarnational'.(85)

These reflections have direct consequences for the issue of 'The Nature and Office of Theological Statements'. What of the characteristics of the sense of God? 'Each of these perceptional modes which goes beyond ordinary sense perception calls for a characteristic response on the part of the recipient.'(89) They require a response. This response is within a long community of faith, in the context of the authority of the Bible.

What is the nature of theological statements? *Deus comprehensus non est deus*. Thomas, Spinoza and Kant are again cited. Of Kant he can say 'he has done more to illuminate our problem than any other single thinker since the middle ages.' Faith is not knowledge. Yet it relates to the practical conduct of life. But we have seen that for Baillie relations with our neighbours are a God-given structure. Therefore for Baillie, Kant's philosophy can be readily integrated with Christian faith.

Hegel provides much less scope for Baillie's reflection. We are dealing here with a period of disenchantment with idealism, associated especially with Hegel. The thought that Hegel might be a fruitful source of intense new doctrinal speculation on the Trinity and on eschatology, in the world of Moltmann and Pannenberg, Rahner and Jüngel, and perhaps most radically and surprisingly of all, in Barth, had not yet dawned. There is a distinct Kantian austerity about Baillie's theology, in contrast to the Hegelian profusion of much of the Continental theology of the next thirty years. If it sometimes fails to reflect the full register of Christian imagination concerning God, at least it respects the mystery. And for Baillie, unlike many of the mystics, the mystery of God is centred in the mystery of Jesus Christ, in grace and gratitude.

John Baillie never produced another systematic christology after the early *The Place of Jesus Christ in Modern Christianity* of 1929, though there are plenty of Christological reflections throughout his writings. Perhaps the fact that he held the chair of divinity, and christology was traditionally taught by his colleague in the parallel chair of Christian dogmatics, or perhaps the existence of his brother Donald's well-regarded *God Was in Christ* may in part have inhibited him. But these are only speculations. Certainly there was scope in his thinking for a fruitful development of the christological dimension of the understanding of God, and perhaps through his devotional writings, of the dimension of the Spirit.

Such developments might have shed light in new directions, unencumbered by the constrictions under which both the disciples of Barth and of the early philosophers of language were to labour in the following decades. We cannot speculate on how this might have been. In the process Baillie's ideas would of course themselves have developed, for he was always sensitive to the state of the art in his field. What we can say is that he made a contribution which remains a benchmark for the future.

IV

I return to some of the epistemological and semantic issues in his philosophical theology. A great deal of work has been done by philosophers since Baillie's time in exploring conditions for truth in statements, and in locating the possible meanings of statements about reality. Debates between realists and anti-realists have reached levels of sophistication unknown to Baillie. There has been, as we mentioned, the rise of the phenomenon of post-modernism in its numerous expressions, and a reaction against the 'foundationalist' views of reality common in the philosophy of the early part of this century. No doubt Baillie would have been a keen observer of these debates, and would have drawn the implications for his theology. But it is worth noting that he had already in 1960 signalled an awareness of the plasticity of the classical laws of physics in drawing attention in several places to the work of Heisenberg. He might have been able to develop the debates surrounding Thomas Kuhn and the structure of scientific inference without great adjustment to the main balance of his theology.

He stressed also that faith involved more than rationalism, and drew attention to the many-layered quality of theological discourse. Here much has been done in recent philosophy as the strait-jacket of early logical positivism has gradually disappeared. In both areas much has been done by Baillie's pupils John McIntyre and Tom Torrance, and by their pupils in the same tradition, though always with a different perspective, since Scottish theology has not been able to afford the luxury of being an insulated or self-sufficient tradition.

Baillie's concern throughout *The Sense of the Presence of God* is to chart the relationship between faith and reason, between philosophy and theology. It is worth comparing this study with more recent work in the field. In seeking a study of a similar high standard and of about the same length, I should now like to look briefly at Ingolf Dalferth's *Theology and Philosophy*, (Oxford, 1988).

Both studies engage in dialogue throughout with the historical tradition in philosophy and theology. Baillie moved from knowledge and certitude to the really real. Dalferth began from the background of the rationality of theology, through theology in the Greek world to early Christian theology. Part I discusses the problem of perspectives, the difference between external and internal views on faith and theology, and the problem of reflection, the difference between faith and theology, between revelation and reflection. Different forms of rationality have been deployed to justify religious belief. Rational theology in the tradition of Aristotle was often preferred to the mythology arising out of religious experience. But Christian faith was more than a rational deduction, and was not easily expressed within the available conceptual options. Christology created a new theological paradigm and generated new modes of reflection.

Part II considers various attempts, all useful but none definitive, to harmonise the perspectives of faith (internal) and reason (external), in Augustine and Aquinas, Luther and the Enlightenment, Schleiermacher and Barth. Barth shows how external perspectives can be interiorised within the language of faith – 'in a very important respect theological attempts to solve the problem of perspective cannot go beyond Barth.' (We may of course reflect on the existence of parallel models for such interiorisation e.g. in Rahner and Tracy. Though Dalferth would doubtless accept that the issues for future development could be framed in alternative forms to that set out by Barth.) The task for the future is to enable translatability between alternative perspectives, in order to move forward, in a harmony without identity.

The third and final part considers how the figurative expressions of faith are to be reconstructed conceptually. Theology 'must explicate the orientational knowledge derived from revelation in a system of doctrines, and elucidate the whole of reality in the light of it. . . . It is the tasks, not their solutions, which constitute the identity of Christian theology'.(x) Theology seeks to be true to God's self-identification in Jesus Christ. All expressions of faith are conditioned culturally, experientially and christologically. Theological statements too must insist on the Gospel of Jesus Christ as the centre of talk about a God who is for us and who is love. Such a perspective 'does not compel adoption of a single version of Christian life but allows for a great variety of Christian existence in the world.'(202) The basis remains the saving love of God in Jesus Christ, appropriated within the life and worship of the Christian community.

It is worth reflecting a little further on the similarities. Both Baillie and Dalferth consider the development of Christian thought within the classic European tradition of philosophy. Both assess the consequences for philosophical theology of the introduction of the new paradigm of Christology into the understanding of God. Both stress the multi-faceted nature of faith, its limitations and also its strength. Both rely on the constructive side of faith to point to ways of coping with the difficulties. At the risk of oversimplification, while Baillie sets out from experience and then qualifies this with christology, Dalferth sets out from christology and qualifies this with experience.

Dalferth's construction clearly owes much to Barth, as Baillie's owes much to Schleiermacher. When Baillie was writing, the exploration of the important differences between these traditions was at the top of the theological agenda. Today the attempt to create a new model beyond Schleiermacher and Barth, taking up the concerns of both traditions, is seen as an important task. To do this through minimisation of the differences would be to waste the creative effort of a century of theological struggle. At the same time, new models may require fresh input from other traditions. The whole question of how to use creatively the various different strands of the European theological tradition in addressing the problems of theology today remains central to the theological agenda.

V

It might be thought that in juxtaposing Baillie and Dalferth I have not yet identified issues which would render Baillie's perspectives entirely obsolete. Deconstructionist and other post-modern philosophies, or perhaps new sociological and anthropological perspectives, create a new agenda for theology. Baillie's framework is simply superseded.

Without question there are important issues for theology which have arisen in the thirty years since Baillie's death. I do not believe that these render all previous work obsolete, but they certainly need to be tackled. And there is a need for a fairly immediate theological response to and development of the most contemporary intellectual issues of the day. Classic theological works always reflect live issues, and this gives them their vitality. But because they are more than simply a commentary on current issues, they do not become dated in the way that instant commentary often does. Indeed, they become themselves a focus for the resolution of issues of current debate, as in Lonergan's study of Aquinas, or Pannenberg's study of Hegel.

Without making immoderate claims, it seems to me that Baillie's work is a kind of classic of a British, and specifically Scottish, approach to theology, in which the evangelical and liberal heritage of the Scottish tradition is both defined and refined. Though he was always aware of developments in current research, Baillie was careful not to let his work depend on any particular current trend or fashion. Open to new ideas, he was prepared to give them time to mature, so that the wheat could be sifted out from the chaff. The last thing that Baillie would have imagined would be that his theology was a final definition of a tradition. But he provided a formidable example of how to produce theology with qualities that endure.

There is a further feature of John Baillie's work to which I wish to draw attention in conclusion, a feature shared with his brother

Donald. I refer to the eirenic quality which characterises much of the Baillie brothers' work, and which enabled them to draw inspiration from many sources, from the theological right and from the left, from different philosophical traditions and devotional traditions, from different cultures. There was nothing here of a fudge, a blurring of issues, of the sort often produced in committee documents. It did not mean that they refrained from adopting a firm point of view, from sharp debate, from agreement and disagreement. But they displayed a rare and remarkable freedom to choose and to communicate with different perspectives. This is not the least of the legacies of John Baillie for anyone willing to attend to what he had to say.

VI

John Baillie was intensively involved with theology. But he did not see theology as divorced from concern with social issues. The 1942 issue of the series of reports which he chaired on 'The Interpretation of God's Will in the Present Crisis', notes that Goebbels had said 'Churchmen dabbling in politics should take note that their only task is to prepare for the world hereafter', leaving the affairs of this world to the totalitarian state. The report then noted that 'It is impossible to read the Bible without realising that there are many issues in our public life which belong to God too'. It had after all been public values, like loyalty, friendship and courage, which had appeared to him to have been significant when doctrines had failed, in his early survey of the attitudes of the troops in the trenches of the First World War, reflected upon in *The Interpretation of Religion*.

Revelation for Baillie came in, with and under, our knowledge of ourselves and of our world. God's self-giving love in Jesus Christ is at one level the clue to the nature of ultimate reality, at another the clue to the understanding of ourselves and the society in which we live. The search for a deeper understanding of God is intimately connected with the search for a society in which God's love as justice, peace and humanity will prevail. Some theologians have illumined our understanding of God without much thought for humane social structures. Others have toiled for a Christian society without too much concern for the complexities of the understanding of God. Baillie reminds us powerfully of the connections. These are neither as indirect as much traditional theology has imagined nor as direct as some modern social theology has decided. But they are there, a challenge to carefully differentiated thought and action.

We have suggested that Baillie's theological position has enduring value for contemporary theological reflection. But of course time does not stand still, and a mere reiteration of his ideas, with a sprinkling of contemporary references and a judicious admixture of the inheritance of the later Karl Barth, would certainly not represent fidelity to Baillie's vision. Baillie was always concerned to remain abreast of the best contemporary thinking, not slavishly imitating but taking cognisance of what seemed to him to be of real value. In the 1990s this would mean taking stock at least of the legacy of Rahner and Schillebeeckx, of Pannenberg and Jüngel, of a wealth of English and American theological writing, and of the whole phenomenon of what is sometimes called liberation theology.

Baillie was well aware that theology has to be done in its cultural context. The post 1918 context was for him a decisive spur to intellectual creativity. The word development is often used in relation to doctrine. It is right to pursue a wise balance, and to respect tradition, as Baillie did. But effective development often calls for more than minor modification. Sometimes a new cultural situation requires decisive change, demolition as well as construction, urgent reappraisal, in order to remain faithful to a living tradition. A tradition unable to engage in energetic criticism and renewal is always in danger of ossification.

It would be comfortable to record that the classic Scottish traditional relationship between theology and church is flourishing and moving steadily ever onward and upward. I am not at all sure that Baillie would have agreed. While the outward appearance of theology and church remains reassuringly familiar, especially on solemn occasions, the gap between tradition and reality in Scotland, as elsewhere, is probably as wide as it has ever been.

For most of the country's population, respect for theology is sometimes tempered by genuine incomprehension, and respect for the church by a lack of a point of contact with their social and their business lives. For many who are single parents, divorced, disabled, unemployed, who do not match the perceived norms of church affiliation, the invitation of the gospel is strangely muffled by our ecclesial practice. The gospel of sheer grace, centred upon the self-giving of God for humanity in Jesus Christ, becomes a coded card which gives access to privileged persons. At this point one might be expected to note that what is necessary is not theory but practice – less theology and more action. Practice is always vital. But I should like to return to theory. Baillie was always aware of the need to think, and to think more deeply in order to reach a deeper understanding of faith. It seems to me in conclusion that Baillie's invitation to pilgrimage is always an invitation to keep thinking, to ask ourselves what we mean by thinking, and to think harder, with honesty and with critical realism.

How are we to forge new perspectives for the understanding of God in an ever changing world? My own suggestion for developing part of the legacy of John Baillie would be on these lines. Faith in God means trust in God for all things. It is from religious experience, as part of our experience of all life, that faith is formed and sustained. This is experience, we claim, not simply of experience but of God. It is based on reflection on experience, ours and that of others throughout history, and it includes other components as well. Faith means trust in one who is in important respects mysterious to us. It involves doubt and uncertainty as well as confidence. Lines of argument come up which count against the existence and activity of such a God. Others count for.

Christians understand God as at once hidden in the process of the natural order and intimately involved in the lives of all individuals in history. God is not aloof from but deeply and personally involved in his creation, he is not present exactly as one human being may be present to another, so that each may be familiar with each other's work and daily engagements diary. God's presence is a hidden presence, not at our disposal for our particular and often self-centred convenience. This is a presence reflected in the numerous world religions, and for Christianity centred in the spirit of the risen Christ.

The God of Christian faith is radically transcendent to the world. In his essential nature love, he is the hidden divine external referent. On him, we believe, the created order depends for its continuing existence. Because of the peculiar nature of divine transcendence, our theories are always underdetermined by the available empirical facts. Transcendence is interpreted in relation to particular cultural traditions within the theological traditions themselves. In this way a multiplicity of often conflicting perspectives arises at the heart of faith's reflection upon God. Faith is driven to deeper understanding among these various perspectives.

God's transcendence is by definition unique. Christians understand themselves to be given some clues to God's nature through grace. Though God's transcendence is unique, our language about it is not. Here is a central paradox about talk of God. In the Biblical narratives, the Old Testament offers accounts of experience of God as the transcendent God who acted through a covenant relationship with his chosen people. Christians have come to trust in this transcendent God through seeing the subjects of the New Testament narrative as the providential culmination of this tradition. They understand God as the self-giving God, whose nature is characterised through the death and resurrection of Jesus Christ.

God's transcendence is a hidden transcendence, and his hiddenness is the hiddenness of presence. The sense of the presence of God is filled out for us in its objective pole through reflection back upon the Biblical understanding of God as Creator and redeemer. The subjective pole in Christian experience is the sphere of forgiveness and reconciliation. Faith believes that God is present to all humanity, even in times of apparent desolation. Wherever there is human suffering God is involved, even if his presence does not prevent the physical or mental consequences of such suffering. Here God is indeed powerless by his own choice, not intervening in the structures of his creation though present to and through them. This powerlessness is emphasised in the parable, which is not just our parable but God's substantially enacted parable, of the experience of God the creator with death on the cross of Jesus. God's power is emphasised in the resurrection of Jesus Christ. Through suffering as through rejoicing, God brings eschatological reconciliation. God is there in suffering, silent identification wherever suffering occurs.

The presence of God may be understood as the presence of the spirit of the risen Christ. Belief in God's providential activity within the created order remains 'against the odds.' The presence of God is mediated through history but may not be 'read off' the course of events, for it is the presence, precisely, of God. God is involved in the history of the created order and in all human history, in general and in special providence. He is engaged in all human life, in its religious and in its secular strivings. He is involved especially in the Judaeo-Christian tradition and in the influence on human life and thought of Christianity across the ages. In this process God uses men and women as the instruments of his love, wherever they are ready to be open to his service. As such God is not simply a matter of academic interest. He is the God who loves, and who continues to invite us to response, to discipleship, to pilgrimage. The theme of *The Sense of the Presence of God* remains a powerful reminder of the debt that Scottish theology continues to owe to the life and thought of John Baillie.

III
CHURCH AND SOCIETY

Chapter 8

THE BAILLIES' CHURCHMANSHIP

Alec C. Cheyne

It was within the context of the Christian Church and (so to speak) for its sake that the Baillie brothers lived their lives and did their thinking.

Even their earliest work manifests a concern for what we might call 'realised Christianity'. At the climax of his argument in *The Roots of Religion* (1926), John reminds the reader that 'To be a Christian is not merely to think this and the other, nor is it merely to do this and leave the other undone; it is rather to have living and personal experience of the fellowship of Christian love . . . It is to know, with all the saints of all the ages, something of the breadth and length and depth and height of the love that was in the heart of Christ and, illumined and strengthened by that knowledge, to place all our reliance upon the love of God and be filled with His fullness'. And the final paragraph of Donald's *Faith in God and its Christian Consummation* (1927), after a reference to the paradox which seems to be inherent in all our speech about God and His purposes, concludes with these words: 'Yet it is not altogether by thinking the matter out, but rather by living it out in daily Christian faith and love, that we shall arrive at a deeper insight. And a book about faith cannot better end than upon this note of hope and expectation'.

The ecclesiastical implications of this emphasis on Christian praxis receive fuller and more explicit treatment in two of the brothers' later writings. The epilogue to Donald's *God was in Christ* (1948) bears the revealing title, 'The Body of Christ', and (in the author's own words) views the landscape thus far traversed 'from the vantage-point of the Church of Christ, since it is the Church that has to tell the story'. Indeed, the closing pages of the book are little short of a rhapsody on

173

the theme of the Church, which is variously described as 'the new People of God, the new Israel, the Ecclesia, the Body of Christ . . . the nucleus of a new humanity . . . God's instrument of reconciliation through the ages.' Still more eloquent is the chapter on this same topic with which John concludes his *Invitation to Pilgrimage* (1942). Arguing that 'It is only in Christ that we can enjoy full communion with one another, and . . . only in our togetherness with one another that we can enjoy full communion with Christ', he offers the following thoughts on Christian community:

> God has apparently done everything He possibly could, short of exercising actual compulsion upon our wills, to prevent us from making our religion a private luxury . . . For what more could He have done than so to order things that men can find salvation only by betaking themselves to one place, where they are bound to meet one another – to the hill called Calvary; by encountering there a single historical figure – the figure of Jesus; by listening to the selfsame story; by reading in the same book; by praying the same prayers in the same Name; by being baptised into the same fellowship and partaking of the same sacred meal – 'all made to drink into one Spirit'; by drawing in fact their whole spiritual sustenance from the same unbroken tradition handed down from age to age? . . . You and I owe all the knowledge of God that we have to our upbringing in the one tradition and our reception into the one fellowship of the Church of Christ, and the only way that is open to us whereby we should bring to others the blessings of that knowledge is by initiating them into the same tradition and receiving them into the same Church.

Against the forceful appeal of totalitarianism, therefore, or what could be represented as the exclusive individualism of the humanist ideal, the Baillies contended (to continue with John's argument) that 'our only hope lies in finding a nobler form of community which will unite us in a stronger solidarity, and call forth a more deep-seated and passionate devotion than even our [wartime] foes can claim to possess.' And so the ardent apologetic of *Invitation to Pilgrimage* closes by taking us, as it were, to the very door of the Christian Church: 'I hope, then, that I have provided sufficient reason why we should all seek the fellowship of the Christian Church, there to rekindle our ideals and rehabilitate them in a solidarity that is stronger than all the solidarities of earth. There may be many that have lately been saying of themselves, with Coleridge's Ancient Mariner,

> this soul hath been
> Alone on a wide, wide sea,
> So lonely 'twas that God himself
> Scarce seemed there to be.

But I hope I have given good reason why they should now decide, again with the Mariner,

> To walk together to the Kirk
> With a goodly company.

> To walk together to the Kirk
> And all together pray,
> While each to his great Father bends,
> Old men, and babes, and loving friends,
> And youths, and maidens gay.

Some idea of the kind of churchmanship to which such finely-expressed convictions gave rise may be obtained by considering three aspects of the Baillies' distinctive contribution to Christian faith and life during the '20s, '30s, '40s and '50s of this century: their style of preaching, their approach to social questions, and the ways in which, as increasingly enthusiastic supporters of the Ecumenical Movement, they sought to do justice to both Catholic and Protestant elements in the Christian tradition as a whole.

(a) Preaching

Since the Reformation, the sermon has never ceased to occupy a central place in Scottish religion. It is hardly surprising, therefore, that some of the Kirk's ablest theologians have also been among its most effective preachers – or that the Baillie brothers should deserve inclusion in the latter as well as the former category.

Donald's reputation as a prince of the pulpit has perhaps stood higher than John's in recent years. That this is so is no doubt at least partly due to the very deep impression made by *To Whom Shall We Go?* and *Out of Nazareth*, two volumes of the younger brother's sermons which were posthumously published in the nineteen-fifties. Each of these won glowing opinions for its author's skill in handling the profoundest and most difficult topics without subjecting his audience to overly demanding dogmatic disquisitions or exegetical exercises. (In this connection, special notice might be taken of the sermon on 'The Glory of the Cross' in the earlier volume, and that on 'The Mystery of the Trinity' in its sequel.)

There is always something indefinable about preaching power, but two aspects of Donald's unusual effectiveness spring immediately to mind. The first is the beautiful simplicity of structure and language which characterises all his work. In this regard, the Memoir by John Dow which forms the prefix to *To Whom Shall We Go?* contains an interesting reminiscence of Donald's early years. 'Donald', we are told, 'knew from the beginning what a sermon should be. I can recall his first student "outline". We wondered what this brilliant philosophy student would produce. A magnificently articulated structure with four heads and many subsections like a class essay? No, we saw on the blackboard a model outline of attractive simplicity and directness. And so his sermons continued all along.' One or two examples from the published sermons should illustrate what John Dow meant. The sermon for Palm Sunday on Matthew's citation of Zechariah 9:9 ('Thy King cometh unto thee, meek, and sitting upon an ass') sub-divides as follows: '(1) What did it mean for the man who first wrote it? (2) What did it mean to the people who thought of it that day, hundreds of years later, as Jesus rode into Jerusalem? (3) What did it mean to Jesus? (4) What does it mean for us, after 1900 years?' The sermon on Election from Matthew 4:18–20 (the call of Simon and Andrew) makes four points: '(1) God always chooses us before we choose Him. (2) God does not choose us because we deserve it. (3) God does not choose us to be his favourites, but to be His servants. (4) When God chooses and calls us, we also have to make our choice.' The New Year sermon on Jeremiah 9: 23,24 takes each clause of its text in turn: '(1) Let not the wise man glory in his wisdom. (2) Let not the mighty man glory in his might. (3) Let not the rich man glory in his riches. (4) But he that glorieth, let him glory in this, that he understandeth and knoweth Me, saith the Lord.' And that on 'Thy Father which is in secret' (Matthew 6:6) expounds what are called 'three simple truths about the spiritual life': '(1) Every man's soul is his own secret. (2) There is One who knows all our secrets. (3) There is One who can lead us into the secret of God.'

Alongside the simplicity bordering on elegance, of the structure and language of Donald's sermons, mention should also be made of their other peculiar strength: the striking appropriateness and practicality of the illustrative material used to drive the message home. Perhaps the most memorable instance of this – though too long for quotation here – occurs in the title sermon of *Out of Nazareth*. But two others may be cited. The first comes from what was probably a Whitsunday sermon on Joel 2:28: 'Your sons and your daughters shall be prophets.' Towards its close, the preacher remarks:

That [the story of Pentecost] is a very old story. Can we translate it into the language and interests of our own modern world? Let us try, with the aid of a little imagination. (1) You take your seat in a railway compartment. In the opposite corner sits a labouring man, reading his newspaper. You look at him, and try to picture the life he leads. A rough, bare life, you think; hard work all day, a quiet pipe in the evening, a football match to watch on a Saturday afternoon; and if he is a particularly decent man, he goes to church once in a while on a Sunday morning. So you sum up his life. Is that all? I wonder. When the man puts down his paper and leans back and shuts his eyes, what is he thinking of? Perhaps he is thinking of GOD. Perhaps he is bringing the light of his faith to bear upon the great issues he has been reading about in his newspaper – labour troubles, party politics, war and peace among the nations. Perhaps he is connecting all those things with the God he believes in. Why not? He is a working man. So was Jesus. And you don't know what depths of Christian faith there may be in the heart and life of that man. (2) Or you go into a shop in the city. A girl at the counter serves you. What does she care for, except to get on as well as she can in her own line, and meanwhile get as much fun as she can out of her wages when working hours are over, a round of rather selfish and empty pleasures filling up her evenings and weekends. And that is all. Is it? It may be. But it may also be that that girl has visions and dreams that would go straight to the heart of Christ Himself. It may be that behind the scenes of what seems a very common-place existence there is a brave unselfish life of burden-bearing for other people, sustained perhaps by the fellowship of the Church of Christ and by a living faith in God.

The second example of felicitously down-to-earth sermon illustration and application comes from a communion address on 'Christ washing the disciples' feet.' It runs as follows:

Through many of the days of our lives, we Christian men and women are pretty uninspiring. We haven't much of the heavenly vision, we let it fall away and come to be content with a very mediocre Christian life. The world has its claims, and we become preoccupied with them; and our neighbours may be difficult, and we become loveless towards them; and our devotions sometimes seem a waste of time, and we become slack about them. And so the days run on, and we are living on a pretty commonplace level, though perhaps we hardly know it, with only half our hearts in the service of Christ. And suddenly perhaps (it sometimes happens at a communion season) we get a glimpse of the poor lives we are living, and we also get a glimpse of the beauty of holiness, the glory of a real genuine whole-hearted Christian life. Yes, and lest we should be discouraged, we at the same time get a glimpse of the wonderful, infinite love of God in Jesus Christ, and His power to help us, and His high purpose for us, that we should be perfect as He is perfect. Then we are fired with holy enthusiasm and aspiration. We resolve in our hearts that henceforth we will not go back nor turn from God at all. Our hearts leap out in faith to God, cast themselves upon His grace, consecrate themselves to His will, dedicate themselves to His service. Our whole hearts go out to Christ our Master. They were indeed His already, but we remember it now in a fresh moment of self-dedication: 'Lord, not my feet only, but also my hands and my head'.

Although John's sermons are not quite so readily accessible as his brother's, a few of them appear in the little collection edited by John McIntyre and published in 1962 under the title, *Christian Devotion*, while others are to be found in the Baillie papers at New College, Edinburgh. In their own way they are as impressive as Donald's: more academic, certainly, in expression, but equally thought-provoking and perhaps more unusual. This is particularly true of a sermon on 'the conversion of the mind' which was preached at Great St Mary's, Cambridge in November 1944. The text – 'Bringing every thought into captivity to Christ' (2 Corinthians 10:5) – gave rise to a meditation on all those thoughts, little ones and great ones, fleeting fancies and ruling ideas, which according to the apostle must be subjected to his Lord. In the course of it, the preacher had much that was both psychologically wise and spiritually discerning to say, including this on our 'little thoughts':

If anybody were to ask you what you have been thinking about today, only one or two things would at first occur to you. They would be what I should call your officially acknowledged thoughts; they would no doubt concern matters of public or professional or family importance, and though not always very weighty, they would at least be eminently respectable. These are the thoughts that pass what the psychologists call the "Censor". But we know that our minds are also at all times giving hospitality to all sorts of unofficial contents. What was in my mind as I waited for the bus at the corner? What visions did I see in the clouds of my tobacco smoke, as I leaned back in my chair to enjoy my after-dinner pipe? What were my thoughts as I lay awake in bed last night? What were my dreams when at last I went to sleep? And what my day-dreams during my idlest waking hours? – If the soul is really dyed the colour of its leisure thoughts [the reference is to an aphorism of Marcus Aurelius] then it is clear that a man is not really converted until his leisure thoughts are converted . . . He [Christ] is . . . as interested in my idle moments as my busy ones, as much in my reveries as my resolutions, as much in my castles in the air as in the more solid edifices of my public and professional life. No man is really Christ's until his day-dreams are Christ's – aye, and his night-dreams too, if they are anywise subject to his control.

Two other sermons from the years immediately after the Second World War take us very near to the heart of Baillie the believing academic. In 1949 (the year before he became Principal of New College) John preached in Belfast on the occasion of Queen's University's centenary celebrations. Taking as his text the words from Luke 12:48, 'For unto whomsoever much is given, of him shall much be required', he offered his hearers a meditation on university life under three heads: its responsibilities, its temptations, and its limitations. What he had to say on the last of these sounds a note which we can recognise as distinctively his own.

'The special responsibilities', he observed, 'all presuppose, and do not in the least degree replace or mitigate the one fundamental responsibility which we share before God with every member of the human race. You and I are men and women first, and students only afterwards, and therefore in the first instance it is exactly the same demands that God makes on us all. Surely our Puritan fathers were right when they said that on the Day of Judgment we shall stand before God, stripped not only of our earthly possessions and dignities, but stripped also of our accumulated learning. They were right, because that is how we stand before God **now**. There is one demand God makes on us all. And we all know what it is. It is to do justly and to love mercy and to walk humbly before Him all the days of our life. It is to give our souls without reserve to His keeping. It is to put our whole trust in the merits of His blessed Son. Nothing else matters until that has been settled. All our high culture, all our specialist knowledge, is so much useless lumber and rubble, except as it is built upon that foundation and used for its further up-building.

A little further on, there occur these typically Baillian phrases: 'the given truth is that we have all of us more knowledge than we are willing to use, or to use for the right ends. There may be much that we do not know, but we all know enough to be better than we are, and to make our society an altogether better thing than it now is.' And the conclusion is as follows:

I believe that we shall stand firm only if, in cultivating our intellects, we take heed not to lose our souls; only if, while becoming ever more complex in knowledge, we remain simple at heart; only if, as sinful men and women, whose lives stand naked in His sight, we first put ourselves right with God, and then bring every thought, all our knowledge and all our learning, into captivity to the obedience of His Christ.

Three years earlier, in the Great Hall of Birmingham University, Baillie preached a sermon on Martha and Mary with the title, 'Only one thing is necessary'. It ended with some phrases which sum up his message not only on that occasion but in many others:

The one thing needful, then, is not money or power or fame or a successful career. And . . . I hope I may assume that it is not what we call culture – a cultivated mind . . . We should be fully prepared for the discovery that the one thing needful is **the same for everybody** – the same for peasant and plutocrat, the same for household drudge and high-born student, and (incidentally) the same also for students and professors. Further, we should be prepared to learn that it is something of an entirely non-competitive character, and in no sense a limited commodity of which somebody else must have less because I have more. What is it then? What is this pearl of great price? What is the one thing needful, the good part which Mary chose? The story puts it quite simply: 'she sat at Jesus' feet and heard His Word.' And that is what it is.

No doubt the Baillies will be longest remembered for their theological work. But at least from the mid-thirties, by which time John had begun teaching in Edinburgh and Donald in St Andrews, they were widely regarded as being among the most distinguished preachers of their generation. Churches and university chapels across the English-speaking world vied with each other for their services; and in the light of the sermons we have looked at, as well as many others, equally worthy of consideration, which are still available in printed or manuscript form, it is not hard to understand why.

(b) Social attitudes

'A concern for social justice lay very near to the core of his understanding of Christian faith.' With these words (to be found in the biographical essay which he prefixed to Donald's posthumously-published *The Theology of the Sacraments*) John introduced the most explicit account anywhere available of his brother's attitude to social questions. He continued as follows: 'He was zealous not only for religious but for political and especially **economic** freedom; zealous also for equality, not in a doctrinaire understanding of it, but in the sense of the removal of the many unjustified inequalities with which he felt our society to have traditionally been burdened. He was thus inclined rather strongly to the left in his political convictions, about which he was always outspoken, though refusing to sell out to any single system of economic doctrine and hesitating to attach any label to his views. He would say, "I don't know whether I'm a socialist or not, but I do certainly think, etc." . . .'

As will presently be seen, there is little doubt that the biographer shared the views he was describing. For both brothers were very much the heirs of a revolution in social attitudes which had taken place within the Scottish Churches during the closing decades of the nineteenth century and the opening decades of the twentieth – the very period in which John and Donald Baillie came to maturity and did a great deal of their most strenuous thinking. In the words of one recent historian, Scotland in the years before the First World War witnessed 'the first significant break from traditional Christian social concern based on an acceptance of the existing order, and which expressed itself in charitable and reclamation work, and a new Christian social concern based on a suspicion or rejection of the existing order, and which expressed itself in social criticism and in more dynamic and radical forms of social action.'

The process of deepening social concern and intensifying social criticism· which had marked the late-Victorian and Edwardian periods looked for a time like being carried even further by the impact of the 1914–18 War, that shatterer of nineteenth-century complacency. As everyone knows, of course, end-of-War hopes soon ran into the sand, and were succeeded, as the '20s gave way to the '30s, by a reactionary mood of disillusionment, cynicism and opportunistic self-interest. Yet the set-back proved remarkably temporary. The onset of the Second World War precipitated another tremendous surge of questioning and heart-searching, not least in the Churches; and among the advocates of reconstruction – along with his contemporary, William Temple, Archbishop of Canterbury from 1942 to 1944 and author of an immensely influential paperback *Christianity and the Social Order* – was John Baillie. A relatively recent homecomer to Scotland (in 1934), he soon acquired a considerable reputation as thinker, teacher and administrator – a reputation which in May 1940, that month of supreme crisis, led to his appointment as convener of the General Assembly's special 'Commission for the Interpretation of God's Will in the Present Crisis'. That body's formidable task was defined as 'to seek reverently to guide the Church in the interpretation of the Holy Will and Purpose of God in present-day events, and to examine how the testimony of the Church to the Gospel may become more effective in our own land, overseas and in the international order.' During the succeeding quinquennium it produced a series of searching and wide-ranging reports which marked a kind of high-water mark in the social thought of twentieth-century Scottish Christianity.

The 'Baillie Commission' (as it was often called) had to handle a vast array of complicated and controversial topics, and sub-committees were set up to deal with Church Life and Organisation, Social and Industrial Life, Marriage and the Family, and Education. But in every case their handiwork was discussed and licked into shape by the parent body, while plenary sessions considered the more fundamental theological problems that arose along the way, together with matter bearing upon the future task of International Reconstruction. Five annual reports were made to the General Assemblies of 1941 to 1945 inclusive – three of these being made available for a wider public by the SCM Press under the titles *God's Will in our Time*, *The Church Faces the Future*, and *Home, Community and Church*. In 1946, after the Commission's discharge, a composite volume, containing whatever seemed likeliest to be of permanent interest in its findings, came out under the title *God's Will for Church and Nation*. Excluded from this compilation was a good deal of material relating to the internal life and organisation of the Church of Scotland, as well as sectional reports on such topics as 'the Feeding of Europe, the Treatment of the Vanquished Nations, our Duty to the Jewish People, Religious Freedom, and so on' which (in the convener's words) had been 'left behind by the march of events'. But what remained – the real legacy of the Commission's work – amounted to a remarkably comprehensive epitome of responsible and forward-looking thought in the Kirk.

John Baillie's personal responsibility for the conclusions reached by his committee cannot, needless to say, be established in any detail.

But those who were acquainted with his confidence in the face of reasoned argument, his ability to combine the over-all view with regard for particularities, his coolly balanced way of presenting a case, and his lucid, rather 'literary' style – as well as his somewhat imperious manner, which allowed little scope to obstructionism or ill-considered dissent! – readily gave him much of the credit for both the form and the content of the Reports. All the more interesting is it, therefore, to discern the general direction in which their analysis of society pointed.

After distinguishing between 'ultimate spiritual principles' and 'secondary and more specialised principles which exhibit the relevance of the ruling principles to the particular field of action in which guidance is needed', the 1942 Report laid down the following 'relevant middle axiom' for the proper conduct of socio-economic affairs: 'Economic power must be made objectively responsible to the community as a whole. The possessors of economic power must be answerable for the use of that power, not only to their own consciences, but to appropriate social organs'. Such a position no doubt appeared startling enough to conservative-minded churchmen like Dr John White of the Barony in Glasgow; but greater surprises were to come. Building on the 1942 axiom, the Commission asserted two years later that 'the common interest demands a far greater measure of public control of capital resources and means of production than our tradition has in the past envisaged.' And it then went on to sketch an understanding of things whose 'left-wing' or 'socialist' tendencies are sufficiently conveyed in four quite radical subheadings: 'The Tyranny of Private Interests', 'The Necessity of a Greater Measure of Communal Control for the Rehabilitation of our Social and Industrial Life', 'The Necessity of Communal Control for the Conscientious Discharge of our World Responsibilities', and 'The Necessity of Communal Control for the Revitalisation of our Democracy'.

Of course, Baillie and his associates were careful not to suggest that the implementation of their proposals would inevitably bring about a kind of heaven on earth. 'Even democracy built round the idea of common control has no inherent certainty of curing our disease', they conceded.

It is sometimes claimed by the secular theorists that such a construction would, by the mere planning of production for use, lead to the guarantee of employment for all, to the removal of the fear of bankruptcy, to the disappearance of the anxiety and bitterness associated with competition, to the limitation of production to socially valuable commodities, and to the equal sharing both of necessary suffering and of the achievements of social development. The Christian will make no such claim, and will indeed doubt whether so Utopian an ideal is ever likely to be realised on earth.

Yet they immediately went on to assert that 'this deeper insight does not release the Christian from the obligation to put forward such claims as **can** be substantiated, viz., that failing a greater measure of public control, and its resolute development as a soil not inimical to the nurture of Christian faith and life, economic chaos must inevitably issue in an end of such limited democracy as our nation has already enjoyed.' And their survey culminated in the following indictment – firmly if cautiously phrased – of the way things were ordered in the industrialised West

What men want is not a Utopia, but an objective that is really obtainable, though not without a hazard; a fair chance without too much disfavour; a cause not devoid of idealism. For such they are still prepared to accept discipline. But our present economic life no longer provides a recognisable objective; it denies a fair chance in life to a multitude of our citizens and a fair chance of leadership to those with the will and capacity to lead; and our democracy lacks a cause such as we can follow confidently and with all our heart.

It was in the 1942 Report, however, that the Commission, while discussing 'The Nature and Extent of the Church's Concern in the Civil Order', delivered its most telling reply to the view that Christians depart from their essential task whenever they turn their attention to questions of social justice.

'Christians have often failed' (so the message ran) 'to distinguish adequately between the religious and political spheres, and have thus misled the Church into making pronouncements on questions which it only imperfectly understood. But we hold it as certain that the greater harm has come about through the opposite error – through the indifference of Christians to the maladjustments of that civil ordering of society in which they like others have a part, and the consequent failure of the Church to bring its own light to bear upon the problems so created. If it were merely that Christians were so exclusively absorbed in heavenly things as to be indifferent to the earthly ills of themselves and their neighbours, that alone would spell a serious falsification of the true Christian temper; but it is to be feared that many of us must plead guilty to the even more damaging charge of complacently accepting the amenities, and availing ourselves of the privileges, of a social order which happened to offer these things to ourselves while denying them to others . . . There can be little doubt that it is to the failure of Christians to realise and act upon these social implications of the Gospel that the present weakness of the spiritual life in our land must in no small part be attributed. We long for a revival of spiritual religion, but there are many who suspect the spirituality to which we call them of making too ready a compliance with a social order that for them means only hunger, slum conditions, unemployment, or sweated labour . . . Selfishness is of the very essence of the sin from which, in any revival of religion, men need to be redeemed; but what if there be no particular form of this sin from which we more need to be redeemed today than a complacent indifference to the social evils that surround our comfortable lives?'

There is some reason to think that the stance adopted by the Commission helped not a little to bring about the almost seismic shift which took place in the social thinking of this country as the War drew to its close – the shift epitomised in the Beveridge Report of 1944 and the inauguration of the National Health Service four years later. Today, politicians and historians alike are deeply divided about the wisdom or otherwise of the revolution that ushered in the Welfare State, and churchmen and theologians would seem to be in similar case. Yet nearly all of them would probably concede that the modern world has not seen very many instances of Christian leaders giving more strenuous – and influential – thought to social and economic problems than was given by the Baillie Commission in the period between 1940 and 1945. For the dominant part he played in its labours, almost as much as for his contribution to 'pure' theology, John Baillie may be said to have earned a secure place in the history of twentieth-century Scottish religion.

(c) Loyalties – Reformed, Catholic and Ecumenical

Seekers for a concise yet comprehensive account of the doctrine of the Church which underlay the Baillies' life's work can hardly do better than turn to the pronouncements of the Commission just mentioned, and in particular to that portion of its 1943 Report which was republished three years later under the heading, 'The Church of Christ – Its True Nature and its Universal Mission'. It is a document which may confidently be taken as presenting the views not only of the Commission as a whole but especially of its masterful convener, whose clarity of thought and incisiveness of judgment are discernible in almost every phrase.

'The Church', it begins, 'is essential to the Gospel. Apart from the fellowship which we are privileged to enjoy within it the Christian salvation and the Christian way of life cease to have real meaning.' Then follows a description, on fairly traditional lines, of the Unity, Sanctity, Catholicity and Apostolicity of this indispensable institution. On its Unity, attention is drawn, in phrases which echo some of the most favoured affirmations of the Ecumenical Movement, to what St Paul had to say on the subject:

> (a) He stresses not only the one Spirit, but also the one body; not merely the spiritual but also the corporate unity of Christ's Church . . . (b) He does not speak of the unity of the Church as an ideal; he speaks of it always as a reality . . . (c) He always thinks of this unity as a sacramental unity, signed and sealed by baptism and participation in the sacred meal.

On its Catholicity, the Commission contends that:

> To say that the Church is one is at the same time to say that it is universal . . . The later usage of the term to distinguish one section of the Church, claiming to be alone orthodox and legitimate, from heretical and schismatic bodies, marks a shift to both a more intellectualistic and a more hierarchical emphasis . . . When the Church was first rent asunder by schism, and throughout the greater part of its subsequent history, the various resultant bodies tended each to exclude the others as not belonging to the true Church of Christ, which they conceived themselves alone to represent; but in our own day a more tolerant and charitable view is widely taken, the former mutually exclusive 'sects' being regarded rather as differing 'denominations', all of which are recognised as 'branches' of Christ's Church. Nevertheless the existence of such disunity within the Body of Christ gives rise to grave problems.

On the Church's Apostolicity, the Commission makes the following comment:

> This means that it is continuous with the Church of the New Testament, and founded on the witness of the Lord's first disciples . . . The means by which this apostolic succession has been maintained and transmitted have, as is well-known, been the subject of much controversy, but of the reality and importance of the succession itself there can be no doubt . . . Like the Ephesians to whom Paul wrote in the first century, we also in Scotland in

the twentieth century, 'are built upon the foundation of the apostles and prophets, Jesus Christ himself being the chief corner stone'.

On its Sanctity, finally, the judgment made by the Westminster Divines that 'The purest churches under heaven are subject both to mixture and to error' leads on to a declaration that

> the Church on earth is a society, not of the just but of the justified, not of the righteous but of the forgiven and the redeemed. And it is itself a redeemed society – no mere collection of redeemed individuals, a society entrance into whose fellowship constitutes the salvation of the individuals comprising it.

Building on these convictions, the Commission went on to discuss a host of related topics; and a few of its more revealing comments deserve to be recorded. Referring to Cyprian's *'extra ecclesiam nulla salus'*, the Report observes, felicitously, that 'The truth is not that adherence to the Church (still less to one branch of it) is a formal precondition of salvation; the truth is rather that entry into the divine-human fellowship is what salvation **means**.' The case for infant baptism is strongly argued, with conspicuous dependence on Calvin and the Westminster Confession, and the Commission's views on both baptism and confirmation are summed up as follows:

> What is important is the recognition that there is an age to which . . . individual testimony is proper, and also an age before which it would be unnatural and hurtful to demand it, and that, nevertheless, those of earlier age may be just as truly beloved servants of Christ, yielding to Him the only kind of service of which they are capable or which at that age He desires from them, and accepted by him as cherished members of His mystical body.

And there is an interesting section on 'The Church of Faith and the Church as Viable Institution', in which the course of thought is traced from the New Testament through Augustine, the catholic orthodoxy of the Middle Ages, Wyclif and Hus, Calvin and the Westminster Divines to the present day, and approval given to J. H. Oldham's assertion (in one of the Oxford Conference volumes of the nineteen-thirties) that 'Within the Church as a organised society the true Church has to be continually recreated.'

Against this doctrinal background, it is possible to discern the presence of two strands, not necessarily compatible with each other in every respect, in the churchmanship of the Baillie brothers. On the one hand, from childhood upwards their outlook bore the unmistakable imprint of Reformed Protestantism, and even in their maturer years they never ceased to be deeply involved in the life of their own communion, the Church of Scotland, and passionately concerned for its welfare. On the other hand, with the passage of time their catholic sympathies came increasingly into view, and from the nineteen-thirties to the nineteen-sixties there can have been few Church leaders who surpassed them in enthusiastic advocacy of the Ecumenical Movement and whole-hearted participation in its activities. Each of these strands – the denominational, that is, and the ecumenical – requires to be examined before a fully rounded picture of the Baillies' contribution to mid-twentieth century ecclesiastical life can be drawn.

First, then, the denominational strand. Enough has already been said, elsewhere in the present volume, about the tradition of Calvinist theology and Reformed churchmanship to which both John and Donald fell heir. It is, however, worth emphasising that throughout their active ministries each played his full part in the life of the congregations with which he was associated, as well as in the proceedings of the lower and higher courts of the Church – kirk session, presbytery and General Assembly. The clearest instances of their congregational and parochial involvement are provided by Donald's ministries at Inverbervie, Cupar and Kilmacolm, as well as his service on the kirk session of Martyrs Church, St Andrews during his tenure of the Chair of Systematic Theology at St Mary's College. Their service on the courts of the Church reached its peak when John, who had already made a unique place for himself as convener of the 'God's Will Commission', was called in 1943 to the office of Moderator of the General Assembly of the Church of Scotland.

Nor is it without significance that under John's leadership the Baillie Commission balanced its world-wide vision with a solicitous regard for the state of ecclesiastical affairs in Scotland itself. The 1943 Report, in particular, looked with an affectionate if critical eye on such matters as the recruitment, supervision and training of ministers, the use of personnel generally, worship, evangelism, preaching. While much in Scotland's religious inheritance was gratefully acknowledged (not least the parochial system, the eldership, and the centrality of 'the preaching and teaching function of the ministry'), quite radical changes were also suggested. Some of these, such as the composition of a new catechism or the revival of 'superintendants' to oversee the work of parish ministers, did not ultimately commend themselves to the Kirk. But others – closer oversight, from the centre, of every aspect of ministerial life; a probationary year for young ministers and a fixed retiring age for their seniors; greater frequency of communion; above all, admission of women to the eldership and even, conceivably, to the ministry of Word and Sacraments – were to be acted upon by the next generation.

Even the Commission's final Report (submitted to the General Assembly of 1945 and entitled, 'The Conclusion of the Whole') sounded a note of unapologetic admiration for the Church of Scotland and its heritage in worship, government and doctrine:

> By the use of the simplest means its mode of worship has, at its best, been marvellously effective in creating a sense of awe and reverence in the presence of God. Its system of government by a series of church courts from General Assembly down to kirk session has so successfully provided for united consultation and action on the national scale that it has served as a model for many communions. Its emphasis on sound doctrine, which has given a certain theological quality to the proclamation of its message, has saved it from absorption in the cultivation of subjective emotion and has enabled it to keep the Faith once delivered to the saints.

Nor did it manifest any inclination to submerge regional peculiarities or denominational distinctiveness in a blandly uniform, icily regular super-Church – as the very next sentences made abundantly clear:

> None of these elements in our heritage must in any wise be surrendered, but they must rather be thought of as constituting the most valuable contribution we have to make to the spiritual enrichment of the greater Church for which we pray. The way to a reunited Christendom is not through a weakening of the distinctive witness of the separate communions, but rather through such a convinced and convincing exposition of each as will prompt those who represent the others to think whether they have not here something to learn as well as to teach. Nor can we hold it desirable that even the completest possible pattern of future reunion should involve the ironing out of all such regional and sectional divergencies of tradition. The disappearance of such diversity of usage and of emphasis could, at least under earthly conditions, only spell impoverishment.

Alongside this denominational strand in the Baillies' thinking, and in a kind of contrapuntal relationship with it, there is always present the other – ecumenical – strand. We have seen how eloquent the God's Will Commission could be in its praise of the Presbyterian heritage; but the eulogy just quoted was immediately succeeded by a solemn warning:

> Such ecclesiastical patriotism is not enough . . . A world situation demands a world church . . . Because the situation facing us all is so largely a single situation, we can meet it only by presenting to it an united Christianity. We desire therefore to record in the strongest possible terms our sense of the duty now laid upon our own Church to throw itself with single-minded zeal into the convergent efforts now being made towards the development of a true ecumenical consciousness throughout the whole Body of Christ.

'A world situation demands a world church.' The simple phrase expresses a belief by which both John and Donald seem to have been inspired throughout their adult years, and it would hardly be an exaggeration to say that neither of them could have loved the Scottish Kirk so much had he not loved the *Una Sancta* more – or equally, at the very least.

Their strongest early stimulus to interest in the world-wide Church apparently came from 'Edinburgh, 1910', the great World Missionary Conference of which John R. Mott was the chairman and J. H. Oldham the general secretary. Indeed, one of the most telling passages in the Baillie Commission's 1948 report on 'Division and Unity' might almost be taken as the convener's recollection – after more than thirty years – of what he had heard at the meetings of that never-to-be forgotten assembly:

> When European missionaries and indigenous Christian leaders of all denominations [in the younger Churches overseas] discuss the main problems of their work, two main questions are constantly raised. The one is whether the younger Churches can thrive and grow as a mere loose federation, each part of which continues to parade as the reason for its separate existence beliefs and practises which it does not itself regard as being of really vital importance. The other question challenges the Churches of the West. Can they hope to carry out effectively their preponderant part in the fuller evangelisation of the world, unless they confront men with a unity of witness and a cohesiveness of effort which cannot be attained so long as present divisions prevail?

For well over twenty years after 'Edinburgh' (at which, of course, they were no more than onlookers), the brothers had little or nothing to do with high-level inter-church relations. Only when John moved from America back to Scotland, and Donald from the parish to university teaching did their growing reputation as theologians combine with their enthusiasm for Christian unity to bring them to prominence in the ecumenical movement. Then – half way through the nineteen-thirties, that is – they both began to be actively involved in what was familiarly known as 'Faith and Order'. Donald played a major part in the Edinburgh Conference of 1937. John, who had been a member of the British Council of Churches almost from its inception in 1942, was elevated to the Central Committee of the World Council of Churches at the first great Assembly held in Amsterdam in 1948. The second Assembly, at Evanston in 1954, appointed him – a signal honour – one of six World Presidents. Donald's last important contribution to the Movement was made at Lund (Sweden) in 1952; but for a long period before then he had served as Chairman of the sub-commission on *Intercommunion,* whose Report with that title was published the previous year.

On the home front, Donald was serving as convener of the Church of Scotland's Inter-Church Relations Committee at the time of his death; while John was a member of the panel of Church of Scotland negotiators who, after protracted conversations with their counterparts in the Church of England, the Scottish Episcopal Church and the Presbyterian Church of England, produced the controversial 'Bishops Report' in 1957.

It is not so easy to detect John Baillie's hand in what was officially called 'Relations between Anglican and Presbyterian Churches' as in the Reports of the God's Will Commission. For one thing, he was not the permanent chairman of the Church of Scotland panel. (Donald had originally been nominated for that office, but he died in October 1954. Thereafter it was held in rotation by John, Professor William Manson and Dr 'Archie' Craig.) For another, the Church of Scotland representatives were much less free to determine their agenda, and much more circumscribed by their association with the delegates of other communions, than the Baillie Commission had been. Nevertheless, one cannot but think that Scotland's most eminent theologian – Principal of New College, ex-Moderator of the General

Assembly, and one of the leading figures in the World Council of Churches – must have had a very considerable say in the debates and been in general agreement with the conclusions as published.

Throughout the conversations, a central question had been whether oversight in the Church should be conciliar (as in Presbyterianism) or individual (as in Anglicanism): by presbyteries, synods and General Assembly, or by bishops. In the end of the day – and there were some at least who regarded this as a notable break-through – the negotiators opted for an answer which could be described as embodying the 'both . . . and' rather than the 'either . . . or' approach. In the words of Archie Craig's biographer, Elizabeth Templeton, they recommended that 'all the participating churches should recognise this diversity and catholicity of the Church, and should show that recognition by incorporating in their structure the modes of participation which were cherished by both. Thus, the Presbyterian churches would modify their structure in the direction of adopting a form of episcopacy which was acceptable to both, while the Anglicans would develop a form of order in which ordained ministry and laity would be more closely linked in decisions concerning government and doctrine.'

The fateful recommendations, acclaimed by some as displaying statesmanlike resourcefulness and denounced by others as either devious or hopelessly unrealistic, were published at the end of April 1957. They were then subjected – in Scotland, at least – to lengthy and intensive scrutiny; and it was not until the General Assembly of 1959 that the Kirk's final verdict was given. By a majority of 34 in a total vote of 566, the fathers and brethren declared their opinion that (in the phraseology of the victorious motion) 'the proposals are unacceptable in that they imply a denial of the Catholicity of the Church of Scotland and of the validity and regularity of its ministry within the Church Catholic.' The tide of inter-Church rapprochement, which had been flowing in Britain ever since the nineteen-thirties, looked as if it might be on the turn; and the immediate resignation of Dr Craig, the convener of the Assembly's Inter-Church Relations Committee, seemed to mark the end of an era.

At the time of the crucial debate John was out of the country on a lecture tour in the United States, and one can only guess at the difference which his presence might have made. In any case, it has to be remembered that his best days were now in the past: in 1954 he suffered a devastating blow in the death of his brother, and two years later he retired from New College at the age of 70. On his return to this country he soon became seriously ill, and his depleted energies were spent in the preparation of his Gifford Lectures rather than on the defence of a lost cause. We may, however, be sure that he deeply regretted the failure of the most determined effort yet made to end the age-old conflict (one of the most profound and protracted in Christian history) between Episcopacy and Presbytery, and that if anything could have disturbed the remarkable serenity of his last days it would have been a realisation that the high-water mark of ecumenical advance in the twentieth-century had already been reached – and perhaps passed.

Like his brother, Donald spent a great deal of time and energy in the committee work which was (and is) such an essential part of the Movement. Yet conceivably his most enduring service to the cause was made neither in the Inter-Church Relations Committee of his own denomination nor on the Faith and Order Commission of the World Council of Churches but through the pages of his posthumously-published lectures on *The Theology of the Sacraments*. There, more than anywhere else, is made plain his passionate desire to reconcile warring traditions and, if possible, to blur the edges of conflicting orthodoxies – to attain (as he says in the opening chapter) 'such a deeper and more Christian understanding as could draw together those of the Catholic and those of the Protestant tendencies.'

The first half of the book considers the nature of the sacraments in general, and their place in the life of faith, before going on to outline a defence of infant baptism which – while drawing on the insights of recent New Testament scholarship – does not deviate in essentials from traditional orthodoxy, Catholic or Reformed. Throughout these chapters the author's conciliatory temper is constantly in evidence. After discussing whether the principle of a 'sacramental universe' (so dear to theologians from the Catholic wing of the Church) can be reconciled with the Reformed belief that a sacrament depends entirely on the divine word of promise, he concludes: 'It is only when God speaks and awakens human faith that the natural object becomes sacramental. But this can happen to material things only because this is a sacramental universe, because God created all things visible and invisible.' On the relationship between faith and grace in the sacraments, he rejects both the *ex opere operato* doctrine of medieval Catholicism and the popular Protestant view that the efficacy of the sacraments depends on the faith of the receiver, preferring to say that they operate **through** human faith. 'God', he writes,

> works faith in our hearts. He bestows on us the gift of faith, gaining our confidence, not forcing it. His graciousness overcomes our mistrust, His grace creates our faith, so that when we come to Him it is really **our** faith, and we come willingly. In order to bring about this end He uses means – words, smiles, gestures, symbolic gifts, which we call sacraments.

He will have nothing to do with the 'Catholic' view of the sacraments as extensions of the Incarnation (arguing that incarnation did not go on for ever, but came to an end, and that since then the divine Presence is with it in a new way through the Holy Spirit working in the Church by means of Word and sacraments); but at the same time he is concerned to emphasize that Incarnation and sacraments are inseparable. 'It is', as he puts it,

> of the essence of the Christian sacraments that they could not have existed but for the historical incarnation. They have continuity with it, they point straight back to it, they can only be celebrated in the redeemed community which it created, and only by those who within that community have been set apart in a succession which connects us through the ages with the origins of our religion.

It is, however, in the second half of the book that Donald Baillie's eirenic spirit is most potently obvious. 'Doubtless', he remarks at the outset to his Presbyterian audience,

> we should all wish to criticise the Anglo-Catholic doctrine of the eucharist . . . But if we cannot get beyond a merely negative criticism, we may, when asked for our doctrine of the Lord's supper, be found offering a stone instead of bread . . . Surely if we criticise Roman or Anglo-Catholic eucharistic doctrine it will be because we claim that we have some better and richer and higher belief about what God gives us in the sacrament. But I am not mainly concerned to criticise the doctrines of those other traditions, or to make a gulf between them and our own views: I would be much better pleased if it emerged from my discussion that they and we are nearer to each other than we sometimes think.

After an interesting examination of 'the **dramatic** symbolism of the Lord's supper, in which sympathetic use is made of modern Catholic insights and stress laid on the fact that 'the eucharist consists of a complex of elements, words and actions', he goes on to ask, 'What are the realities that it [the sacrament of the Lord's supper] ought to symbolise if it is to be true to the Gospel of Christ? . . . What are the things signified?' His answer involves a discussion of two 'elements of meaning' that have traditionally been found in the sacrament: the Real Presence and the eucharistic sacrifice.

On the former, he begins by reminding his audience that when we speak of God's presence (whether in creation as a whole, to humankind, to believers, or in the sacrament) we must think not of a local or spatial presence but of a spiritual, personal relationship. In their theology of the sacraments, he contends, all the Churches, Lutheran and Reformed as well as Roman and Anglo-Catholic, have periodically offended against this principle; indeed, he draws attention to certain crudities in thought and expression of which one or other has been guilty. Nevertheless he believes that every tradition at its best has clearly desired to avoid such crudities, and that in essentials they are all of one mind and heart. His considered – and reconciling – judgment, therefore, is as follows:

> Surely what the Roman doctrine at its best is struggling (with a very inadequate metaphysic) to conceive is the reality and objectivity of the divine presence as something prevenient and given, if only we will accept it.
>
> And surely it is the same truth that we Presbyterians are endeavouring to express in a safer and surer way when we say that in the sacrament Christ is as truly present to the faith of the receiver as the bread and wine are to his outward sense. 'Present to the faith of the receiver' – that is the most real presence conceivable for a divine reality in this present world. The most objective and penetrating kind of presence that God can give us is **through faith** . . .
>
> This does not mean that somehow we conjure up the divine presence by believing in it, or that we produce the faith out of our own resources, and that in response to our faith God gives us His presence. Nay, God is prevenient, and faith depends on His actions; He calls it forth, and that is His way of coming to dwell in a man or a company of men. That is what He does when He uses the symbolism of the bread and the wine, the words and the actions, to give Himself to us in the sacrament of the Lord's supper.

On the eucharistic offering (perhaps an even more controversial aspect of sacramental doctrine), Baillie is concerned to suggest that,

apart from Rome, the difference between the Churches 'may not be
so extreme as is often supposed.' Both the 39 Articles of Anglicanism
and the Westminster Confession of the Reformed tradition repudiate
the sacrifice of the mass. Yet their violent reaction against medieval
abuses and superstitions should not prevent us from asking whether
the sacrament of Holy Communion, properly and fully understood,
does not contain something of the element of oblation, sacrifice or
offering – and Baillie's answer is a very positive one.

Among the arguments which he advances are these. First, all our
worship may be regarded as an offering to God (cf. the Shorter
Catechism on prayer as 'an offering up of our desires unto God').
Second, while condemning the 'Popish sacrifice of the mass' the
Westminster Confession itself speaks of the communion service as
including 'a **spiritual oblation** of all possible praise to God'. Third,
'while in the sacrament it is profoundly true that God is the giver and
we are the receivers, it is also true that receiving God means giving
ourselves to Him; and indeed . . . God's giving of Himself to us and
our giving of ourselves to Him are but two ways of describing the
same thing'. Fourth, in offering our prayers, our praises and ourselves
to God we also recall Christ's self-offering, without which we can do
nothing – and of course that sacrifice of His, made once on Calvary,
is also an **eternal** sacrifice, having 'its divine, "vertical" relation to
every moment of our sinful human history'.

Gathering together his entire argument so far, Baillie believes that
we may say something like this on the whole subject: 'in the
sacrament, Christ Himself being truly present, He unites us by faith
with his eternal sacrifice, that we may plead and receive its benefits and
offer ourselves in prayer and praise to God.' And if we **can** say that,
'then surely we Protestants, we Presbyterians, have our doctrine of
eucharistic sacrifice'. Whether or not this interpretation finds favour
with theologians from the warring traditions is perhaps doubtful,
though it is impressively supported by references to Roman and
Anglo-Catholic writers, as well as John Calvin, which purport to show
that the gulf between 'Catholic' and 'Reformed' may not be so wide as
is often imagined. At any rate, we may hope for general sympathy with
Baillie's passionate anxiety, revealed again in the closing pages of *The
Theology of the Sacraments,* to minimise the differences and maximise
the agreements between the various ecclesiastical traditions. Stressing

the corporate nature of the communion, and alluding – with some pride? – to Archbishop Brilioth's opinion that the Reformed Churches' most distinctive contribution is to be found in their emphasis on the note of fellowship at communion, he ends with a statement and a question: 'Unless our sacramental service maintains at its very heart that note . . . of Christian solidarity, of fellowship in the body of Christ, it will not be the holy communion at all . . . May it not be that both the doctrine of the Real Presence and the doctrine of the eucharistic offering begin to come right and to take their true shape when they are controlled by the idea of the sacrament as a corporate act of the one body of Christ?'

'Christian solidarity' and 'fellowship in the body of Christ': in phrases such as these may be found the most convincing explanation open to us of the ecumenical commitment of both John and Donald Baillie. But no study of their churchmanship should end without a word concerning the personal piety which inspired and sustained it. In John's case, it is necessary only to refer to his *Diary of Private Prayer* (which since its first publication has sold more than 125,000 copies in Britain alone, and has been translated into over a dozen languages), and to Isobel Forrester's reference in 'A Cousin's Memories' to the 'three clear focal points' in his study at Whitehouse Terrace, in Edinburgh: 'the big, uncluttered desk by the window', 'the big leather chair, where he often sat far into the night reading' – and 'the prayer desk by the window with its little pile of well-worn versions of the Scriptures and of devotional books' where in solitude he read and thought and worshipped. As for Donald, John Dow's reminiscence of him has a few sentences whose truth many contemporaries have confirmed:

> Nothing but the peremptoriness of an early morning train could persuade this man of God to omit family worship at his own table. Unfailingly by 8.40 each week day down College Street came the familiar figure in the old mackintosh, gown over his arm, often looking pale, ill and fragile, on his way to morning prayers in the University Chapel: others might steal a morning off, he with more excuse would not. When he was a worshipper, there was the promptness of the real participant in every response. When he himself conducted the service, we could not but be drawn closer by the tones of his voice and the sincerity of his words. In addressing a newly-ordained minister his final stress was on the danger of letting carefulness about many things cut out the one thing needful – personal devotion.

The brothers' last substantial contribution to scholarship, John's Gifford Lectures, ended by quoting Kierkegaard's dictum that 'Truth is not an objective statement about certain relations of being, but a form of existence in which such relations are actualised', followed by a prayer from Henry Vaughan. It was a peculiarly appropriate conclusion; for in their preaching, their application of the Faith to social issues, both to the Church of Scotland and to the ecumenical Christian community, as well as in their theological teaching and writing over some forty years, John and Donald Baillie provided their contemporaries and posterity with an impressive example of theological truth embodied in life, and piety and learning harmoniously combined.

Chapter 9

JOHN BAILLIE
AND 'THE MOOT'

Keith W. Clements

Studying the work of important theologians usually involves discovering what they read, and when. Less often do we attend to the company which they kept with other living people, but even just to know what that company was, and its circumstances, can be illuminating. It is well worth asking what may be learned about a Scottish Professor of Divinity who over a period of seven years – most of them under the tiresome and distracting conditions of wartime – would travel two or three times a year to the south of England, to spend a long weekend in discussion of Christianity and the future of western society. Those bare facts alone indicate an unusual degree of commitment to a long-term goal. When one learns that the company he kept on these occasions included figures as diverse as a Jewish sociologist of international reputation, a poet and literary critic approaching the peak of his output and fame, a university grants administrator, a professor of philosophy, and a writer-cum-farmer of unconventional (not to mention communistic) tendencies, our curiosity is properly aroused. Such was the company John Baillie kept, from 1938 until the end of the Second World War, in the discussion group known as 'the Moot'.

The Moot was the child of J. H. ('Joe') Oldham (1874–1969), the extraordinary pioneer of so much ecumenical endeavour and organization, British and international, for the greater part of the first half of this century. Oldham was a Scot whose formative student years at Oxford had been moulded by the dynamic, evangelical and interdenominational Student Christian Movement of the 1890s. After missionary service with the YMCA in India he took the theological degree at New College, Edinburgh, and then studied in Germany

199

during 1904–05. For a time he was intending for the ministry of the United Free Church of Scotland but it was as a lay person, albeit always in full-time work for the churches, that he was to use his considerable organizing abilities and impressively original mind. He was appointed Organizing Secretary for the Edinburgh Missionary Conference of 1910, now by common consent the first great landmark in the modern ecumenical movement, becoming the secretary of its Continuation Committee out of which was born the International Missionary Council, and founded and edited the *International Review of Missions*. Gifted with exceptional clarity both of perception and expression, he was to prompt much vital new thinking on the missionary calling of the world church in relation to social and political problems, especially as he saw that the colonial era in Asia and Africa must inevitably be drawing to a close. Of his many writings none was to be more timely, or prophetic, than *Christianity and the Race Problem* (1926).

By the 1930s Oldham was wrestling with the challenge which modern secularism was posing for the Christian mission, and he was among the first to insist that that mission consists not of drawing the world into the church but in releasing the power of Christian faith – especially through its lay members engaged in their secular responsibilities – into the world. From 1934 he was chairman of the research committee of the Universal Christian Council for Life and Work, another of the three great strands of the ecumenical movement which were to flow into the formation of the World Council of Churches, and so was intimately involved in preparations for the Conference on 'Church, Community and State' at Oxford in 1937. By now the totalitarian threats to any kind of 'Christian' order in society were all too real, both from the neo-pagan fascist regimes of Europe and the atheist Marxist state of Soviet Russia. Oldham was among those in Britain who believed that political resistance to such external threats would not by itself save western society. Rather, British society was itself in deep crisis without any adequate spiritual foundation for tackling its social, economic and political problems. Oldham voiced these fears publicly in a letter to *The Times* just after the Munich crisis in 1938, touching many nerves and prompting a number of others to identify with his sense of impending catastrophe, for example T. S. Eliot whose reflections took the form of his lectures *The Idea of a Christian Society.*

Meanwhile, Oldham was already engaged in his own response. For some time, evidently, he had been convinced that the necessary changes in society, if they were to have a genuinely moral and spiritual basis, would have to be pioneered by committed people in key positions of secular responsibility in politics, the civil service, the universities, education, broadcasting and the like. Such people would need a strong sense of loyalty to a common ethical enterprise. They would, in short, need to constitute an 'order' devoted to the renewal of the common life. Such an order would in turn require, at its core, a group of thinkers committed to wrestling with basic social issues in the light of Christian faith.

Thus was conceived Oldham's idea of 'the Moot'. Today it would doubtless be called a 'think-tank', witnessing to the take-over of our social imagery by a pseudo-technology. But the name 'Moot', deriving from the Old English word for an assembly, a *meeting-point* for debate, was not an incidental choice by Oldham, and here is already a clue to a probable reason why Oldham invited John Baillie to be one of the original members: a shared interest in the personalist philosophy of encounter and human relations, exhibited especially by such continentals as Buber, Ebner and Grisebach. For Baillie, this had been a relatively recent discovery during his time in the United States. It was under his encouragement that the English translation of Buber's *Ich und Du* was undertaken by one of his New College students, Ronald Gregor Smith, in 1937, and the personalist strain becomes fully evident in Baillie's *Our Knowledge of God* of 1939, which includes lecture material from 1936 onwards. Oldham, for his part, had had his interest in the personalist approach kindled as early as his student days in Germany during 1904–06. *Real Life is Meeting* was his own paraphrase of Buber's dictum *Alles wirkliche Leben ist Begegnung* – and formed the title of his influential little book of 1942.[1] But the relationship between the two Scotsmen in fact went back nearly thirty years to the Edinburgh Missionary Conference of 1910 at which the young Baillie, then a student, was one of the stewards.

Significantly, the other 'academic' theologian – in the sense of being a university teacher – whom Oldham invited to join the Moot

---

[1] *Real Life is Meeting* (Christian Newsletter Books, Sheldon Press, 1942)

was likewise Presbyterian and likewise a powerful exponent of the personalist element in religion: H. H. Farmer of Westminster College, Cambridge.[2] Farmer, however, was able to attend only two early meetings of the group and had to withdraw. Also Presbyterian was the young Eric Fenn, who had been Oldham's organizational assistant at the Oxford Conference of 1937, and who was now working for the BBC Religious Broadcasting Department. The younger generation was also represented by the Anglican Alec Vidler, editor of *Theology* and from 1939 to be Warden of St. Deiniol's Library, Hawarden. Vidler had been staunchly Anglo-Catholic in his early days of parochial ministry in Newcastle and Birmingham, but was becoming steadily more sympathetic to the neo-orthodoxy of Barth and Brunner, and the social teaching of Reinhold Niebuhr.

Baillie, Fenn and Vidler in fact were the only ordained clergy among the regular attenders of the Moot. Theological ability, however, was also amply to be found among the lay majority, and not only in Oldham himself. H.A. Hodges (1905–76), Professor of Philosophy at Reading University since 1934, and an authority on Wilhelm Dilthey, was a devout Anglican deeply interested in the interaction between philosophy and religious belief. T. S. Eliot had made a notable conversion from agnosticism to orthodox Christian faith and its high Anglican version, and, as noted above, and as evidenced in much of his poetic and dramatic output from the early 1930s onwards, was exploring the proper spiritual basis of social and cultural, no less than personal, life. Baillie, himself a lover of poetry, had been on friendly terms with Eliot since his New York days. At the farthest imaginable pole from Hodges and Eliot, temperamentally as well as in intellectual outlook, was John Middleton Murry (1889–1957), a highly unconventional figure who had worked variously as journalist, art-critic, wartime censor and editor of diverse journals, and was now a farmer leading an experimental community which practised a kind of Christian communism. His leading passions were the practical application of the teachings of Christ, a radical understanding of democracy, and the works of Katherine Mansfield. Yet another strand of Christian lay commitment was represented by (Sir) Walter Moberly (1881–1974), who after a

---

[2] Cf. H. H. Farmer, *The World and God* (Nisbet, London, 1935)

distinguished career in teaching political science and as administrator at various universities, was from 1935 Chairman of the University Grants Committee. He had also, as a young Oxford don, contributed two essays to the controversial volume of liberal theology *Foundations,* in 1912.

Perhaps Oldham's most surprising invitation, yet one which had immensely creative results, was to Karl Mannheim (1893–1947) who as a Jewish refugee from Nazi Germany had been teaching at the London School of Economics since 1933. His writings on the sociology of knowledge had already set an immense agenda in that field, but he was equally concerned with the empirical problems of society and politics, and especially with the increasingly planned nature of modern society and the values motivating it.

The Moot first met on April 1–4 1938 at High Leigh in Hertfordshire. It was to meet two or three times a year, usually over a weekend, until just after the end of the war, the venue being in London, or more frequently Oxford or somewhere in the home counties. The pattern remained consistent. Before each meeting, papers written by one or more members of the Moot, but sometimes commissioned from other writers or extracted from their works, would be circulated and these provided the substance for discussion in the meeting. The meetings were chaired by Oldham himself, and were necessarily highly disciplined affairs in view of his acute deafness, each member having to speak in due order so that Oldham could position himself alongside each in turn. The minutes, usually taken by Oldham's wife Mary, are virtually verbatim accounts of the proceedings.

The most frequent attenders, apart from Oldham himself, were Hodges, Mannheim, Moberly, Vidler and Fenn. The agenda was usually firmly set by Oldham. The most industrious producers of papers were Hodges and Mannheim – especially the latter, some of whose papers were in fact on the way to becoming books such as *Man and Society in an Age of Reconstruction.*[3] Hodges, Mannheim, Moberly and Murry also did most of the talking.

John Baillie was present at that first meeting in April 1938 and for the next four meetings, until the one held September 23–24 1939. By

---

[3] *Man and Society in an Age of Reconstruction* (Routledge and Kegan Paul, London, 1940)

that time of course war had broken out, and soon afterwards Baillie went to work for the YMCA in France. On his return in 1940 he visited the United States, and not until the twelfth meeting, August 1–3 1941, was he in attendance again. The fact that while in France he kept up correspondence with the Moot – often from uncongenial huts and canteens – indicates his commitment, as does his readiness to rejoin the group when opportunity returned. There was a shorter period of absence during his Moderatorship of the General Assembly of the Church of Scotland, when he missed three meetings from June 1943 to January 1944. In all he attended eleven times.

'He was one of the more silent, but also one of the most regular, attenders at the Moot', recalls Eric Fenn of John Baillie.[4] The first meeting must have impressed him with the feeling that, for all its mixed oddity of outlook, with its intellectual and ethical passion the Moot was going to offer a rare opportunity for anyone seeking to relate Christian belief to the public world of the day. Oldham himself had prepared a paper on the growing divorce between the churches and the contemporary world. As usual when groups of this nature meet for the first time, this session was occupied a good deal with hearing how each member in turn saw the situation. Moberly made the first comment on 'The Nature of the Crisis' – 'the whole traditional relation between church and community had become unreal – e.g. the Coronation or the contrast between a Cathedral city and a new housing area.' Baillie spoke second, and readers familiar with his life and thinking in the later 1920s and 1930s will not be surprised at his own, more historically conscious, assessment:

> John Baillie said that he had been conscious in previous experience of similar groups prior to the Oxford Conference that the real problem was not the relation of church to community but a division in the Christian mind itself. He instanced the conflict in his own mind on going from a Calvinistic home in a Highland village to a school based on humanistic culture. What is the relation of the secular to the sacred? How far was humanism as it has emerged from the Renaissance wrong? How far was it fine and right and something to be woven into a future Christian tradition? On the other hand, how far does the fault lie on the side of religion which may need cleansing?[5]

[4] Interview with author, 25 October, 1991
[5] Minutes of 1st. Moot Meeting, p. 2. These and other 'Moot Papers' are largely unpublished and held in private collections.

This, Baillie's first intervention in the Moot, was to prove typical of his overall contribution, in its display of large-scale consciousness of the history of western thought, its tensions peculiarly experienced by him personally. The larger historical frame of reference did not come naturally to all members of the group. This first meeting, and several subsequent ones, spent much time discussing Oldham's scheme for an 'Order' of lay people in key public positions committed to working for a more Christian society. The discussions became tortuous: How many members would be required? How would they be recruited? What kind of publicity should be produced? What relation would such an Order have, either to the churches as such, or to the Moot itself? But the Order never materialised, and at times the Moot seemed on the point of degenerating into yet another coterie of intellectuals forever talking about action but never acting. The discussions however were not completely sterile. What did emerge, less ambitious but with genuine influence, were the *Christian Newsletter* of the war years and, subsequently, the Christian Frontier Council. Baillie, while not dissenting from any of the proposals for joint action, does not seem to have been particularly interested in them. His interventions came largely when the more fundamental questions of the nature of society, Christian ethics, and the questions facing belief in God, were on the agenda, and his own priorities as they appeared to him in April 1938 were stated in his last contribution in that meeting:

> John Baillie said that he had had in mind for some time the writing of a book on 'The Theory of Ethics'. For the last two and a half centuries Ethics had been taught as detached from Theology and Religion. It was necessary to return to the view of Ethics as part of Theology – in fact to the Theology of Sanctification.
> The most important problems seemed to him to be:
> (a) The Christian judgment on the Renaissance and the relation of Christian faith to modern thought.
> (b) Education [6]

To the Moot as a whole, the challenge of the fascist and communist totalitarian revolutions, and the future of western democratic society in an age of social and economic planning, were of rather more immediate moment than the Renaissance. Baillie accepted this. But

[6] ibid., p. 13

his Moot interventions were typically to be in the form of qualifying and cautionary remarks in response to what he regarded as oversimplifications or one-sided statements of a case. Nor was this due solely to his historical perspective on ideas. Karl Mannheim of course brought his central European background with him, as did Adolf Löwe, another exile who attended several meetings. T. S. Eliot, however anglicized he aspired to be, could not entirely expunge his American beginnings. But Baillie had a wider first-hand experience of the contemporary western world and acquaintance with its thought, than had any of these. He had both studied in Germany and taught in America, and had remained closely in touch with theological movements on the continent and with the German church scene in the Third Reich. In an age of undeniable crisis, when many souls (including some in the Moot) were periodically gripped by a near-apocalyptic dread of imminent catastrophe, he was inclined neither to romanticize nor to write off prematurely the western world and its intellect. He therefore played the role of the wise one who, in the midst of vigorous debate on any particular topic, gently suggests that there may yet be more to be said. That subject might be the significance of Rousseau for the modern debate on totalitarianism and democracy[7] or the relations between the 'scientific' and 'Christian' world-views (where Baillie was critical of Hodges for implying that these were the only options on offer,[8]) or the relative effects of totalitarian and democratic societies on academic activity, or a comparison of Chinese and Greek understandings of law in relation to religious belief.[9]

There is not space here to do more than mention some of the areas where such input was made by Baillie. He was at his most assertive, however, when there impinged on the discussion the issues of the relation between belief in God and moral values, and between the moral values held specifically by Christians and those held more widely in society. Obviously for a group such as the Moot, setting itself to consider how Christian understanding and commitment might be instrumental in achieving wider social change, this was a

[7] Minutes of 2nd. Moot Meeting, p. 7
[8] Minutes of 14th. Moot Meeting, p. 3
[9] Minutes of 16th. Moot Meeting, p.15

vital underlying question. Thus for example at the second meeting, in September 1938, where much time was spent discussing just what might be meant by a Christian ordering of society, Baillie takes John Middleton Murry to task for positing too uncritically in his introductory paper the 'national church' idea. The national church, said Baillie, might easily become nationalistic, and Murry seemed to ignore the fact that 'the Christian Church was necessarily wider than the single nation and should not confine its mission to the nation'.[10] Perhaps here one can detect strong echoes of Oxford 1937. Equally, Baillie was critical of Hodges, who had stated that 'to conceive and work for a Christian social order can hardly be the central task, because a social order is not an end in itself; it is merely an adjustment of social forces which is maintained for the sake of an end beyond itself.' This, to Baillie, was 'misleading and ambiguous as it confused ethical and technical elements',[11] that is, it could lead to the effective banishment of all ethical considerations from 'social' issues. Rather, Baillie thought more useful a distinction made by Oldham between two uses of the term 'society': first, the 'full and distinctive personal relationship', and second, 'the series of social arrangements necessarily only partially personal.' The first meaning gave a criterion for judging how far the second was in accord with Christian principles – but both were to be assessed ethically. Indeed, on several occasions in the course of Moot meetings, Baillie expressed unease with the apparent acquiescence of some Christian thinkers in a divorce between ethical principles and their concrete applicability. For the first meeting, Oldham had posited four aims of national life as springing from Christian faith, though not exclusive to Christians:

1 A social environment in which the gospel of God's love for men is reflected at least fitfully in the actual conditions of their lives and does not appear in relation to those conditions a hollow mockery.

2 A society in which men can live as those who are responsible to God and consequently to one another, and who have, therefore, the opportunity of responsible choice.

3 A society in which there is a growing realisation of our membership one of another.

[10] Minutes of 2nd. Moot Meeting, p. 2
[11] ibid., p. 3

4 A society which has a respect for the claims and rights of all men, as created by God and the objects of His redeeming love, and has as its purpose the service and well-being of mankind.[12]

This met with the general criticism from the Moot, that similar statements had often been made before but with little result. Oldham replied that merely as a statement it had no value 'but if the formulation had a group of people behind it with a common understanding of what it meant then the situation would be different.' Baillie's concern was with concreteness:

> John Baillie said that his difficulty arose because the statement was not detailed enough and he felt that the Church ought to be able to give much more detailed guidance. Such guidance was available on the basis of the Catholic doctrine of natural law and the Protestant doctrine of the orders, a full statement of which was to be found in Brunner's book Das Gebot und die Ordnungen. The suggested formulation here was short and vague. Our question was what to show in place of the mediaeval statement of natural law and deistic theory of the rights of man which stood essentially on the same ground.[13]

Baillie also made clear that, as with Murry and Oldham, his understanding of a Christian society had to do with the actual behaviour of people and institutions within it and the ethical principles governing that behaviour. William Paton, making his only appearance at the Moot, had queried the Moot's anxiety about a 'Christian society' and had pointed to, for example, the strength of the established church and its place among public institutions, the significance of the recent coronation, and so forth. Baillie retorted brusquely that these examples 'showed rather a concordat between the State and the Cultus, whereas Murry (and by implication he himself) was pleading for public policy directed by Christian principles. The fact was a deep separation between politics and religion.'[14]

Some members of the Moot, such as T. S. Eliot, were concerned to underline the necessity for Christian dogma as the only sound basis for any Christian morality, social as well as individual. Others like

[12] J. H. Oldham, 'The Problems and Tasks of the Council on the Christian Faith and the Common Life', p. 5 (Moot Papers)

[13] Minutes of 2nd. Moot Meeting, p. 14f.

[14] ibid., p. 11

Murry were concerned to identify the specifically Christian ethic. Baillie did not disagree with either approach, but was more phlegmatic. He protested

> against making the distinction between the converted Christian with a theological background and the unconverted in society too sharp. The real distinction seemed to him to be between those who accepted Christian dogma and those who did not, and this was a matter of gradation. We had a society in which some took a negative view (atheism) and others a full catholic conception. The bulk of the population lay in between these two extremes. He was anxious to keep this fluid in thought because of the growing tendency to believe that one cannot support ethics without a dogmatic background. . . [15]

Shortly afterwards, in response to Alec Vidler's question on how much more is meant by a Christian society than a just or a good social order, Baillie said that 'if a social order was good then it was surely also Christian. Christianity could not be better than the good.' Vidler commented that he meant good 'in the sense of as good as possible in a fallen order', to which Baillie replied that this implied the distinction between revealed and natural law. Two orders were connected with Christianity, one of which was less than ideal, as implied also in the two terms 'Das Gebot' and 'Die Ordnungen'.[16] But Baillie was always uneasy if it was ever implied that the 'less than ideal' represented a compromise on fundamental moral order and values. This came out particularly sharply at the thirteenth meeting in December 1941 during discussion of Karl Mannheim's paper: 'Towards a New Social Philosophy. Part II: Christian Values in the Changing Environment.' Mannheim's paper opens by declaring its central problem to be the finding out 'how the application of fundamental Christian values changes with the social and economic environment' and proceeds to explore how, if at all, social planning can be applied to religion, conceived of as those primary experiences from which radiate the most formative motivations of morality and spirituality. Inevitably, he has to deal with the basic issue of the relation between religion and morality – an area which John Baillie had of course trodden thoroughly in his own way. Mannheim remarks that an immoral man may sometimes have deep religious

[15] ibid., p. 16
[16] ibid., p. 17

experience and that through the notion of natural law Christianity has acknowledged 'a form of uprightness not permeated by the spirit.' Mannheim continues:

> . . . Christian values will have two facets – one which makes the values appropriate devices for regulating behaviour and conduct, and another which is the expression of a basic experience that need not be shared by everybody. To put it another way, I should say that given values can always be interpreted both as a means of adjustment to real situations and at the same time as types of adjustment which are directed by a particular *Weltanschauung*. The adjustment character of values makes it imperative that they should change to a certain extent with the social environment.[17]

The Christian, says Mannheim, differs from the pagan in that '[he] does not want simply to adjust himself to the world in general, but only to do so in terms of an adjustment which, among many other possible adjustments, is in harmony with his basic experience of life.'

It was Baillie who made the first comment on Mannheim's paper, stating frankly that 'he felt the paper gave no real answer to the question, what were the values of democratic civilisation and what was the nature of the specifically Christian interest in those values.' Mannheim replied saying that it was useless to draft a list of democratic values such as had derived from the French Revolution. A new start had to be made by a community of persons working at concrete issues and his paper had been intended only to prepare the ground for such a task. The discussion quickly seized on Mannheim's whole notion of 'adjustment'. Gilbert Shaw asked whether the attitude of the Early Church to slavery was an instance of 'Christian adjustment'. Baillie intervened to suggest that this provided an instance of 'compromise with a deeply rooted system', prompting Mannheim to say that 'as soon as the early apocalyptic hope faded, compromise, or adjustment became inevitable.'

But to equate 'adjustment' with 'compromise', was felt by Walter Moberly and Gilbert Shaw to be skirting round the whole area of nature and grace. Baillie strongly agreed: 'There were two types of adjustment – the first involved the interpretation of a clear principle in relation to circumstances, and the second involved the

[17] Mannheim's paper, p. 8

compromise of Christian principles to fit external needs. We badly
needed a Natural Theology . . . to help disentangle the issues'.[18]

Next day Baillie determinedly returned to the point, expressing
puzzlement on 'the need to adjust values to circumstance. He held
that the Christian had certain eternal values to which circumstances
must be adjusted, though these values must be implemented and
expressed differently in different ages.'.[19] T. S. Eliot and others felt
that Mannheim's paper as a whole met this point. Baillie however
insisted 'that there was a fundamental difference of view here, though
it might not be proper to discuss it now.' Mannheim attempted to be
conciliatory: 'To him and to those who shared his approach, eternity
was not an archetype of higher value than change. In application
there would be little difference, and with the admission on his part
that no concrete expression of change could be perfect there was
ground for co-operation.' Baillie was unconvinced – 'the difference
lay not in our attitude to Plato, but in our attitude to Christianity and
the immutability of God.'

It was Walter Moberly who had the last, and in the circumstances
perhaps the wisest possible, word on the issue in suggesting that the
main question concerned the amount of variation permissible in
values in determining what might need to be done. 'If we took the
empirical approach some variation was inevitable.' Maybe that
remark best indicates what was going on in this discussion: an
encounter between the sociologist assessing the possibilities of co-
operation on concrete enterprises, and the philosophically-minded
theologian primarily exercised by 'how things are' in time and
eternity.

That 'fluidity' between specifically 'Christian' values and the wider
moral values of the human community, which Baillie had earlier
spoken of as important to maintain, was for him a consequence of the
hierarchy of values whose ultimate source and end is God. For the
Moot meeting of September 1942 Baillie wrote a short paper,
'Approach to a Deduction of Values'.[20] It is quintessential Baillie, in
its reassertion of the Shorter Catechism's dictum that man's chief end
is to glorify God and enjoy him for ever, and that 'All other values are

[18] Minutes of 2nd. Moot Meeting, p. 3
[19] ibid., p. 5
[20] Moot Paper dated 28 August, 1942

valuable only as contributory to this ultimate end; whether directly or indirectly; whether as means to its attainment or as ingredients in its fulfilment.' But equally these 'other values' *do* serve the end of ultimate divine glorification, the *summum bonum,* whether as knowledge of the world, communion with others or aesthetic enjoyment. So also all service must ultimately be conceived as the service of God, while at the same time its various forms are to be allowed their relative independence.

There is no record of subsequent discussion of this paper by the Moot. It probably received an appreciative nod, but as should have become clear by now the members of the group would long have been familiarised with its approach by Baillie's presence and verbal interventions. But we have yet to mention what were effectively Baillie's two most substantial contributions to the Moot. Typically, these did not involve attempts to inject his own views, but rather invitations to attend to the thought of two other contemporary figures whom he considered of vital significance for any serious address to the issues of Christian belief and ethics in the modern world. Also characteristically for John Baillie, they were two figures who would not usually have found sympathetic ears on the same head: Jacques Maritain and Karl Barth.

Jacques Maritain, the French Roman Catholic philosopher and social thinker, had set out his vision for a reintegration of Christian belief and social order – as integrated as was the mediaeval world-view but on a quite new post-Enlightenment and post-Marxist Catholic basis – in his *True Humanism* which appeared in English in 1938.[21] It was a call for Catholic social morality to find embodiment in secular movements for genuinely communal and personalist forms of social order, with equal justice given to freedom and mutual responsibility. Maritain's approach was already appealing to Oldham, for Maritain no less than Oldham saw the Christianisation of society as being the vocation of the Christian *laity* in their secular involvements, and Oldham's vision of an 'order', largely of Christian lay people committed to social change was at the very least strongly reinforced, if not actually inspired, by Maritain. Oldham was therefore anxious that the Moot in its early stages should read and digest Maritain. John

[21] *True Humanism* (Geoffrey Bles, Centenary Press, 1938)

Baillie for his part had little need of persuading, for one can imagine the approbation with which he would have read passages such as:

> The Christian knows that God has infinite resource; and that the possibilities of good faith stretch further than men imagine. Under many names, names which are not that of God, in ways known only to God, the interior act of a soul's thought can be directed towards a reality which in fact may truly be God. For, as a result of our spiritual weakness, there can easily be a discordance between what in reality we believe and the ideas in which we express to ourselves what we believe, and take cognisance of our beliefs. To every soul, even to one ignorant of the name of God, even one reared in atheism, grace offers, at the moment when the soul deliberates with itself and chooses its final end, grace offers as an object, something to be loved above all things, under whatever name the soul describes such an end to itself . . .[22]

In fact Baillie cites these words as part of an extended quotation in *Our Knowledge of God* (p. 93f).

At Oldham's request Baillie wrote an extended review and critique of *True Humanism* for the third Moot meeting in January 1939,[23] and all members of the group were invited to submit in writing their own comments. Baillie was chosen as interlocutor precisely because it was felt he was not predisposed to agreement with Maritain by the tradition to which he belonged. One might therefore expect Baillie to be offended by Maritain's negative stance towards the Reformation and Karl Barth: '[Barth's] error is that of Luther and Calvin: it is to think that grace does not vivify'.[24] Some British reviewers, notably John Macmurray who detected in the book an elevation of Aristotle to being a source of Christian revelation, reacted strongly against such sweeping anti-Protestant polemics and were consequently inclined to dismiss Maritain altogether. Baillie however provided the Moot with a patient and fair exposition of the book, and argued that Maritain's criticisms of the Reformation and its heritage were not central to the main thesis. In a telling and revealing paragraph he states:

> Doubtless I am less opposed to Aristotle and the Greek tradition than were Luther, Ritschl, Harnack, Karl Barth . . . yet I am very conscious of the wrong-headedness of the kind of synthesis between Aristotelianism and Christianity attempted by St Thomas. But I do not feel that Maritain's

[22] ibid., p. 56
[23] John Baillie, 'Paper on Maritain's True Humanism' (Moot Papers)
[24] Maritain, op. cit., p. 63

proposal in this book depends on Aristotelianism or Thomism at all. Naturally enough he makes the most of the Thomist affinities of his proposal . . . But though I myself reject the Thomist doctrine of the *analogia entis* as an account of the nature of our knowledge of God (and each winter devote four lectures to its demolition!), the use here made by Maritain of the principle of analogy appears to me quite innocuous. I am able, then, to accept the meaning of this book while still holding . . . to the essential justice of the Reformers' protest. . . If I agree . . . with most of Maritain's criticism of Luther and Calvin in this book, it is because what he here criticises is not the true heart of their witness, namely their doctrine of justification by faith, but their conceptions of freedom and the relations of sacred and secular . . . [25]

With Maritain's diagnosis of the inner history of Europe, of the fatal modern divergence between secular and Christian ways of thought, Baillie expresses himself in profound agreement, as well as with many of Maritain's perceptions of the contemporary scene, such as that while communism is avowedly atheist in its ideology, there is more *practical atheism* in fascism. But Baillie's final question is: How far has Maritain really succeeded in attaining a clear view of the relation of religion to politics? Here, once again, Baillie reveals himself troubled by the apparent tendency of contemporary Christian ethicists to countenance a necessary *compromise* between the ethics of the kingdom of God and the possible ethics of the kingdoms of this world. Maritain, in Baillie's view, champions this doctrine of necessary compromise – but at least is preferable to Reinhold Niebuhr (erstwhile colleague of Baillie at Union Seminary, New York and for whom Baillie had a continuing and warm personal regard) who insists that in the political sphere the goal is justice, with all its finite constraints, and not love. But *why*, asks Baillie, is this necessary compromise required? He finds no clear answers in Maritain. It is significant that at least he was troubled by the question which, albeit in rather different form, has re-emerged in those recent Third World liberation theologies which express dissatisfaction with the 'eschatological reserve' of western political theologians in the Niebuhr tradition. Whatever this final doubt, there is no question that Baillie's overall endorsement of Maritain greatly encouraged the Moot in its endeavour to find a new social manifestation of Christian belief.

[25] Baillie, op. cit., p. 2

Baillie's role in the presentation of the thinking of Karl Barth to the Moot was less direct, but still crucial. It has been said that Baillie's own commitment to neo-orthodoxy reached its peak during the war years.[26] In fact he never represented himself as a 'Barthian' in the Moot, but on many occasions we find him saying something like '. . . whereas Barth would say. . .' He was concerned that the group should take seriously the challenge of Barth's radical questioning of all human endeavour, even and especially religiously-inspired endeavour, in the cause of the kingdom of God, not necessarily because he identified wholly with Barth but because he felt that his questions needed to be answered. Of the other members of the group, probably only Alec Vidler and Oldham had really thorough and first-hand acquaintance with Barth's (and Brunner's) work. Baillie's concern was strategic as well as strictly theological. He was increasingly concerned that the general theological tone of the Moot might find itself out of touch with the younger generation of theologians such as he was nurturing at Edinburgh, who by now were rejecting the liberalism of their parents and taking their cues much more from neo-orthodoxy. If the Moot wished to be heard by the likely leaders of Christian thinking of the future, they likewise would need some familiarity with Barth and company.

Baillie felt this particularly at the twelfth meeting of the Moot in August 1941, at which a paper by H. A. Hodges, 'Christian Thinking Today' was discussed. Hodges in effect called for a new Christian philosophy, which could provide the basis for a Christian 'world-view': 'Our problem is . . . in the first instance that of making Christianity visible again, of making people see it as a really possible way of looking at things. Secondly, we have to try to make it intelligible, so that anyone who sees it as a vision may be able to assure himself that it is not a mirage. . . [The] third task which faces us [is] to make it desirable; to discover and draw out those impulses in humanity which it is meant to satisfy, so that the relevance and excellence of it may be felt.' Red rags to Barthians indeed! At Baillie's suggestion, it was decided to invite a younger theologian of the neo-orthodox school to write a response to Hodges' paper, and on Baillie's

[26] E.g. D. S. Klinefelter, 'The Theology of John Baillie: A Biographical Introduction', *Scottish Journal of Theology*, 22, 1969, p. 430

recommendation it was Thomas F. Torrance who met this request with seventeen erudite and closely-argued pages[27] which gave no quarter to the desire for a 'cast of mind' as a basis for Christian belief. 'The idea of an *anima naturaliter* contradicts almost every page of the New Testament. A Christianity with a Cross at its heart is not by any means something congenial to the natural man'.[28] 'Christianity is the message of death and resurrection. To return to an old analogy, if the spokes of the wheel actually converge at a point, then the wheel is useless. A hole must be knocked clean through them before the axle may bear upon them in such a way as to make the hole useful and significant. So Revelation knocks the bottom out of our natural thinking to make room for a new orientation'[29]

In turn Hodges wrote a reply to Torrance, 'Barthianism and Christian Thinking' The paper is a stout defence of the role of philosophy in the knowledge of God. Hodges was somewhat irritated by what he considered to be exaggerated claims by Torrance at certain points to fundamentally different approaches between them, and even more offended at apparently being dismissed as a 'liberal'. Barthianism, suggested Hodges in turn, is yet another manifestation of the widespread desire to find certitude through dogmatism. 'It has the weakness of all dogmatisms, that there is no reason why anyone else should believe what it says.'[30]

Torrance's paper was discussed at the next Moot meeting in December 1941. Baillie felt it necessary to explain his choice of Torrance as respondent, in that he was an extreme but a true representative of the younger theologians, and that most younger ministers (of the Church of Scotland at any rate), while they might not agree wholly with him, would none the less 'agree in substance.' Hodges referred to his reply to Torrance, and his original paper, and was anxious to stress that between the two of them there was greater common ground than might be supposed. All Hodges felt he was trying to do, was to identify the human elements in the communication of belief. In fact what emerged out of this discussion – in part thanks to Baillie's pointing out that the central issue as with

[27] Thomas F. Torrance, 'Christian Thinking Today' (Moot Paper)
[28] ibid., p. 13
[29] ibid., p. 15
[30] H. A. Hodges, 'Barthianism and Christian Thinking', p. 5 (Moot Paper)

Maritain was the relation of Christianity to culture – was agreement on a highly interesting project, to be undertaken largely by Hodges, on the nature and role of those 'archetypes' of religious significance in society. While some members of the Moot may have felt that the Barthian intrusion into their agenda was a waste of time, in fact it sharpened greatly their recognition that easy continuities could no longer be taken for granted in the communication of belief in modern society.

John Baillie thus played a self-effacing but significant role in the Moot, less concerned to thrust his own views than to widen and deepen the discussion to include the contributions of past and present figures whom he considered it was essential to hear. Without him, the Moot would have been deprived of the counsel of a good deal of the Christian theological tradition and the contemporary theological scene. It might also have been less earthed in mundane experience. Sociologists, even, do not always have the last word about society, and Baillie had his ear very close to the everyday sounds of the world, whether in the huts and canteens of the YMCA in France or in the streets of Edinburgh.

What, in turn, did Baillie gain from the Moot? Clearly, a good deal of satisfaction and stimulus both intellectually and in terms of fascinating human company. When Oldham finally closed the Moot down – the death of Karl Mannheim in 1947 was the decisive factor in this decision – Baillie no less than the others must have felt that a uniquely enriching chapter in his life had come to an end. Indeed, apparently, Baillie objected to this termination on the grounds that the Moot was unique in the kind of freedom it enjoyed, in not being beholden to any church or quasi-ecclesiastical body, neither the British Council of Churches nor even the Christian Frontier Council.[31] But there was also a particular need which the Moot served to meet as far as Baillie was concerned. At the last session of the thirteenth meeting in December 1941 the members shared their individual experiences of conflict and difficulty in the areas being addressed by the Moot. Baillie for his part confessed to 'The difficulties involved in formulating official advice to the Christian

---

[31] I am indebted to Professor Donald MacKinnon, who joined the Moot in its later years, for passing on to me this observation of the late Kathleen Bliss, and for other helpful comments and reminiscences concerning the Moot and John Baillie.

Churches on the interpretation of the Will of God in the present crisis'.[32] What he was referring to most immediately, of course (though not exclusively), was the Commission for the Interpretation of God's Will in the Present Crisis, set up by the General Assembly of the Church of Scotland in May 1940, and of which he was Convenor. There was of course much common interest between the Moot and the Commission on many issues, and in the Commission's Report of 1942 some sections of Chapters I and II, dealing with the breakdown of secularism, the need for true community, the ideals of western civilization, the problems of applying New Testament teaching and Christian values in a 'mixed' society and the meaning of 'middle axioms', are to say the least strongly redolent of the Moot papers and discussions.[33] An enquiry into the actual relationship between the Moot and the Commission would involve some detailed source-criticism, but there can be scarcely any doubt that Baillie found the Moot a rich and encouraging resource for handling and furthering the investigations of the Commission under his charge. It is also impossible to imagine that the writing of *The Belief in Progress* and *What is Christian Civilization?* did not owe much to those years in the Moot.

It was in fact through its resourcing of the particular responsibilities and initiatives of its individual members, that much of the external influence of the Moot took effect – the writings of Mannheim and Hodges in their respective fields of sociology and philosophy for example, or Vidler in social theology, or Eliot, Moberly and Oldham himself in the *Christian Newsletter* and the thought-provoking writing which that journal inspired and enabled from many other pens during the war years. Baillie likewise both gave to and gained from the Moot and by his participation in this imaginative exercise of restoring Christian engagement in social thinking, enabled his Church to gain from it too.

The papers and minutes remain, for our enrichment in our own time. Of course nothing that survives in the files can ever completely convey what must at times have been brilliantly flashing moments of verbal encounter and insight, passionate refutation and conciliatory

[32] Minutes of 13th. Moot Meeting, p. 121
[33] For the collected reports see *God's Will for Church and Nation* (SCM, London, 1946)

openness. Not to mention wit. One would have given a lot to have heard the tone of voice in which John Baillie, at the second meeting, apropos of the deep contemporary separation between politics and religion, drily remarked that people were 'equally horrified at hearing Christianity doubted and at seeing it practised.'[34]

[34] Minutes of 2nd. Moot Meeting, p. 11

Chapter 10

GOD'S WILL IN A TIME OF CRISIS: JOHN BAILLIE AS A SOCIAL THEOLOGIAN

Duncan B. Forrester

Was John Baillie a Social Theologian? The obvious answer might be an unqualified 'no'. Only one of his books – *What is Christian Civilization?* (1945) – can count as social theology. Very few of his articles are on Ethics or Applied Theology. It is true that many of his writings from *An Interpretation of Religion* (1929) show much concern with questions of value, and the relation of religion and ethics, but this was no more than was characteristic of liberal theology of the time. On the face of it, John Baillie has far less claim to the title of social theologian than his friend, Reinhold Niebuhr, or Reinhold's brother, Richard, let alone contemporaries such as William Temple, A. D. Lindsay, Emil Brunner and Karl Barth. Craig Beveridge and Ronald Turnbull may well be right in linking him with John Macmurray, Ronald Gregor Smith and John Macquarrie as 'Scottish Personalists',[1] in pointing out that John Baillie had a steady concentration on moral experience right up to *The Sense of the Presence of God* (1962), and asserted the reliability of moral knowledge: 'There is nothing of which I am more assured than that I must not exploit my fellow man in the interest of my own selfish gain, but must seek his own good no less than my own and, if need be, at the cost of my own. There is nothing of which I am more assured than that Hitler was wrong in attempting to exterminate the Jews.'[2]

[1] Craig Beveridge and Ronald Turnbull, *The Eclipse of Scottish Culture* (Polygon, Edinburgh, 1989), p. 99
[2] *The Sense of the Presence of God* (Oxford University Press, 1962), p. 28

But this in itself does not make John Baillie a social theologian. For that side of his contribution we must look elsewhere.

It has often been said that the Baillie brothers divided the nascent Ecumenical Movement between them: Donald was an influential and long-term member of 'Faith and Order', whereas John served on 'Life and Work' and later became a President of the World Council of Churches. John's 'Life and Work' involvement took him to the 1937 Oxford Conference on Church, Community and State, where he shared in leading the opening worship and worked in the section on 'Economic Order' along with R. H. Tawney, John Macmurray, T. S. Eliot, V. A. Demant, Paul Tillich, and Reinhold Niebuhr, among others. He was already by that time a prominent and respected member of an influential, international and ecumenical network of people concerned with church and society issues, and had a distinguished and stimulating roll call of dialogue partners. And he was an heir of the developing tradition of ecumenical social ethics in which his friend and fellow Scot, J. H. Oldham, was the pioneer. 'Life and Work', and the Oxford Conference in particular, influenced him profoundly and ensured that as a social theologian he was to be radical and ecumenical. The Oxford preparatory documents, particularly W. A. Visser 't Hooft and J. H. Oldham's volume, *The Church and its Function in Society*[3] shaped his thinking about society decisively and provided the base for the development of his own thought during the war years.

Baillie's time in North America ensured that he knew Social Gospel liberalism from the inside, but he was notable among theologians in America at the time in his awareness of the challenge to liberalism presented by the new 'dialectical theology' or 'theology of crisis' from the continent of Europe. Baillie did much to mediate a critical account of what was going on in German theology to the English-speaking world. He was himself closer intellectually to Brunner than to Barth. His close friendship with Reinhold Niebuhr, from Baillie's arrival at Union Theological Seminary in 1930, encouraged Niebuhr towards a more serious and less pragmatic and episodic approach to theology. As Richard Fox, Niebuhr's biographer, puts it, 'Baillie

---

[3] Visser 't Hooft and J. H. Oldham, *The Church and its Function in Society* (George Allen and Unwin, London, 1937)

vindicated theology in Niebuhr's eyes because he preserved the standard liberal starting point of man's own natural potential for knowledge of God. Here theology was not a flight to other-worldly dogmatism, but a discriminating study of concrete man in relation to the transcendent. Baillie's thoughtful critique of Barthianism showed Niebuhr the way to the more sophisticated level of theological reflection that he reached during the 1930s.'[4] But as a continuing dialogue partner, Niebuhr also influenced Baillie. In particular, the impact of Niebuhr's Gifford lectures on *The Nature and Destiny of Man,* delivered in Edinburgh in 1939, is everywhere evident in the productions of 'The Baillie Commission', which I will discuss later.

John Baillie's social theology, like so much other significant theology, was elicited by a crisis. In his case the crisis was not simply the Second World War, although that was seen as the climactic explosion of problems and uncertainties which had been building up for several generations. The war was a symptom of Christian civilization, as he argues in his little book, *What is Christian Civilization?,* published at the end of the war; a crisis as profound and devastating as any in recorded history. Just as the First World War stimulated Barth to make a clean break with his liberal past, and convinced him of the political significance of theology and of the theologian's unavoidable political responsibility, so the Second World War crystallized Baillie's mind and made him endeavour with a new earnestness to discern the signs of the times.

In recent days *The Kairos Document*[5] from South Africa has helpfully analysed the nature of a kairos/crisis and the kinds of theology that it may elicit:

> A crisis is a judgement that brings out the best in some people and the worst in others. A crisis is a moment of truth, that shows us up for what we really are. There will be no place to hide and no way of pretending to be what we are not in fact. At this moment in South Africa the church is about to be shown up for what it really is. No cover-up will be possible.[6]

A kairos/crisis is 'the moment of grace and opportunity, the favourable time in which God issues a challenge to decisive action.' It is the stimulus which may enable us to hear the Word of God and

---

[4] Richard Fox, *Reinhold Niebuhr* (Pantheon, New York, 1985), p. 125
[5] *The Kairos Document* (British Council of Church, London, 1986)
[6] ibid., p. 1

distinguish it from the noise with which it is surrounded. But three kinds of theology may result, according to the authors of the Kairos Document. What is called 'state theology' is simply the vindication of the status quo and the ideological justification of the powerful. Secondly, there is 'church theology' which puts near the top of its concerns the institutional security and the unity of the church. Church theology, the Document says, may criticise a system such as apartheid, but it does so in a cautious and formal way, repeating slogans about reconciliation and non-violence, but never endangering the institutional interests of the church. It appeals to the powerful to bring about reforms, but 'God does not bring his justice through reforms introduced by the Pharaohs of this world.'[7] It does not understand the mechanisms of injustice and oppression and in fact gives 'tacit support to the oppressor, and a support for brutal violence'. The preferred option of the *Kairos Document* is 'prophetic theology'. Based on social analysis and biblical insights, it will *denounce* sin and *announce* salvation. But to be prophetic a theology must name the sins and evils which surround us and the salvation we are hoping for. Prophecy must name the sins of apartheid, injustice, oppression and tyranny in South Africa today as 'an offence against God', and point to the measures which must be taken to overcome these sins and the suffering that they cause.[8] On the other hand, prophecy will announce the hopeful good news of future liberation, justice and peace as God's will and promise, naming the ways of bringing this about and encouraging people to take action.[9] Now, just as Barth developed in the 1930s a *Church Dogmatics* which was both challengingly prophetic and profoundly ecclesial, so I would want to argue that John Baillie, through the work of the Baillie Commission, developed a theology which affirmed that the church, in its being as well as in its statements, was called to be prophetic, and rejected by implication the common suggestion that only individuals can be prophetic. And in its method the Commission strikingly anticipated the U.S. Catholic Bishops' Pastoral Letters on War and Peace and on the Economy. The Baillie Commission pioneered a process of widespread consultation and discussion over a period of years as part

[7] ibid., p. 12
[8] ibid., p. 15
[9] ibid., p. 18

of the way in which the Church made up its mind on what had to be said in this particular kairos.

The Commission for the Interpretation of God's Will in the Present Crisis was established in May 1940, 'the hour of our nation's greatest peril', by the General Assembly of the Church of Scotland under the convenorship of Professor John Baillie – hence it was popularly known as the Baillie Commission. Its task was, on the assumption that 'God is speaking to mankind in the solemnising and chastening events and experiences of our day, to seek reverently to guide the church in the interpretation of the Holy Will and purpose of God in present-day events, and to examine how the testimony of the church to the Gospel may become more effective in our own land, overseas and in the international order'. The members were a representative selection of the leadership of the church, including several well-known theologians, together with a minority of distinguished elders with varied experience of public life. There were no women members. There is no doubt that John Baillie's influence was paramount, especially in the general orientation of the Commission and the method it adopted in its work. Unfortunately, details of the Commission's discussions and the drafts of reports are not available, so we have to rely on the printed reports and the minutes of Assembly discussions. Internal evidence may suggest that key passages in the reports were written by Baillie himself, and he was happy to put his name to all the reports, to 'possess' them and to defend them vigorously in public. These reports were delivered annually to the Assembly from 1941–5 and attracted considerable attention and stimulated much discussion outside as well as within the Church of Scotland. Several study guides were published; the main reports were circulated widely by SCM Press, and in 1946 a volume, *God's Will for Church and Nation*[10] containing extracts from all the reports was issued and was widely circulated.

Baillie was clear about the nature of the crisis. In his speech presenting the Report of 1942 he said: 'Long-established prejudices are being disturbed. Long-cherished opinions are being revised. People are ready to raise new questions and think new thoughts. The old watchwords are being re-examined'. People are asking questions

---

[10] *God's Will for Church and Nation* (SCM, London, 1946)

about freedom, about democracy, about justice and community. Everyone knows that the life of Britain, and indeed of all Western nations, is going to be very different after the war. There is an opportunity for the Church to make its voice heard and make a contribution to the discussion of the future. 'Surely ...', he concluded, 'it is time that the Church was beginning to make its voice heard. These are matters in which moral and spiritual issues are profoundly concerned; surely the Church has something to say about them for the guidance of its people'.[11] In this time of crisis for the Church and for Christian culture there is a need for the renewal of faith and for openness to new ideas. But above all, the need is for the discernment of the signs of the times, so that the Church may respond in faith to what God is doing in the world. This task was an evangelical one: how to understand and proclaim the Gospel in current circumstances. The Gospel cannot be separated from Christian values, nor can either be presented in abstraction from the problems of the world. 'How', asked John Baillie, 'can man be drawn to a Gospel whose one practical expression is serving Christ by serving the least of his needy brethren, if we preach it in abstraction from the crying needs of the poor and oppressed of our own society?'[12]

The Baillie Commission Reports addressed theological issues quite directly, and see theology as the foundation of the whole project. The central controversy is understood as being about the doctrine of man. The liberal optimism of the 19th century having faded, it is necessary to re-affirm that 'any ordering of society must in the last resort be governed by some conception of the chief end of man, and, if the Christian view of this end be the only true one, then the first thing needful for the solution of the world's problems is an enlargement of the number of those who live by the light of it'.[13] Such a 'true anthropology' would emphasise the limited and dependent status of human beings as creatures, as well as social solidarity – 'our inter-dependence is given in the very nature of our being'. People are created in the divine image, but fallen, sinful. Hence human nature

[11] J. G. Riddell and George M. Dryburgh, *Crisis and Challenge: Studies on God's Will in our Time* (Church of Scotland Committee on Youth, Edinburgh, 1942), pp. 113–123
[12] ibid., p. 121
[13] *God's Will for Church and Nation*, op. cit., p. 15

requires to be remade. Everywhere in the modern world people are seeking for true community. While welcoming 'the returning spirit of community after the long reign of individualism',[14] neither secularism nor totalitarianism have been able to deliver a sustainable pattern of community. Humanity needs a community that 'claims man's total devotion', and this can only be the Christian church, where community is based on 'something that transcends community', and an authentic understanding of inter-dependence. There are obvious echoes here of Reinhold Niebuhr's *The Nature and Destiny of Man*, particularly in the precedence given to anthropology, and the emphasis on sin.

What is the relation of such theological foundations to ideals and to war aims? Whatever may have been the case in the past, it is clear to the Baillie Commission that in modern times the relation between fundamental convictions on the one hand and values and principles on the other has become complex. Secularization has meant that for many people ideals are now detached from their historical rooting in the Christian faith, and notions of the sacredness of the human person, human rights, freedom, justice and equality have become free-floating. This, the Commission argued, meant that such ideals were in danger of losing their grip over people's minds because of their separation from passionately held convictions and dogmas. In addition they suffer 'change and deterioration'. Only the Christian faith can clarify and renew such ideals, and explain why they are so important.

Although it is also true that secular idealists have opened the eyes of Christians to implications of their principles and ideals, and challenged them to take these things more seriously, 'all our ideals and standards must once again be related to a true conception of man's chief end'.[15]

This concentration on ends is crucial to the central argument of the Commission's Reports, and is explicitly related to the first question in the Westminster Shorter Catechism: 'What is man's chief end? – to glorify God and enjoy Him for ever.' The Church thus claims privileged access to issues of teleology, which are inherently

---

[14] ibid., p. 21
[15] ibid., p. 28

spiritual matters. Problems in the public realm are seldom if ever capable of a purely technological solution. They always involve questions of end and of purpose, and therefore a spiritual dimension, in which the Church and theology have a peculiar competence. Thus 'there is no problem about which (the Church) should not have something to say, although there is also no problem about which it is in a position to say all that must needs be said'. There is a place for the expert and for technical knowledge, but 'there is no single social issue which it is safe to relegate *entirely* to the expert specialism of our political and economic knowledge. No department of life must be governed in the last resort by merely departmental considerations'.[16]

This is, of course, another way of affirming the sovereignty of Christ over the whole of life, but it also suggests a demarcation between the secular and the sacred which is markedly different from that proposed at the same period by William Temple. The Commission is claiming that a theological voice is relevant in virtually every issue and is wholly unabashed in making quite specific comments and suggestions on a very wide range of matters. It draws the boundaries of the Church's competence far more widely than does Temple, and there is no trace of Temple's rather apologetic tone when making Church pronouncements on public affairs. Although the Commission recognises that the Church needs to distinguish its own actions from those of the State – theocracy is explicitly set aside – there is a recognition that the individual Christian acts as both a Christian and a citizen and is called to bring all his thoughts and actions - 'into captivity to Christ'. Accordingly, there is not nearly as sharp a distinction as that to be found in Temple between what the Church and its leaders may say, and the more partial and partisan views that an individual Christian might adopt. Temple in his immensely influential *Christianity and Social Order* (1942), put in an Appendix the policies that he as an individual wished to promote, on the ground that these matters would be likely to be controversial whereas the main body of his argument, he hoped, would be generally acceptable to Christians. The kind of issues Temple relegates to the Appendix are for the most part dealt with directly by the Baillie Commission, which successfully persuaded the Church of

[16] ibid., pp. 38–9

Scotland to endorse some fairly specific policy proposals. The fact that it did not confine itself to generalities but argued that the principles it advocated could be expressed in specifiable policies and practices is one of the most distinctive features of the Baillie Commission. The Commission thus practised R. T. Tawney's dictum 'to state a principle without its application is irresponsible and unintelligible'.[17] But the Commission still believed it was observing a limit, a frontier between the role of theology and principle on the one hand, and that of technique on the other. 'We have striven', said John Baillie, 'to abide by the principles as to the limits of the Church's concern and competence that we have laid down for ourselves. We make no political recommendations, we discuss no economic theory, we confine ourselves to laying down certain prior conditions which must be observed by any political or economic programme, no matter by what "ism" it calls itself, or does not call itself, to which Christians living in the present situation can give their assent. For instance, we say that "economic power must be made objectively responsible to the community as a whole"; but we do not attempt to say, because it is a matter to which the Christian revelation does not extend and on which the Church as such has therefore no right to speak, whether or to what extent this must involve the direct ownership by the State of the means of production and distribution.'[18]

The Baillie Commission espoused the middle axiom approach, gave it a distinctive interpretation, and produced one of the very best instances of this way of relating to public affairs and doing social ethics. The middle axiom approach was developed in the ecumenical movement, and found its classical expression in Oldham and 't Hooft's *The Church and its Function in Society*.[19] The Commission affirms that while all Christian principles are available in the New Testament, there are problems in applying these principles in the very different circumstances which face us in the modern world. Hence there is a need for 'certain secondary and more specialised principles which exhibit the relevance of the ruling principles to the particular field of action in which guidance is needed. "Middle axioms" they

[17] R. H. Tawney, *The Attack and Other Papers* (London, 1953), p. 178
[18] Riddell and Dryburgh, op. cit. , pp. 121
[19] I have discussed middle axioms more fully in Chapter 2 of my *Beliefs, Values and Policies* (Clarendon, Oxford, 1989) which gives references to the current debate.

have been called. . . . They are not such as to be appropriate in every time and place and situation, but they are offered as legitimate and necessary applications of the Christian rule of faith and life to the special circumstances in which we now stand'.[20]

The Commission suggested a range of specific middle axioms. The most interesting of these was first formulated in the 1942 Report as follows: 'Economic power must be made objectively responsible to the community as a whole. The possessors of economic power must be answerable for the use of that power, not only to their own consciences, but to appropriate social organs'.[21] After much discussion the Commission sharpened the axiom in 1944 by adding: 'The common interest demands a far greater measure of public control of capital resources and means of production than our tradition has in the past envisaged'.[22] This is, of course, close to being a quite specific policy commitment to some form of public ownership. But the details of implementation and the choice of specific ways ahead, even here, were left open, as long as the medium term goals were accepted.[23] The industrial sections of the reports started from a shrewd critique of the existing industrial order, citing mass unemployment, the dominance of the profit motive, the growth of inequality, and lack of participation as major defects. Recognising that an economic system is concerned with wealth creation, the Commission urged a broader understanding of the nature of wealth, and suggested two over-arching ethical principles – justice and community. This led to the presentation of three specific middle axioms:

(a) Extreme inequalities in the possession of wealth are dangerous to the common interest, and wise measures should be sought by which they may be controlled.

(b) It should be our aim to provide the fullest opportunities of education for all children, in accordance with their differing capacities.

(c) The opportunity to lead a useful social life must be ensured for every adult active citizen, together with a living

[20] ibid., p. 35
[21] ibid., p. 62
[22] ibid., p 157
[23] ibid., p. 171

wage appropriate to the present stage of economic development.[24]

Middle axioms are thus, in the Commission's view, both critical principles against which existing institutions and processes must be judged and positive values on which policy should be based.

The Baillie Commission gave detailed attention to a wide range of specific issues relating to the life and organisation of the Church, education, and marriage and the family. In particular it was clear to the Commission that the life of the Church was of peculiar importance in this context for two particular reasons. First, it was only possible for the Church to address the State with suggestions about the principles that should be expressed in public policy if the Church showed that it took these same principles seriously in its own life. Ideally the life of the Church should demonstrate the attractiveness and viability of what it was advocating in the broader society. In the second place, the Commission saw its role as in a real sense evangelism – the announcement of the Gospel as it affects the whole of life. The Church had to be aware that judgement begins with the household of faith, and that the life of the Church should confirm the Gospel it proclaims.

The Baillie Commission and its various reports are, I believe, of continuing importance for three reasons in particular. In the first place, the Commission showed an exemplary theological seriousness and determination to ground its work in carefully thought-through theology. This makes its reports one of the small number of really distinguished examples of the middle axiom approach. It also highlights weaknesses in some other middle axiom studies, in particular the tendency to evacuate the conclusions of theological content, and to assume a rather benign consensus on values between Christians and others in our society. The Baillie Commission was aware of problems and possibilities arising from the secularisation of values which were derived from the Judeo-Christian tradition, and consistently argued that the Christian message was radical and challenging, in relation to values as to policies. The Commission's Calvinist heritage reinforced by the influence of Reinhold Niebuhr made it see sin as the central problem, not just with individuals, but

[24] ibid., p. 63

with structures, systems and institutions, and this made it impossible
for it to adopt the optimism and progressivism either of theological
liberalism or of philosophical idealism.

Secondly, the Baillie Commission was an official Church of
Scotland body and its reports were received and approved by the
General Assembly. It encouraged and enabled a major denomination
to take quite specific positions on a range of issues affecting its own life
and the life of the nation. It meant that the Church of Scotland was in
fact committing itself to the need for a new social and economic order,
and outlining what the principles and some of the structures of that
order should be, as well as providing these with a theological rationale.
The Church of Scotland, as as result of the Baillie Commission, clearly
affirmed that out of post-war reconstruction it hoped to see something
emerge that was very like the programme of the Labour Party for the
establishment of an egalitarian welfare state and a responsible
participative industrial system.[25]

Thirdly, the Baillie Commission had considerable impact on
public opinion throughout Britain. Its critics suggest, and suggested,
that it did little more than reflect, with a theological top-coating,
radical opinion of the sort that swept the Labour Party to power in
1945. It is difficult to refute convincingly such allegations, because
there was a considerable overlap between the emerging radical ideas
about post-war reconstruction and the proposals of the Commission
in relation to public policy. It would, however, not be inappropriate
to compare the Baillie Commission's reports with the Beveridge
Report, the blueprint for the Welfare State. Both rode a tide of public
expectation of a better future and a hope for radical change in post-
war Britain. But each shaped and fed the public's expectations, and in .
the case of the Baillie Commission strongly influenced *Christian*
opinion in favour of radical social change and provided a well-
thought out theological and ethical undergirding for post-war
reconstruction.

These were no mean achievements, and point firmly to John Baillie
as a social theologian of real eminence, if too seldom recognised as

[25] On this, see further my *Christianity and the Future of Welfare* (Epworth, London,
1985), pp. 38–41. The best – and only – recent assessment of the Baillie Commission is
Donald C. Smith, *Passive Obedience and Prophetic Protest* (Peter Lang, New York, 1987),
pp. 372–383

such. Contemporary social theology has lessons still to learn from him and from the reports of his Commission. The Baillie Commission responded to a kairos/crisis with a 'church theology' which was also prophetic, and in important ways anticipated both theological declarations such as the *Kairos Document* and recent 'theologies of nation-building' in Africa and Asia. The legacy of the Baillie Commission has been too much neglected in Scotland.

Chapter 11

CHURCH AND SOCIETY
IN THE THOUGHT
OF JOHN BAILLIE

James A. Whyte

I

The sources of John Baillie's social thought are not easy to come by. Little of his work is explicitly addressed to the social question. But his friendships with Reinhold Niebuhr and J. H. Oldham, and his commitment to the developing ecumenical movement kept bringing this question to the fore.

Above all there was the need to give leadership to the Church's thinking during the Second World War. In 1940 the General Assembly set up a special commission on The Interpretation of God's Will in the Present Crisis, with John Baillie as its Convener. Substantial reports were presented between 1942 and 1945, and these were subsequently edited and published under the title *God's Will in our Time*. The Baillie Commission was a weighty body and its reports were wide-ranging. One cannot assume that the Convener was responsible for, or even in agreement with, all of the writing. Only the Commission's papers could tell us which drafts were written by John Baillie, and research has so far failed to find a copy of the papers of the most important Church Commission this century. Internal evidence suggests that he was possibly responsible for the first two sections of the 1942 Report, on The Presentation of the Christian Faith in the World of Today, and The Nature and Extent of the Church's Concern in the Civil Order, and that he was not responsible for the section on Education in the 1943 report, or that on Marriage and the Family in 1944. But one cannot be certain of this, nor about the extent of his involvement in the sections on The

235

Church of Christ (1943) and Social and Industrial Life (1942 and 1944).

The lectures which he gave during and after the war, *Invitation to Pilgrimage* (1942) and *The Belief in Progress* (1950) also give insights into his social thought, but the clearest statement is in the three lectures entitled *What is Christian Civilisation?*, given in 1945 as the Riddell Lectures in the University of Durham. In the second edition (1947) he added an appendix on Kierkegaard, Barth and Brunner on the Practice of Baptism. This chapter will reflect mainly on the viewpoint of that little book, and consider its relevance for our time, forty-five years later.

The point of departure is a remark made by Winston Churchill in 1940, before the Battle of Britain. 'Upon this battle depends the future of Christian civilization.' Baillie says 'It is this concept of Christian civilization that I should like to discuss. I desire to ask in what sense any possible civilization can be said to be Christian, how far either any past order of things or our present one merits such a description, and what the prospects are for the future.'(7)

The word Christian was first applied as a nickname to the Christian community at Antioch. 'There is therefore no doubt that a community, as well as an individual, may be rightly spoken of as Christian. Our question is only how the word may be applied to a civilization.'(7–8)

The problem of the first Christians was how to relate their tiny Christian community to the vast community around them, professing a different religion. The first solution is found in Romans 13; Paul's belief that Roman law represented in large measure God's gracious and restraining hand upon the sinfulness of men. However, when the church ceased to be a Jewish sect and lost the protective umbrella of the *religio licita* 'Christians were constrained to distinguish the area of their rightful obedience from that of their necessary disobedience.'(11)

The idea of their influencing or reforming pagan civilization could not occur because of their powerlessness and voicelessness and because their own hopes were set on the coming Kingdom, not on the improvement of earthly society. But then, from being a small and insignificant minority the Christian community became a large and influential minority, and finally became the religion of the rulers of the Empire.

'In the ancient world the effects of such an event could not fail to be dramatic, for a community religion was in those days so integral a part of its general life that the conversion of the rulers inevitably meant the conversion of the community as a whole.'(14)

Baillie does not deplore the Constantinian settlement. He sees it as inevitable, given the conditions of the time. 'It was taken for granted that a state must have an established religion.'(ibid.)

More significant for him is the ninth century reconstitution of the Empire under Charlemagne, with the vision 'of a universal civilization whose unity should be that of "one Lord, one faith, one baptism".' Here is 'the first clear concept of a Christian civilization.' (15–16) As this developed, Church and Empire are seen as 'two organs of a single society conceived as definitely and universally Christian.'

'Christianity is now compulsory . . . Every member of society is obliged to make Christian profession; and exclusion from the sacraments carries with it the loss of civil rights . . .'

The Protestant Reformation did not change this. The Empire broke up, but in lands that accepted the Reformation, whether Lutheran or Calvinist, the situation remained the same. 'Both systems continued to demand that all children be baptized in infancy, so that the whole population was included in the Church's membership. Both systems made the observance of divine ordinances compulsory, and absence a punishable offence.'(18)

But the growth of tolerance brought compulsory Christianity to an end. 'It still remained true that membership of an national community almost automatically involved baptismal membership of one branch or another of the Christian Church. Thus a new type of Christian civilization here makes its appearance upon the stage of history – what I shall call an open as contrasted with a compulsive Christian civilization.'(19)

This process of development was never without protest. From Tertullian, who in the second century inveighed against the worldliness of the church and against infant baptism, on through the centuries there have been movements of protest. The medieval church domesticated the monastic movement through the 'double standard.' Baillie compares the distinction between the religious and the secular life to the honours and pass degree in Christianity. The Reformers swept away the double standard, but retained the idea of a church which would embrace the whole community. 'Their aim was not the creation of a sect which would achieve purity by separating itself from the life of the community, but a thoroughgoing reform of the community itself.'(22) But movements of protest continued, in the Radical Reformation, such as the Anabaptists.

How far was society itself transformed by its membership of the Church? In its structures, it seems, very little. There were some early changes to the legal structure of the Empire, but no idea of radical reform. The civil order was seen as embodying Natural Law. Yet in spite of this, through the Christian centuries, culture came to be impregnated with Christian belief and Christian standards.

Calvinism had a much more comprehensive idea of an ordering of society according to Biblical principles. 'Nevertheless,' says Baillie, 'the application of this ideal was apparently not conceived as involving any great interference with existing arrangements. . . The attempted sanctification of the economic life too often degenerated into a mere sanctioning of the existing structure. . . Nevertheless the germinal idea of Christian social reform was here present, making it no accident that the modern movements in that direction should have principally made their appearance, and secured their following, within those lands which Calvinism has most deeply influenced. I believe also that the public life of these lands in times near to our own has approached closer to the true type of what I have called an open Christian civilization than that which has elsewhere been enjoyed.'(28–9)

Since the 18th century we have a new phenomenon – 'millions of men and women in all our communities who profess no religious faith, take part in no religious observance, and have connection with no religious institution.' There are millions more whose adherence is minimal. Yet of each of these it can be said that 'the print of Christ's hand is still upon the customary framework of his life and upon the ideas in his mind.'(30–1)

The roots of this detachment from the church lie in the Enlightenment, but even more in the Industrial Revolution. (There are echoes here of the sections on Social and Industrial Life in the reports of the Baillie Commission.)

Baillie looks at the responses to this situation. Some demand 'the frank recognition of the Church's minority position within a society no longer Christian in any recognisable sense.'(36) Others go further and say that that has always been the case. With Constantine and Theodosius it was the world that conquered the Church rather than the Church the world. Others, while not going so far in their rejection of the Christian centuries, believe that we have inoculated men with a mild form of Christianity so as to render them immune to the real thing. Such views are found in Roman Catholicism and in the Anglicanism of the Oxford Movement, but have found their strongest expression in the Lutheran and Calvinist lands of continental Europe.

In German theology the Ritschlian movement of the nineteenth century reacted against the Church's compromise with the world, a compromise which, as they rightly saw, goes back beyond the first Christian emperors. The alliance of Patristic theology and Greek philosophy, the transformation of Church order to conform to the social structure of the Empire, and the Church's acceptance of natural law were all rejected by Ritschlianism, and these views were inherited by Barthian theologians, however much they rejected other aspects of Ritschlianism. 'It is within this movement that we find the strongest expressions of the minority position of the Church and the most outspoken repudiation of the idea of a Christian civilization.'(39)

Given Hitler's attempt to make the Church subservient to Nazi ideology, the response of the Confessing Church was both courageous and necessary. But is it, he asks, appropriate to our situation? In general he believes, as Reinhold Niebuhr does in regard to pacifism, that the movements of protest have their place in the providential ordering of things. We need them to stab our consciences and to prevent us from being lukewarm. But he cannot accept that they have the whole truth. 'The question ultimately turns on the measure in which we believe the Church to have been justified in the principles governing its admissions to baptism in the various periods.'(41)

Before going on to deal with this salient point in his argument, Baillie insists on his distinction between 'the open Christian civilization of the modern period and the compulsive or conscriptive civilization that preceded it. It is only the former that any of us is likely to be found defending at this time of day.'(41)

Central to Baillie's argument is the importance of baptismal practice. 'It has long seemed to me,' he says, 'that the element of truth to which too little weight is given by the protesting movements is that contained in the Christian doctrine and practice of the baptism of families – a doctrine and practice which, very significantly, was the main target for the criticism of some of the most extreme of these movements, from Montanism to Anabaptism.'(41–2) 'The insight enshrined in this doctrine and practice is that the most likely way to bring men to an individual decision for Christ is to nurture them within a Christian community.' 'Just then as it is wrong to think meanly of the Christianity of children before they reach the age of personal decision and are confirmed in the faith, so I believe it is wrong to hold as of no account the Christianity which pervades the life of a community before it is confirmed in the personal decision of every individual citizen. It is very evident, for instance, that Calvin's defence of paedobaptism and his championship of community religion were ultimately rooted in a single principle in his mind.'(42)

T. S. Eliot defined a Christian society as a society 'of men whose Christianity is communal before being individual.' In the mission field, many come into the Church before they have experienced any inward transformation of their lives. The problem is not resolved by restricting membership of the Church to 'select companies of the twiceborn.' 'For . . . we Westerners owe the people of these missionary lands not only the presence in their midst of such select companies, but also the provision of a Christian community life and a Christian culture to take the place of the indigenous life and culture we have so rudely destroyed. . . . Can it possibly be our duty to offer to these peoples a Christian church which guards its purity by restricting its numbers and confining itself to a narrowly conceived evangelism, *plus* a purely secular civilization?'(43–4)

Turning the same argument to the home front, he points out that the indigenous religions of western and northern Europe were destroyed through the success of the Christian mission. 'Christianity has therefore a responsibility towards the general society of the West such as it would not have had if the old religions had retained their place in that society. . . . For in such measure as the Church should now, by withdrawing into itself, seek to disclaim the regions of its more diffused influence, in that measure it would be abandoning the civilization of the West to a secularist condition which was, in part at least, the creation of its own earlier missionary activity.'(44–5)

'If Christian ideas do not regain something of their hold upon our national life, we shall sooner or later fall victim to such pagan ideas as have lately been resuscitated in Germany.' 'For the fact that this stage has not been reached . . . seems to me to provide the Church with an opportunity which may not again occur – an opportunity which the Church can grasp, not by retiring into itself as a self-conscious minority within the nation and separated from the great sweep of national life, but rather by endeavouring to strengthen the things that remain, building upon such diffused Christian sentiments as still exist in the public mind and not resting until this has been fortified into genuine Christian conviction.'(46)

In 1943, the centenary of the Disruption, John Baillie had been Moderator of the General Assembly, and in his closing address he quoted Thomas Chalmers, who in 1830 had said 'I hold the Establishment to be not only a great Christian good, but one indispensable to the upholding of a diffused Christianity throughout the land'. Baillie comments 'What has happened between his day and ours is that the public standards of conduct have been more and more divorced from the creed and the worship. Diffused Christianity today means only the surviving influence of moral ideals after the impulse of worship has failed and the belief has grown dim and shadowy.' Yet this is important. Baillie refers with respect to the many 'who neither worship nor believe but whose lives are in many respects a continual judgment on my own.' These are not pagans. 'It is Christian virtues they are practising, while their spirituality is at least more Christian than it is anything else.' And Baillie suggests that if the Church is to nurture this 'diffused Christianity' into living faith, a new strategy is required. 'Scotland may indeed be threatened with a reversion to paganism, but it is not pagan yet, nor can I think that a wise strategy will address it as if it were.'

The closing address to the General Assembly was adumbrating the ideas to be developed in the Riddell lectures. There he points out that the alternatives facing us are not between being Christian and being pagan, but between belonging to the Church and belonging nowhere. He quotes T. S. Eliot, 'A society has not ceased to be Christian until it has become something else.' Baillie's own birth had been 'not only into a Christian family . . . but also into a civilization whose laws, manners and public standards had at least been deeply affected by the impact of Christian truth.' The hope of the future lies in a reinvigoration of this civilization, and that 'can result only from its regained hold upon the fundamental Christian ideas.'(47)

The eternal hope must always be the soul's chief anchor for the Christian, 'but willingly to surrender the lesser hope, while there remained a prospect of its being in some measure fulfilled, would be sadly to restrict the possibilities of his earthly walk and conversation.'(48)

In the final lecture Baillie returns to the criticism that Christian civilization has never been more than a facade and that true Christians have always been a small minority. What this criticism misses is the fact that public opinion counts for more than legal compulsion. 'The powerful encouragement of Christian profession by public opinion preceded by many centuries the legal enforcement of it, and was always the real power behind such enforcement . . . The most important fact about the ages of conformity, therefore, is not that Christianity was then established by law, but that it was then favoured by public opinion.'(52)

The Christian civilization of the past was one where nearly all acknowledged the authority of Christian truth and Christian standards, however far they were from living by them.(54) Baillie takes issue with Gilbert Murray and others like him, who think that you can keep the standards without the belief, the myth. 'There must be a return to the integrity of the Christian outlook or a still further disintegration.'(59) But he sees signs of hope. 'A generation long accustomed to be fed on the ideal begins again its quest for the real. And here, if anywhere, I hold our hope to lie. For only thus can the West again come to understand that what Christianity did was not to set before men new ideals, a new system of ethics, or a new law to replace the old, but rather to give them a new conception of reality, a new access to reality, and a new assurance of the grace of God, from whom all reality proceeds; and that therefore while indeed there is a Christian ideal and a Christian ethic, the secret of obedience to them lies in the humility engendered by the knowledge that we must trust for our ultimate salvation not to the measure of our own goodness but to the unmeasured divine forgiveness of our sin.'(59)

'All earthly civilization, including that which has been most permeated by Christian influence, becomes subject to ultimate criticism as falling under the final judgment of God.'(63) We cannot rest content with a society which has simply 'a Christian tone'. But disengagement from the problems of society is not possible for Christians today. Neither the monastery nor the catacombs would be possible without evasion of duty, still less the complacency of accepting without protest the privileges of a cruelly unjust society. 'Christians who today defend the Church's slowness to concern itself with social reform by standing fast on the distinction between "religion and politics", or between "religion and economics", too often find themselves in the same camp as those men of the world whose opposition to projected reforms proceeds only from the defence of their own vested interests in the existing order.'(63–4)

He dismisses the view that the Church's criticism of the social order must confine itself to a merely negative role. That would be to destroy without helping to rebuild. It would be equally bad 'were the Church to align itself with a particular party programme; for party government is of the essence of the liberal order, and while anything of that remains, the distinction between the spheres of religion and of politics must retain a large measure of validity.'(64) But the real danger is that 'by allowing the political and economic order to take care of itself, the Church of Christ will tragically fall short of its duty of bringing the light of the Christian gospel to bear upon every activity of the common life.'(64–5)

Yet true justice does not exist on earth, for 'every earthly civilization is a civilization corrupted by sin, and the only justice it knows is therefore the kind of justice which can exist in a society of men who remain largely unjust in their own individual desires.'(65)

This insight was to some extent preserved during the Christian centuries by the distinction between the absolute and the relative Law of Nature, but that tended to an uncritical acceptance of force, property relations, slavery, the class ordering of society, etc.(66) Better is Reinhold Niebuhr's understanding of a dialectical relationship between historical justice and the love which belongs to the Kingdom of God. Niebuhr sees, what Brunner failed to understand, that justice may be a necessary instrument of love, and that institutions and personal relations may be necessary to one another. 'There is no institution that can flourish on the basis of legal compulsion alone, dispensing altogether with love; nor is there any personal relationship that is altogether independent of institutions, and into which there enters no element of justice.'(59) This is true of the family and it is true of the Church. So the earthly civilization and the Christian ideal of community do not stand in simple antithesis to one another. Their relationship is dialectical, as is the relationship between our eternal hope and our temporal hope. 'In proportion as a society relaxes its hold upon the eternal, it ensures the corruption of the temporal. All earthly civilizations are indeed corruptible, the *pax britannica* no less than the *pax romana,* and Christendom no less than Babylon and Troy. But if most have perished prematurely, it was largely as a result of their own proud illusions. And if our Western civilization is to prove more durable, it can only be in the strength of this more chastened estimate of its own majesty, and this knowledge that "here we have no continuing city."'(70)

So ended the Riddell lectures. When a second edition was published in 1947, Baillie added an appendix on Kierkegaard, Barth and Brunner on the Practice of Baptism. This underlines the link that he discerns between the practice of infant baptism and the idea of a Christian civilization. He quotes Barth. 'Am I wrong in thinking that the real basis of the practice of infant baptism both among the Reformers and ever since has been that neither then nor now was one willing under any conditions or at any price to surrender the position of the Protestant Church within the Constantinian *corpus Christianum?'* And Baillie comments 'We might ask in reply whether we are wrong in thinking that the real basis of these three writers' difficulty with the practice of infant baptism is that they are unwilling at any price to *accept* the position of the Protestant Church within the *corpus Christianum*'.(85)

II

Forty-five years have passed since Baillie wrote. Do his arguments for an open Christian civilization still have validity, or has the situation changed irrevocably since his time?

Changes there have certainly been, but it may be argued that they have not been in the direction of secularism. Immigration since the

1950s has produced a sizeable Muslim minority within Britain, who bring with them attitudes – as seen in the Rushdie affair – which strongly reject the post-Enlightenment tolerance with which we have comfortably lived. In most of the conflicts of our time people identify themselves not simply by the national communities to which they belong, but by religious communities. At the time when Baillie wrote the received wisdom in the Church – in, for example, the Foreign Mission Committee – was that the future lay between Christianity and Communism. The old religions of the east were regarded as spent forces. But now it is Communism which has dramatically collapsed and the old religions are full of confidence. It is not clear whether Christianity shares that confidence. Is there any future then for Baillie's advocacy of a Christian civilization?

It can be argued that in spite of the changed situation that option has not yet been removed from the board. But it must be recognised that the idea of a Christian civilization has been under attack more from within the Church than from outside of it. Many of our modern arguments are there in Baillie's writing, but his quiet voice of reason has not been heard.

There are two surprising omissions from his argument. First, in speaking, as he does, of the print of Christ's hand upon the life of modern man, he does not speak of our literary and artistic heritage – the life of the imagination. The symbols of our culture are Christian symbols, and writers, artists and film-makers who would not consider themselves to be within the Christian church find themselves using Christian symbols – indeed, are sometimes fascinated by them.

Secondly, and strangest perhaps for him, in speaking, as he does, of the need to reinvigorate our civilization with the understanding of Christian reality – the reality of grace – he does not speak of the intellectual task before the Church, to understand and interpret its faith so that it can speak with intelligence and integrity to our contemporaries. It may be argued that the weakness of the Church lies partly in its failure to take that task seriously and to develop a public theology.

In an article published in 1952 in *The Frontier,* and entitled 'The Theology of the Frontier', John Baillie considered the problem of the frontier, in the sense in which Paul Tillich had used the term in his autobiographical sketch, *On the Boundary.* The frontier with which we are concerned is with those whose thought 'shows some traces of Christian parenthood.'(216) 'For us in this country it is seldom a frontier between Christianity on the one hand and either an alternative religion or even anything that is sufficiently definite to do duty for an alternative religion on the other. We have to face doubt and negation rather than counter-affirmation; agnosticism perhaps, but seldom an alternative gnosis.'(217)

He looks at the Barthian response to this situation – a 'No' to culture, an insistence on proclamation rather than argument, and he suggests that this 'is closely related to a much more widespread tendency which has manifested itself quite independently in this country – the tendency of fully observant Christians to close up their ranks, to advertise their minority position in the community, and to deny the application of the adjective "Christian", in any important sense, either to the society in which we live or to those members of it who are not fully observant churchmen.'(220) 'The corpus christianum, it is said, never was an authentic thing. True Christians always were in a minority. And true Christians are the only kind of Christians there are.'(220)

The alternative strategy which Baillie considers is that of The Latent Church, as outlined by Tillich and exemplified by Simone Weil, but he also looks sympathetically at Bonhoeffer's 'religionless Christianity', and at Jacques Ellul's *Presence au Monde,* both of which suggest a rapprochement between the Barthian strategy and a more liberal one.

The rejection of the *corpus Christianum* has certainly been a very insistent, if not dominant note within the Church in the decades since Baillie wrote. One can see this in different forms.

First, there is, as he pointed out, the influence of Barthian theology. One of the most striking points in his argument is the strong connection he makes between the practice of infant baptism and the idea of a Christian civilization, and the way in which Barthian theology is hostile to both of these. It is noteworthy that for most of its existence the General Assembly's Panel on Doctrine has been dominated by this theology, often in alliance with Scoto-Catholicism.

The exponents of this theology in Scotland have not gone so far as Karl Barth himself in rejecting infant baptism, but their concern for the purity of the Church leads to exclusive attitudes. The Special

Commission on Baptism (1953–62) was a particularly weighty expression of this, using the type of biblical scholarship which goes with that type of continental theology. The practical outcome of the Commission's labours was an act, Act XVII of 1963, regulating the admission of infants to baptism, which was so restrictive as to make it difficult for the Church of Scotland to function as a national Church. In terms of this Act the Church is most readily seen as a fortress within a hostile society rather than as the heart of society.

This exclusiveness links up readily with those who, for other reasons, wish the Church to reject infant baptism altogether. That which Baillie saw as the mark of a Christian civilization is becoming an issue within the Church of Scotland.

This new sectarian protest, which Baillie so accurately described in the passage quoted above ('True Christians are the only kind of Christians there are'), denies the name of 'Christian' to all except the twiceborn. Its roots appear to be less in continental theology than in American revivalism. But it has certain characteristics in common with the others – it is authoritarian, uncritical in its use of the Bible, and has a pure church ideal, though it is individualistic in a way that Barthianism could never be, and largely unaware of the wider tradition of the Church. But taken together, these movements represent a rejection of the idea of a Christian civilization, and with it, that of a national Church.

If these movements, together with the tiny but influential Scoto-Catholic group, represent a conservative rejection of the *corpus Christianum,* there is also a radical rejection of it, which is essentially anti-Establishment. The beginnings of this are very accurately observed by John Baillie, but for its development since his time we might look at Denis Munby's *The Idea of a Secular Society* (1953), an answer to T. S. Eliot's *Idea of a Christian Society* (1939) (the book with which Baillie was so much in agreement) and, even more, at the wide influence of the book by Harvey Cox, *The Secular City* (1965).

Munby proposed a society essentially neutral, without standards and symbols, but tolerant of all – not an 'open Christian society' such as Baillie defended, but simply an open society. The question was whether this was a real possibility, but it was an ideal which attracted some liberal minds. Cox, on the other hand, hymned the anonymity of the city as the matrix for a new freedom in human life, where everything was a matter of personal choice. It is difficult not to see him as contributing to the removal of religion from the public arena.

The secularization theory, which properly concerned the removal of areas of life (e.g. social welfare, education) from ecclesiastical control (a process quite consistent with Baillie's 'open Christian society'), came to be widened to mean a decline of religion, and of its influence, in society. It has been taken for granted, among sociologists and among some theologians, that ours is in fact 'a secular society'. Yet evidence has never been lacking for what has been called 'the strange persistence of religion', and its continuing influence not only in private life but also in public affairs.

Professor Duncan Forrester begins his book *Beliefs, Values and Policies* (1989) with these words 'We live in a plural society in a secular age. One would expect the influence of religion in the public realm in such a context to be vestigial. But almost the opposite appears to be the case. Not only among Islamic Fundamentalists and the Moral Majority in the United States, but in countries where organized religion is in sharp decline conviction politics has had an amazing renaissance. Politicians increasingly speak in theological language, and church leaders and theologians surprisingly frequently make significant contributions to public debate.' He concludes, 'The role of theology in the public arena calls out for analysis and evaluation.' (p. 1) One need not quarrel with that, and Professor Forrester makes a valuable contribution to such analysis, but one might have expected him also to be led by the evidence he cites to examine his assumption that ours is a secular age. He does not do so, and the sub-title of his book is *Conviction Politics In a Secular Age*.

There are, of course, hidden agendas in theological writing, and theologians sometimes wish to believe that this is a secular society because they themselves have a pure Church idea and are opposed to the Establishment. Baillie noted that the Ritschlians whose attitudes lie behind much of the Barthian opposition to a Christian civilization were not so naive as to believe that before Constantine all was well with the Church. It is not uncommon to find modern writers, however, suggesting that the Church was pure until it fell from grace by accepting the apple presented to it by the serpent Constantine. This is an attitude which I have called 'pre-Constantinian romanticism'. This may be seen in the book by Professor Alistair Kee

Constantine versus Christ: the triumph of ideology (1982), written to prove that Constantine never was a Christian, that Eusebius was a liar, and that the Church has been made captive, ever since, to the power-structure of the Establishment. In his concluding chapter Professor Kee shows his motives for interpreting the history in the way he does. He wishes to deliver Christianity from what he sees as the deadening effects of the establishment of religion, and to permit the flowering of a prophetic protest, through a political theology embracing Marxism as its ideology. Freedom from one ideology means captivity to another.

Opposition to a Christian civilization is found also among some devotees of the ecumenical movement, who see in Third World Churches – notably the Church of South India – their idea of a pure Church. Their ideal Church is therefore a tiny minority within a pagan society. Closer inspection of Third World churches might reveal that this is also a form of romanticism. But the situation in Britain and Western Europe is, as Baillie saw, radically different from that, so that the South India model is misleading for a mission strategy in this country,

John Baillie never despised what he called 'the protest movements', from Tertullian on. Today we may have to distinguish between what is genuinely prophetic protest and what is trendiness. Perhaps the true prophet today is the one who is not seduced by the sectarianism either of the right or of the left, any more than by the complacency of a lukewarm establishment. But if he or she wishes to strengthen the things that remain and to seek an open and genuinely Christian civilization, they will find no better inspiration than John Baillie.

IV
PERSONAL REMINISCENCES

Chapter 12

JOHN BAILLIE AT PRAYER

Thomas F. Torrance

One day at Lambeth Palace during a session of our conversations between the Church of Scotland and the Church of England John Baillie told us that his father, the Rev. John Baillie, never read the Holy Scriptures without first putting on black silk gloves. Some years later when attending worship in the Free Church at Gairloch, Wester Ross, which had been built by John Baillie's father many years before, I was startled to hear the minister declare that while the Church welcomes everyone, Jesus Christ receives only the elect. Those two instances have much to say about John Baillie himself, for he inherited his father's deep reverence for all things divine and holy, and recoiled from the rather harsh conception of God and the divisive doctrine of double predestination that prevailed in Westminster Presbyterianism. From the very roots of his being he worshipped God with his heart and his mind, and was so tuned into the grace and love of Christ that he constantly sought to live out the revealed mind of God in his open relations with others within and without the Church.

This deeply theistic and Christian openness of John Baillie was nowhere more evident than in his wholehearted commitment to the ecumenical movement. Due to his reaction from traditional Calvinism and his rational way of believing influenced by Neo-Kantian and Neo-Hegelian philosophy he reacted rather critically toward what he held at that time to be the teaching of Karl Barth. But I recall a change in his personal attitude toward Barth, when following upon the founding of the World Council of Churches at Amsterdam, he and Barth were thrown together in theological dialogue about differences in unity and unity in differences, and engaged in common acts of worship. What impressed Baillie, he told us when he came back to Edinburgh, was the theological reverence of

Barth and the unrestrained joy and fervour of Barth in worship, not least in his praise of God in hymns. Like Barth, Baillie was convinced in his examination of European thought that the ages of faith were not man-centred but God-centred, and that man cut off from God lapses into unreason.

Unlike Karl Barth, John Baillie was deeply influenced by liturgical worship, and in particular, partly through his wife who was a descendent of the Reforming Bishop Jewel of Salisbury, by the Anglican Book of Common Prayer. It is in and through regular worship that the human mind becomes centred and formed in God. It was a rich blend of the profound sense of the majesty of God in the God-centred worship of the Free Church of Scotland deriving from John Calvin and the ordered beauty of classical liturgical worship that characterised John Baillie's own conception and practice of prayer. He had a profound sense of the beauty of holiness and an innate feeling for personal decorum and propriety in forms of thought and speech before God. This was apparent in his liturgical use of prayer in public worship when he conducted Holy Communion Services in New College. He greatly prized the theological and liturgical form and completeness of the Eucharistic Service in our Church of Scotland Book of Common Order, which was heavily indebted to his colleague William Manson. Deep feeling for mystery and beauty in the orderly worship of the Triune God was also very marked in his habit of private devotion as reflected in his prayers for all the mornings and evenings of the month published in *A Diary of Private Prayer*, still used by myriads of people and available in many languages across the world. All his prayer in public and private alike was breathed out of a deep well of mental longing and an intimate waiting before God. How typical are the sentences with which he concludes the prayer for the First Morning:

> O God, who hast been the Refuge of my fathers through many generations, be my Refuge to-day in every time and circumstance of need. Be my Guide through all that is dark and doubtful. Be my Guard against all that threatens my spirit's welfare. Be my Strength in times of testing. Gladden my heart with Thy peace; through Jesus Christ my Lord. Amen.

And the evening prayer of the Fifth Day:

> Almighty God, in this hour of quiet I seek communion with Thee. From the fret and fever of the day's business, from the world's discordant notes, from the pride and blame of men, from the confused thoughts and vain

imaginations of my own heart, I would now turn aside and seek the quietness of Thy presence. All day long have I toiled and striven; but now in stillness of heart and in the clear light of Thine eternity, I would ponder the patterns my life has been weaving.

During my own years of teaching theology in New College when I was a colleague of John Baillie, and afterwards, I used to ask myself two questions about students as they completed their training: whether they had tuned into knowledge of God in their studies so finely that they had attained a theological instinct for divine truth, and whether their conduct of public worship reflected the habit of private prayer. They were much more important for the holy ministry, I felt, than clever essays, profound learning, or brilliance in examinations. Fine-tuning of the human mind in the knowing of God and direct personal communing of the human spirit with God lie at the very heart of theological understanding, and bear decisively not only on the vocation of the pastor but on the vocation of the theological professor. It would not be too difficult to show that the changes in John Baillie's own thinking from a sceptical strain evident in his early books to a more positive strain are not unconnected with his increasingly liturgical interest in worship and his greater commitment to the general framework of classical Nicene theology. His participation in conjoint acts of worship in the Ecumenical Movement in which the Nicene Creed was often very central, as among Anglicans and Orthodox, reinforced this development considerably.

I recall vividly the first time my eyes fell on the prayer-desk John Baillie had in his study, and realised that it was there on bended knee that he daily opened his mind to the self-disclosure of the Lord God and allowed it to direct and shape his teaching during the day. 'Prayer, after all, is but thinking towards God.'[1] And what is Christian theology but prayerful thinking toward God, as Karl Barth used to insist? Baillie, for his part, was acutely conscious of the need for truth in the inward parts of our being (Ps. 51:6). That is what God desires and what we so seldom give him, he once declared in his Alexander Robertson Lectures in Glasgow. 'The one great difficulty which confronts God in his desire to reveal himself to you and me, that

---

[1] *Christian Devotion*, p. 23

thereby he may save us, is the difficulty of cutting through the dreadful tangle of dishonesty and lying self-deception and pathetic make-belief with which we all the time surround ourselves.'[2] What burdened him in the class-room was not only the need for truth in his own inward being, but the need for truth in the souls of future ministers and the eternal destiny of the people, men and women and children, to whom they were sent to minister the Gospel. How could he himself engage in true theological thinking and how could he communicate theological truth faithfully without the preparation and guidance of prayer in which his own soul was constantly opened toward God? 'Blessed are the pure in heart, for they shall see God.'

The place of a prayer-desk in the midst of his books and adjacent to the desk where he penned his lectures and composed his books reveals the importance John Baillie gave to the bearing of prayer upon what he liked to call, citing from St. Bonaventure, 'the journey of the mind into God' (*itinerarium mentis in Deum*). And so we find he used to pray:

> Give me an open mind, O God, a mind ready to receive and to welcome such new light of knowledge as it is Thy will to reveal to me. Let not the past ever be so dear to me as to set a limit to the future. Give me courage to change my mind, when that is needed. Let me be tolerant to the thoughts of others and hospitable to such light as may come to me through them.[3]

John Baillie was essentially an intellectual who appreciated the pensée of Blaise Pascal, that compared to all else in nature 'our whole dignity consists in thinking', but who also held with Pascal that man is as nothing compared to the Infinite. Prayer was thus for Baillie the spiritual act whereby on the one hand he took refuge in the thought that God is utterly beyond the comprehension of his mind but whereby on the other hand he yielded his mind to the mystery of God whose transcendent light in Christ Jesus breaks through the incapacity of our finite minds and illumines them with his presence.

> O God above me, God who dwellest in light unapproachable, teach me, I beseech Thee, that even my highest thoughts of Thee are but dim and distant shadowings of Thy transcendent glory. Teach me that if Thou art in nature, still more art Thou greater than nature. Teach me that if Thou

[2] *Invitation to Pilgrimage*, p. 20
[3] *Diary of Private Prayer*, The Fourteenth Evening

art in my heart, still more art Thou greater than my heart. Let my soul rejoice in Thy mysterious greatness. Let me take refuge in the thought that Thou art utterly beyond me, beyond the sweep of my imagination, beyond the comprehension of my mind, Thy judgments being unsearchable and Thy ways past finding out. O Lord, hallowed be Thy name.[4]

For John Baillie, then, prayer had to do with the stretching and cultivation of his mind for the apprehension of divine truth. Yet that was not just an intellectual exercise, for to refer to Pascal again, as he often did: 'Human beings must be known in order to be loved, but divine things must be loved in order to be known.'[5] In other words, it is not only with the top of our minds but with the bottom of our hearts that we may truly believe in God and know God. It is just such a combination of the mind and the heart that we find informing John Baillie's teaching about prayer and his actual prayer. It must be said of John Baillie that he prayed and lived as he prayed; he thought and wrote as he prayed in a modality of what St Paul called 'rational worship' (Rom. 12:1). Rational worship of this kind is in no sense an abstraction, but the directing of the whole being upward toward God within the concrete situations of our daily life and work in space and time where God has placed us.

In no theologian of our time has the contemplation of God been so wedded to a beauty of form deriving from rational worship. It flowed over into his appreciation of all lovely creatures and of the works of God's children, whether in music or drawing or porcelain or verse; but is most manifest in the form of his thoughts and the corresponding form of his writing. We have rarely known such theological prose as flowed from the pen of John Baillie – even his writing was a worshipping and honouring of God in the beauty of holiness.

> Grant unto me such a vision of Thine uncreated beauty as will make me dissatisfied with all lesser beauties.[6]

Here we have echoed the deep Augustinian strain in Baillie's understanding of the love of God. 'Late have I loved Thee, O Beauty,

---

[4] ibid., The Seventeenth Morning
[5] De l'esprit géométrique, cited in *The Interpretation of Religion*, p. 364f.
[6] *Diary of Private Prayer*, The Fifth Evening

so ancient and so new, late have I loved Thee! For behold Thou wert within me, and I outside; and I sought Thee outside and in my lovelessness fell upon those lovely things Thou hast made. Thou wert with me and I was not with Thee. I was kept from Thee by those things, yet had they not been in Thee, they would not have been at all.'[7] And here, for all the difference between them, even in their appreciation of St Augustine, Baillie and Barth came close together. 'If we can and must say that God is beautiful, to say this is to say how he enlightens and convinces and persuades us. It is to describe not merely the naked fact of his revelation or its power, but the shape and form in which it is a fact and is power. It is to say that God has this superior force, this power of attraction, which speaks for itself, which wins and conquers, in the fact that he is beautiful, divinely beautiful, beautiful in his own way, in a way that is his alone, beautiful as the unattainable primal beauty, yet really beautiful.'[8]

And so John Baillie prayed:

> Give me open eyes, O God, eyes quick to discover Thine indwelling in the world which Thou hast made. Let all lovely things fill me with gladness and let them uplift my mind to Thine everlasting loveliness. Forgive all my past blindness to the grandeur and glory of nature, to the charm of little children, to the sublimities of human story, and to all the dimensions of Thy presence which these things contain.[9]

There are two further features particularly evident throughout *A Diary of Private Prayer* to which attention must surely be directed.

The first feature is the sheer humanity of John Baillie bowed in prayer before God. One of the reasons why this little classic has had such a wide and long appeal is that in these prayers Baillie expresses the very thoughts and desires we all have and want to utter before God when we wake up in the morning and lie down to sleep at night, and expresses them in such a simple and beautiful way that we gladly make them our very own. They are direct and profoundly personal, from the heart of the sinner who penitently claims and rejoices in the forgiving love of God and the grace of the Lord Jesus, but they do not have anything of the matey familiarity that cheapens many modern hymns and religious songs. Nor is there is any loss here of reverence

---

[7] *Confessions* X.27 (Sheed and Ward edition, 1949)
[8] Karl Barth, *Church Dogmatics* II/1 (T&T Clark, Edinburgh, 1957), p. 650
[9] *Diary of Private Prayer*, The Fourteenth Evening

and humility before the transcendent Majesty of God the Father Almighty, Creator of heaven and earth, and of all things visible and invisible. Hence they are helpful aids to private worship each morning and evening which do not seem to grow stale, but may be repeated each month with undiminished freshness. Moreover they are prayers which strike deeply into the hidden depths of the human heart where we desperately need forgiveness and healing, and inward peace. It may well be claimed that *A Diary of Private Prayer* does much more than supply ready-made forms of prayer for all occasions of spiritual and physical need – it is at the same time a manual of pastoral care and evangelical guidance, a vehicle of the Word of God addressed to us in Christ Jesus our Lord and Saviour.

The second feature of these prayers that may be noted is their contemporary setting in people's life and work. In a sermon he preached on the teaching of our Lord that 'men ought always to pray and not to faint' (Luke 18:1), John Baillie laid the greatest stress on the fact that God is far from being unconcerned with our trifling earthly affairs, for he does not want us to bottle up our anxieties in ourselves but bids us speak directly to him about them. To those who feel that they should not trouble God with their trivial earthly affairs, Baillie argued that Jesus would have said that 'if anything is big enough to worry about, then it is not too small to pray about'.[10] It was in the same tenor, he remarked, that St Paul wrote to the Philippians: 'In nothing be anxious; but in everything by prayer and supplication with thanksgiving let your requests be made known unto God.' It was intimate prayers of that kind that Baillie formulated to aid people's private devotions morning and night, putting into their heart and their mouth in express terms what they often hardly dare to think or utter, and thereby to encourage people in their more individual prayers for themselves and for others.

Nothing is overlooked in *A Diary of Private Prayer* regarding the contextual situation in which we actually find ourselves today in the necessities and hurts of our daily life and in the desperate plight of those in dire social or physical need, with respect to which we must take our Lord's teaching about petitionary prayer seriously. Our heavenly Father certainly knows all these worries of ours, but he wants us to tell him

[10] *Christian Devotion*, p. 24

about them, and to direct our petitions frankly to him. To reinforce
that view of prayer, Baillie referred to the statement made by D. S.
Cairns, in his striking book *The Faith that Rebels,* to the effect that
practically all that is said in the New Testament about prayer is said 'not
in the interest of being reconciled to things as they are but in the
interest of getting things changed'.[11] And so Baillie did not hesitate to
shape petitionary prayer for us in such a way within the context of our
modern scientific understanding of the universe and its rational order
that it dares to look for real answers from the Lord and Redeemer of the
created universe. We are told to ask, and seek, and knock, and
encouraged to find, in the belief that God will and does answer prayer
made in the name of Christ, yet always with the humility of those who
are ready to recognise that in the overruling wisdom of God the answers
he gives us may be rather different from what we sought to specify. We
must certainly 'make our requests known to God' (Phil. 4:6), 'but it is
contrary to all true faith to suppose that we may hold him to a
particular way of responding. It would be frightening to take upon
ourselves that measure of responsibility . . . As somebody has put it: "If
God granted me the form of my petition, he would be denying me the
substance of my desire."'[12]

Here now is the evening prayer for the Nineteenth Day which we
may make our own.

> O God the Father, I praise the great and holy Love whereby, when we
> had utterly gone astray, Thou didst diligently seek us out and save us,
> sending Thy wellbeloved Son to suffer and die that we might be restored
> to the fellowship of Thy children.
>
> O God the Son, I praise the great and holy love whereby Thou didst
> humble Thyself for my sake and for the sake of my brethren, consenting
> to share our common life, to dwell in the midst of our sin and shame, to
> endure all the bitterness of Thy most blessed Passion, and at the last to die
> upon the Cross, that we might be released from our bondage and enter
> with Thee into the glorious liberty of the children of God.
>
> O God the Holy Spirit, I praise the great and holy love whereby Thou
> dost daily shed abroad in my unworthy heart the peace and joy of sin
> forgiven, making me a partaker with all the saints in the blessings of my
> Lord's Incarnation, of his Passion and Crucifixion, and of his Resurrection
> and Ascension to the Father's right hand on high.

[11] ibid., p. 22
[12] *The Sense of the Presence of God,* p. 65

O holy and blessed Trinity, let me now dwell in the mystery of this heavenly love that all hatred and malice may be rooted out from my heart and life. Let me love Thee, as Thou didst first love me; and in loving Thee let me love my neighbour; and in loving Thee and my neighbour in Thee let me be saved from all false love of myself, and to Thee Father, Son, and Holy Spirit, be all glory and praise for ever. Amen.

Chapter 13

JOHN BAILLIE – AS A STUDENT SAW HIM

John C. Lusk

I was a pupil of John Baillie at New College, Edinburgh, from 1938–41. At that time the union of the Scottish churches in 1929, and the consequent union of the divinity faculties in the universities, were comparatively recent. John Baillie had returned to Scotland from North America only four years previously in 1934, after spending fifteen years there which were formative of his outlook and during which he published his three early books, *The Roots of Religion in the Human Soul; The Interpretation of Religion; The Place of Jesus Christ in Modern Christianity.* He therefore brought to Edinburgh and New College familiarity with a wider world and some of the sophistication of New York. This made him different from the other professors; and they (some of us felt) did not always appreciate him.

I came to New College as a stranger to Scottish university ways, after school and university in England, and a brief spell as a civil servant. I immediately found John Baillie to be the most congenial of the New College professors. He treated his students as adults, who were seriously trying to think out the problems faith, and who were interested in the world outside university and church.

My mother had been a student in the same philosophy class in Edinburgh University as John Baillie. So I was brought up to respect this great philosopher-theologian, and I was eager to learn from him. The question in his classes always was 'what is the truth?' – not 'what does the Church teach?' nor 'what does Calvin say?' nor even 'what does the Bible say?' He was always trying to show us where nuggets of truth were to be found in a great variety of sources. In his lecture style what we noticed most was the lucidity: he was economical in his use of words. To stimulate us he encouraged questions in class, and was extremely patient even with the most foolish ones.

His most recent book, *And the Life Everlasting*, appealed to me, since my mother had recently died. Some have found in that work the high-water mark of Karl Barth's influence on John Baillie. Professor Cheyne notes that practically all the references to Barth in it are favourable.[1] The preface has a wide-ranging criticism of contemporary philosophers who had written about immortality. Was Baillie moving away from his attachment to philosophy towards 'Barthianism'?

Barthianism was of course the great question of those days. In New College we had to try to swallow G. T. Thomson's lectures as well as John Baillie's. In the summer of 1939 I went to Basel to sample the teaching of Barth. I could not fail to be strongly impressed by his emphatic proclamation of the Sovereignty of God; but the fundamental difficulties of his teaching were not removed. Is human reason really so unreliable?

Back in New College, we listened raptly to Baillie's lectures. His standpoint then was that of *Our Knowledge of God* which he published in 1939, and which has been acclaimed as his most important work. I certainly found it more acceptable than any other standpoint which I knew. According to Cheyne, Baillie was then trying to accept the contribution which Barthianism made, while at the same time correcting its deficiencies.

Baillie's attitude to philosophy had developed out of his parents' Calvinism. In 1957 John Baillie wrote his 'Impression' of his brother Donald as foreword to Donald's *Theology of the Sacraments*. There John emphasises their mother's familiarity with the system of beliefs embodied in the Westminster standards: 'if her sons later developed any aptitudes of a philosophic kind, it was undoubtedly by this home training in theological dialectic that their minds were first sharpened.'[2] It was therefore impossible for John to divorce theology from philosophy.

It has often been remarked that in the 1930s John Baillie was regarded in America as a conservative and in Scotland as a liberal. We

---

[1] *The Transforming of the Kirk* (St. Andrew Press, Edinburgh, 19), p. 211
[2] *Theology of the Sacraments*, p. 14

who rebelled against Barthianism gladly accepted his liberalism. But it would be absurd to think that his liberalism was a watering down or reduction of the Christian faith. He was concerned to expound and explain and justify by rational argument the whole of the faith. He combined in a remarkable way open-mindedness towards new ideas with a very firmly rooted grasp of the faith. Fifty years on I am convinced that his attitude to truth is fundamentally right and important, and a necessary corrective to a flood of false or partial theories.

Some students in New College found John Baillie a little forbidding, remote and difficult to get to know. His manner was certainly reserved. His face often assumed that serious mask which was described as the look of the Highland boy on first seeing New York. But his wit and humour were never far away. He was a delightful teller of stories. When he came to the college lunch, there was always competition to sit next to him, though also some apprehension about the deep waters that conversation might lead into. He and Mrs. Baillie entertained us in their home in Whitehouse Terrace; he evinced an obvious interest in his students and in their concerns and prospects.

In the first year of the war, I had an opportunity to see him at closer quarters. In the spring of 1940 he went to France to take charge of the educational and religious work of the YMCA for the British Forces, hoping to continue the work which he had done in the Great War, in the course of which he had met his wife. He asked me at the end of my second year of the New College course to assist him in this work for a short time. I went to France in YMCA uniform at the end of March, and joined him at Arras near the Army Headquarters. After about ten days there while I learned how the YMCA ran its canteens, he took me to Reims which was RAF Headquarters. We made friendly contact with the RAF chaplains: in his dealings with army and air force officers Baillie had a sure touch: he was quite willing to use his authority as a professor. We opened a YMCA 'centre' in the town of Reims, and he left me there to manage it. A month or so later I got news of my brother's death in the RAF, and Baillie advised me to go home for a brief visit to my father. So I left France by what turned out to be one of the last ordinary commercial flights before the collapse of the country. John Baillie had to arrange for the safety of all the YMCA staff in the general collapse, and came out with difficulty from St Malo. The educational work for which we had gone to France had hardly begun.

When I was driven with him in a YMCA car to visit YMCA centres actual and potential, I saw how thoroughly at home he was in France. His French was perfectly adequate for doing business with plumbers and joiners and all the tradesmen. He had an intimate knowledge of the Cathedrals of northern France. He gave me good advice about what cheeses to choose. He knew how to buy 'gargarisme sec' to treat minor sore throats. In all the difficulties and delays in the work he remained calm and efficient and purposeful, though he must have felt very frustrated.

After this YMCA interlude, we returned to New College, and I completed my final year. I was always thereafter grateful to him, not only for his teaching but also for his friendship.

At this time John Baillie was not I think very prominent in the General Assembly and other church courts and in church politics. But he was clearly a keen and devout churchman. He was probably best known throughout the Church for his *Diary of Private Prayer* (1936) which appealed to many people with its characteristic blend of humility and cheerfulness. My recollection is that after the YMCA experience he was more widely in demand as a preacher: he no longer let his philosophical language spoil his appeal to the unlearned. He was not afraid to give his backing to novel ventures such as the Iona Community.

When he did his great work in the Assembly Commission for the 'Interpretation of God's Will', and in the Moderator's chair in 1943, I was in Canada in the RAF. I was on the Pacific coast when I read eagerly *Invitation to Pilgrimage* (1942). Very often I was asked by Canadian church people to tell them what was happening in the Church of Scotland, and my reply always referred to John Baillie as one of our great men. He together with W. D. Maxwell and George MacLeod seemed to me then to be the most important influences in the Church.

About this time John Baillie was becoming prominent in the Ecumenical Movement. After the war I spent a year on the staff of the Student Christian Movement, with the task of visiting the theological colleges of England and Scotland, speaking about the ecumenical movement, which was then enjoying a heyday, with great things expected from the first Assembly of the World Council of Churches in 1947. I found John Baillie in Edinburgh and Donald in St Andrews very sympathetic and encouraging in the work I was trying to do, to persuade the future ministers of all the British churches to take an active interest in ecumenism. From that time on John Baillie was one of the acknowledged leaders of the movement, highly respected in England and throughout the whole world. Since his death Scotland has never been so influential in this field.

After I had settled into parish ministry, I had fewer opportunities of meeting John Baillie. One meeting in Waverley Station remains in my mind. In conversation he expressed great admiration for John Robinson, whose work as a student he had been examining. Baillie always appreciated a clever intellect, but he could hardly have foreseen what was to come in *Honest to God*.

Throughout my ministry I depended firmly on what I had learned from John Baillie and continued to learn in his writings. *The Belief in Progress* appeared in 1950, and *The Idea of Revelation* in 1956: followed by his great work posthumously published *The Sense of the Presence of God*, 1962.

Six years after his death I went to South Africa for a year to deputise for John Summers (another of John Baillie's devoted pupils) in the training of black divinity students. Teaching 'doctrine' I tried in a small way to follow in the steps of John Baillie: in my mind he lived as the ideal teacher.

Twenty years after his death, I was living in Dunblane in retirement, and became familiar with Scottish Churches House. The room in the house called 'The John Baillie Room', planned as a quiet reading room, with a fine photograph of him over the mantelpiece, is a beautiful memorial in a building which he did not live to see but which is surely carrying on some of his work.

Chapter 14

JOHN BAILLIE
ON ETERNAL LIFE

George S. Hendry

In considering how to offer my tribute to the memory of Professor John Baillie I would like to distinguish between my high regard for him as a man and for the great contribution he made to theology in his (and my) native Scotland, and then to offer some critical comments on positions he took on certain theological questions.

I had the pleasure of meeting Professor Baillie only a few times while he lived in Edinburgh, and I knew him mainly through his writings. I was disappointed that he was so vigorously opposed to Karl Barth; and, while I continued to read his books, I came to feel that he had become obsessed with Barth. If I may explain my position briefly, I had been attracted to Barth's doctrine of the Word of God because it seemed to me to offer liberation from the theory of verbal inspiration and inerrancy, which was held by some evangelical brethren to be the first plank of an evangelical faith. But, on the other hand, although I continued to hold to the Barthian position that the Word of God requires no point of contact (Anknüpfungspunkt) such as natural theology, as I became engaged in teaching I came to like Baillie's way of doing theology because I felt it had its point of contact in the piety of a west Highland manse. Is this something to be ruled out? Another Scottish theologian wrote some years ago:

> I cannot help thinking that, as is so often the case, the theologian is returning to his origins, and that here Professor Baillie is simply trying to find good reasons for a conviction which he had somehow acquired from his earliest days in the Scottish Highland manse where he grew up.[1]

I myself had already gathered from some of the autobiographical allusions in his early books that Baillie received some of what he was

[1] Ronald Gregor Smith, *The Doctrine of God* (Westminster Press, Philadelphia, 1970), p. 127

accustomed to call 'religion' in the west Highland manse which was his home. But who, brought up in such a home, could fail to assimilate some of its religion, even if it were parabolic? If I may be permitted to cite my own experience, I was born and brought up in a lowland Scottish home, and there I had an experience with a religious import which became evident to me only when I grew older. I learned in my childhood what it was like to be told that I was bad and to be reprimanded for my bad behaviour, and on occasion to receive *a posteriori* punishment for it but ('the great But' someone has called it) not to be rejected for it. So, when I grew older and I was confronted with the gospel of sin and salvation, it was not strange to me; I had already experienced it in parabolic form, and I was glad to find the original in the New Testament. 'We have had fathers of our flesh which corrected us and we gave them reverence; shall we not much rather be in subjection to the Father of our spirits and live.' (Hebrews 12:9)

Before beginning to write anything on the theology of John Baillie, I thought it would be wise to turn again to his writings, which I had found so stimulating and instructive when I first read them. In this revisit to what had been familiar territory, I realised that he had written one book which I had never read. It was one of his earliest writings, his early venture into the field of eschatology, which he published under the title, *And the Life Everlasting* (1933). As best I can remember, I think it was the title of the book that put me off; the use of the final phrase of the Apostles' Creed seemed to intimate a study of the idea of the immortality of the soul, which had long been accepted as an article of the Christian faith and widely thought to be taught in the Bible. It was a pleasant surprise to find on reading the book that its purpose was quite different. The main feature of the background against which the book was written was a widespread decline of interest in the hope of a future life, a keen sense of difficulties, philosophical and scientific, in any conception of life after death, and a general turning of human interest from a future life toward the possibilities and prospects of progress in this life. Baillie was keenly aware of the general transference of human hopes from heavenly bliss to better conditions in this world. He would later write a book on *The Belief in Progress* (1950).

To return to his earlier book, *And the Life Everlasting,* the first part is devoted to a study of the idea of everlasting life as it had come to be accepted as an article of Christian faith and had received support from the widespread belief in survival after death, and the belief in the immortality of the soul which had received support from Plato and other philosophers.

In that first part of the book which contained most of his class teaching, Baillie presented a lucid and instructive account of the appearance of belief in life after death in some of the cults of the ancient world and the climax argument for the immortality of the soul by Plato. Baillie did not press Plato's idea of the immortality of the soul, nor the arguments with which he tried to support it. But he held Plato in high regard for his dignification of man; and he made frequent references to Plato in his teaching to the puzzlement of some of his students who expressed their sentiments one day with a ditty which appeared on the blackboard as he entered the classroom.

Baillie, Baillie give me your answer, do.
Why ain't Plato found in the canon too?

In the second half of the book, Baillie turned to a study of the authentic Christian hope, which is designated in the Nicene Creed as 'the life of the world to come', and is now commonly designated in English as 'eternal life'. The term 'immortality' is improper since it means literally immunity to death; and when it is applied to the Christian hope, it had to be restricted to the soul and not applied to the body. Baillie presented his case for the Christian hope of eternal life in a chapter entitled 'The Logic of Hope'. The argument was briefly summarised: 'If it is the purpose of God that our souls should be saved from sin, how can it be his will that they should be annihilated at the death of the body?'[2] It seems strange to describe the action of God in a term from Aristotle. It would surely be more appropriate to use theo-logic, if we may so call the language of the Bible. Such terms are available and appropriate in both the Old Testament and the New. It may suffice to cite one example from each. As regards the Old Testament, intense and widespread interest was aroused around half a century ago when it was shown by some experts in the English language that one Hebrew word which plays an important role in the Old Testament has a nuance which had never been brought out in the English translation. The Hebrew word is

[2] *And the Life Everlasting*, p. 164f.

'Hesed' and in the 1511 translation it was rendered 'loving-kindness'. Not only is this wrong, it sounds too gushy. When the word was analysed, it was found to mean 'faithfulness to a covenant'.[3]

There are in many of the Psalms recitals of many of the benefits which God has given us; but there is none that is more thoughtfully celebrated than the gift of his Word and this is most adequately presented in its great and varied function in the proem to the Gospel according to John. The Word is the thought, plan and purpose of God, and he adheres to it unwaveringly from the beginning to the end of time. This is the faithfulness of God which is much praised in the Psalms. It is on his faithfulness that our faith rests and will continue until the Word, which was in the beginning will come to sight at the end.

In conclusion, let me quote from Karl Barth's treatment of the justice of God and the promise of eternal life.

> The purpose of God in His judgment is the sanctification of man, i.e., his direction, preparation and exercise for the eternal life ordained and promised. . . . Eternal life is man's life in harmony with the life of God and all His angels, but also with that of all the rest of the elect, and, indeed, of all creation: in the harmony in which God saw and willed him when, before the foundation of the world, He knew and willed him in His Word, which is the beginning of all His ways and works.[4]

---

[3] Cf. Norman Snaith, *The Distinctive Terms of the Old Testament* (Epworth Press, London, 1944), pp. 94–142

[4] *Church Dogmatics* II/2 (T&T Clark, Edinburgh, 1957), pp. 772f.

Chapter 15

DONALD M. BAILLIE: A WITNESS TO GRACE[1]

Jan Milič Lochman

TEARS FOR ST. ANDREWS

When thinking of St. Andrews I have often been reminded of the saying: one must weep twice – once, on arrival and again, when one departs. In any event, this was my personal experience. It had not been my original plan or desire to go to St. Andrews to study. From 1946 it was possible for traditional links between the Church of Scotland and Czech Protestants to be re-established, and I gratefully accepted the offer of a scholarship to study in a Scottish university. My wish was to go to Edinburgh since New College was much better known in Czechoslovakia than the oldest Scottish university. Yet in error the names of the bursars were switched, and I was sent to St. Andrews!

For a long time, however, I had no cause to weep. From the very first moment, the town and university won me over. The beauty of the grey-stoned town with the ever-present sea in the background fascinated me, and the university, with its age and its ancient traditions still alive, became an alma mater for me. Above all, the intense theological community of St. Mary's College proved to be a true spiritual home. The times were especially favourable; after the restrictions of the war years opportunities for international exchange between students again became possible, and, young people as we were, we enthusiastically seized this new chance. Everything seemed to blossom, and so it was that my St. Andrews year became one of the happiest of my life.

[1] Translated from the German, 'Eine Zeuge der Gnade: Donald M. Baillie'

IN WEAKNESS STRONG

I recall with gratitude my fellow students at St. Mary's and also others including the SCM group which was very active at that time. Most of them I knew personally, and with some I remained bound in personal friendship over many years. As examples, I might mention the names of two who are now deceased: Donald Mathers, later a professor of theology in Canada, and John Lester, later a parish minister in the Dundee area. Happy memories of my friendship and intense discussions with them and with others have always remained with me.

Teachers naturally have a formative significance in the academic life of students, and there also we were privileged. The names speak for themselves: Principal G. S. Duncan, Professors Dickie, Forrester, Honeyman. . . . Above all, however, it was Donald M. Baillie who was decisive for me. It was not merely that my own interest lay in the field of systematic theology for the quiet, almost shy, teacher stimulated and attracted each one of us. It was an attraction different from that of most of the other great theologians of the day. Indeed, we sampled in St. Andrews this more spectacular type of style when we were visited by two of the most celebrated theologians of the day. I shall never forget the day when Reinhold Niebuhr landed like an intellectual bomb in St. Mary's, and we were also able to follow enthusiastically Emil Brunner's Gifford Lectures. Both these men of genius fascinated us through the vividness and brilliance of their thought and presentation, and, in the case of Brunner, this was enhanced by the ready manner with which he engaged in conversation and dealt with questions posed by students.

Donald Baillie hardly distinguished himself by such dazzling qualities. Both in appearance and in the delivery of his lectures, he created the impression of one who was rather reserved, and he made no attempt emotionally to overwhelm his audience or to sweep them away. He would never thrust his own personality into the centre of the academic scene. He drew our attention more by his presentation of the subject-matter in simple and spare formulations without any 'razmataz'. This renunciation of outward effects was not to conceal his own personal convictions on a topic. His lectures were unmistakably clear but were in no way handed down at second hand or dictated as class exercises. He stood by the content of his teaching which was the product of personal resolution and the quest for precision of expression. It was precisely for that reason that he was credible to us. We also encountered the same shy teacher at daily prayers and at church services. Both his translucent dogmatics lectures and the obvious piety of his conduct of worship complemented one another, and together these formed the secret of the silent power and aura of D. M. Baillie.

The effect was heightened by the perceptible fact that he had struggled with physical frailty. Few in my experience have exemplified as convincingly as this St. Andrews' teacher the paradoxical truth of Paul's words, 'for when I am weak, then I am strong' (2 Cor. 12:10). My first encounter with him is unforgettable. On account of illness his opening lecture could not take place in the university. He was confined to bed, yet he did not cancel the event but summoned us to a lecture in his house. An astonishing sight: students gathered round the bed of their teacher – truly an exceptional scene from academic life. Yet it was precisely in this situation that we saw manifested the seriousness of theology and the personal dedication of the teacher both to his subject and to his students.

THE MYSTERY OF THE INCARNATION

Where the content of the lectures was concerned (in seminars we discussed the Westminster Confession) our year had the good fortune to hear Professor Baillie deliver his christology and soteriology. This was the heart of his dogmatics. He presented to us the material which later formed the central chapters of *God Was In Christ,* an important work still worth reading. These lectures were exceptionally helpful to us. They were delivered concisely, yet they did not in any way simplify his overview of the essential questions of christology. His lectures were set in the context of contemporary theology but they displayed an obvious respect for the achievements of the history of dogma. Here one was able either to learn the essentials or to consolidate one's grasp of them. I remember, for instance, his convincing attempt to map out for contemporary christology a path between the Scylla of docetism on the one side, and the Charybdis of a modern historicism on the other. Even today this attempt to discover a responsible christological orientation is as original and relevant as it was when the passionate debates of the 'new quest of the historical Jesus' first broke out. Again, I can recall his wrestling with the great soteriological question 'Cur Deus homo', and, even today, I can still hear his plea for a trinitarian theology in which he exposed me to the Anglican theology he considered stimulating and of ecumenical significance.

Baillie's lectures produced a creative tension within us and this led to many queries and questions being put to him. He did not seek to provoke us, but he bore our questionings patiently and he took them seriously. I seized this opportunity eagerly, and I played the part of the enthusiastic student troubling the lecturer with his 'misgivings'!

This questioning applied above all to the notion with which Baillie himself was most preoccupied: 'the paradox of grace' as the key to the understanding of the paradox of the incarnation. According to Baillie, as Christians we all understand what Paul recognised of his life of faith, especially where he was partially successful, when he wrote, 'not I, but the grace of God which is with me'. (1 Cor 15:10). This led Baillie to the conclusion, 'that this paradox in its fragmentary form in our Christian lives is a reflection of that perfect union of God and man in the Incarnation on which our whole Christian life depends, and may therefore be our best clue to the understanding of it.'[2]

I would not in any way wish to dispute the pedagogical meaning of this consideration, yet I ventured then (and venture even today) the doubt whether such an account of the uniqueness and sovereignty of the incarnation could really be justified. In its association with general Christian experience does it not encourage a relativizing of the biblical-christological 'God was in Christ' to an anthropological level? In an appreciative and detailed Czech review of the book, I later tried to develop this line of questioning by asking: is our personal experience of the paradox of grace not better presented as an imperfect analogy of the life of the *human* Jesus, rather than an analogy of the actual paradox of the incarnation in all its profundity as the incarnation of *God*.

These were obviously Barthian questions that I was trying to

---

[2] *God Was In Christ* (Faber, London, 1948), p. 147

express in different ways to my teacher, although I did not study under Barth until after my time in St. Andrews. While holding to his own views, Baillie always showed great patience in dealing with my questions. He was never on any occasion resentful or even annoyed at my contentiousness, and, at the end of the course, I was ashamed of the generosity of the report he issued me. I was even more deeply affected when years later, after his death, I learned of his concern about my fate in a homeland which had become subject to Stalinist domination only months after my departure from St. Andrews. He had sent out a message which expressed his desire to enable me to come to Scotland and to find suitable employment there, in the event of my being subject to political pressure and being able to escape from Czechoslovakia. Here was a most impressive demonstration of the trust that this teacher placed in his rebellious students.

LIVING LEGACY

If after 45 years I were to outline the personal significance of my teacher and to state how he had influenced me through several decades of teaching in Prague, New York, Basel and many other places, I would list three main points. These are by no means exhaustive.

1. Both in an academic and ecclesiastical context my life's work has been centred upon systematic theology. One can approach this discipline in a variety of ways, and, indeed, I have always had several different models in mind. For example, it is possible to establish in a comprehensive and coherent manner a complete dogmatics. This has been done in our time with incomparable success by Karl Barth, although even here the task remained incomplete. Yet there are other systematic theologians who deal not with the subject matter in its totality but with particular areas of enquiry. Here I think, for instance, of Reinhold Niebuhr. Again, there are still other systematicians who are totally absorbed in the issues of the day and whose theological work is immersed in real life situations. Here I think of my Prague teacher, Josef L. Hromádka.

Where amongst these models are we to locate a thinker such as Donald M. Baillie? I believe he holds a modest yet significant place in his attempt to teach systematic theology by concentrating upon the essentials, and by encouraging students to focus upon these, instead of being distracted by a misguided concern for more 'relevant' questions. This does not imply a dogmatic minimalism. The wealth and variety of old and new dogmatic themes cannot be ignored. They must be worked through with respect. At the same time, the responsibility of the dogmatician is not exhausted by a study of the winding paths of historical and contemporary discussion. There must also be a process of judgment in which one discerns what is essential and directs one's students towards it. Here priorities must be set. This is risky and one must bear in mind the double reference of the dogmatician: responsibility both to the Biblical message and also to the demands of the time.

For the most part, I have chosen this approach in my own teaching. A preoccupation with the fundamental texts of the faith – the Ten Commandments, the Apostles' Creed, and the Lord's Prayer – has been a priority for me when these are set within the context of the most pressing issues of our day. Looking back, I can say that Donald Baillie was not the only teacher whose personal example inspired me; yet in his concentrated dogmatic work, as exemplified by *God Was In Christ*, he has been the outstanding and, I hope, most formative model.

2. Donald M. Baillie is also a model theologian in his trust of the *classical line of Christendom*, (to use an expression of my Prague teacher, J. L. Hromádka). Of course, the history of Christian theology can never be reduced to a single line as, thank God, there are many lines of theological thought. But not all are of equal weight. There is already a *classical line* in Reformation theology and this should not be neglected even when one is in search of new forms of expression. In Baillie's lectures we were able to become immersed in the Christology of the ancient Church, (especially from Athanasius to Chalcedon), the Church fathers of the middle ages such as Augustine and Anselm, the Reformers, (above all Calvin), and naturally the ecumenical contemporaries such as Barth, Brunner, Niebuhr, and Hodgson.

Yet this approach is not self-evidently the right one; at least, it was not for D. M. Baillie. His heart did not always lie with the classical line. Brought up in a strict Calvinist home, he was exposed painfully as a student to the challenges of a more secular culture within the university. According to the testimony of his brother, he did not cope at all easily with the tension. 'Donald was afterwards to be a valiant defender of the faith. . . but he had to pass through a long struggle from which only slowly he was able to emerge.'[3]

His first endeavours were not surprisingly of an apologetic orientation. Yet his path through many years of faithful pastoral service led him further into the central teaching of the Church. Again we have the evidence of John Baillie: 'In his latter years Donald frequently confessed to me that the focus of his interest had gradually moved onwards from the more general problems of what is usually called the philosophy of religion, such as had formerly occupied him, to the detail of Christian dogmatics.'[4] Nonetheless, on this journey towards the centre there was no decisive break; a sensitive understanding of the difficulties that modern persons felt with dogmatic themes always informed his expositions. It was precisely this that enhanced the credibility of his positive dogmatics. Here also he became for us a supreme example to be emulated.

3. D. M. Baillie is also significant for the manner in which he held in dialectical tension a trust in his ecclessiastical and cultural origins with a genuine ecumenical openness. In him there stood unmistakeably before me a Scottish divine. It may have had something to do with his physical appearance but it was above all his unambiguous rootedness in the inheritance of the Scottish church and its theology. He would gladly share with us reminiscences of his teachers, above all of H. R Mackintosh. And he played a leading part in the struggles of the church in his own day, particularly in renewal movements such as the Iona Community and the Student Christian Movement.

Yet Baillie was open to other types of theological tradition and to the ecumenical movement. It was through his influence that I was motivated to study in depth the Anglican tradition which is little known on the continent. I was impressed also by his attention and openness to continental theology, especially from Germany and Switzerland. The great names of Barth, Brunner and Bultmann featured in his lectures. He always viewed them critically yet never in

---

[3] John Baillie, 'Donald: A Brother's Impression' in D. M. Baillie, *Theology of the Sacraments* (Faber, London, 1957), p. 20

[4] ibid. p. 28

a distorted manner as was sometimes the case in St. Andrews. Karl
Barth was never a theological extremist in his eyes and he never spoke
of a 'Barthian onslaught' in theology and church life.

Thus I have also learned from Baillie (or perhaps I should say that
I was confirmed in a knowledge already gained in Prague) that
responsible ecumenical theology displays a trust in one's own
ecclesiastical and cultural setting alongside a concern to allow other,
and sometimes strange, voices their right and proper place. This
became apparent to me not only in my academic teaching but also
through many years of serving on the Faith and Order Commission
of the World Council of Churches; on which, incidentally, Donald
Baillie had once represented the Church of Scotland.

In my study for several decades, I have kept photographs of men for
whom I have been especially grateful along my theological journey.
Beside my Prague teachers and friends such as J. L. Hromádka, J. B.
Souček, and the philosopher, Jan Patocka and beside my
unforgettable Basel teacher, Karl Barth, there is also a picture from
Scotland of D. M. Baillie. It is an especially beautiful picture. Our
teacher is standing at the centre of a Scottish landscape, by a lochside
surrounded by Highland hills. Someone has described this photo as a
'symbol of the incarnation'. It strikes me rather as a symbol of the
'paradox of grace'. In expression and appearance he is an
inconspicuous man who points not to himself but much more to the
backdrop of God's nature and grace. Yet in doing so he becomes
himself a personal and convincing witness to grace – a graceful man.

Chapter 16

D. M. BAILLIE – AS A STUDENT SAW HIM

Murdo Ewen Macdonald

On the first of November, 1954, Donald Baillie's obituary appeared in the 'Scotsman'. During lunch the phone rang. It was Donald's brother John, Professor of Divinity at Edinburgh University and Principal of New College. He went on to say that while his brother's obituary was factually correct it lacked something. It gave the impression that the person who wrote it did not know Donald very well. Then he asked, 'Murdo Ewen, will you write a tribute to your former Professor and friend to appear in the "Scotsman" tomorrow morning.' Here it is.

Late D. M. Baillie
An Appreciation

The Rev. Murdo Ewen Macdonald, St George's West Church, Edinburgh, writes of the late Professor D. M. Baillie: The first time I set eyes on him was at an evening service in summer with the sun struggling through a stained-glass window. I didn't know who he was, but as he turned to enter the pew in front of me, I was struck by the face, so finely chiselled and by the eyes so curiously shy and sharp.

The next time I saw him was at a meeting in the Students' Union when he was introduced as the Professor of Systematic Theology. It was the same man who had attracted my attention in Church over a year before. I remembered every detail of that first impression, the loose-limbed undulating walk, the lean ascetic face, the indefinable aura of goodness.

Later came his impact as a Professor. From the first we realised that he was a giant and so great was our awe of him that we were in danger of regarding him as an Olympian who dwelt apart. We soon learned that he was the simplest and friendliest of men, the most hospitable of hosts, a born story-teller and a genius with children. As the months passed into years we discovered something else. This man was more than a scholar – he was a saint in whose transparent humility we saw reflected the beauty of holiness.

As a teacher he was supreme. Himself a master of paradox, his lectures had a paradoxical effect upon his students. On the one hand you felt the last word had been spoken on every subject, be it incarnation, atonement or eschatology. On the other hand he stimulated more than he satisfied by opening up wider vistas and horizons. We felt like Keats on first looking into Chapman's Homer.

How providential that he wrote his magnum opus, 'God Was in Christ', before he was called home. It is the work not only of a great theologian, but also of a devout man 'far ben' in the world of the spirit. If the task of the preacher is to take the insights of theology and translate them into the language of the pulpit – a difficult but exhilarating exercise – we ministers will for ever stand in debt to the author of this great book.

To me his death came as a stunning blow, but my deepest emotion is one of profound gratitude. He was my teacher and my friend and knowing him as I did my faith in God was fortified. I believe in immortality for many reasons and desire it because I find life here so significant that I want it to continue. But with Donald Baillie on the other side, the belief becomes even more meaningful. This man of God with the delicate frame and the robust faith left many disciples behind him.

I have had many excellent teachers at the several schools I attended and at my university, but the one who made the greatest impact on me was Donald Baillie. His influence helped to shape all my ministries. The debt I owe him is incalculable.

For one thing he taught me that the preaching, teaching and pastoral ministries along with theology form an organic unity.

There must be no divorce between preaching and theology. 'What God hath joined together let no man put asunder.' To be sure the two disciplines can be distinguished but they can't be separated. Theology can save preaching from subjectivity and amiable sentimentality. Preaching can save theology from stratospheric speculation by tethering it to the solid earth. This proclaimed word points to an Event rooted in history. It relates to the needs of ordinary men and women.

In 1965 at the request of Professor James Whyte of St. Andrews University I became an external examiner of a Ph.D thesis. It was written by an American student, Nicholas Van Dyck. The subject was 'Theological Themes in the Preaching of D. M. Baillie'.

Dr. Van Dyck had at his disposal Professor Baillie's published works and his unpublished lectures, along with two volumes of published sermons and many unpublished ones. He came to the firm conclusion that this renowned scholar communicated his theology more lucidly and more effectively from the pulpit than from the lecture room.

To Donald Baillie theology was not a disembodied system of timeless truths, it was grounded in human experience. Like his brother, John, he took secular culture seriously, history, science, politics, music, literature and the visual arts. In this respect he had much in common with Paul Tillich.

For another thing, Donald Baillie taught me practically all I know about the art and craft of sermon construction. This is how it all started. In the first term of my second year in St Mary's College, I found myself preaching in Martyrs' Church, morning and evening. Sitting under me were three of my professors, Donald MacPherson Baillie, Edgar Primrose Dickie and William Roxburgh Forrester. The sight unnerved me. I was more nervous than I was when years later I was dropped behind the enemy lines.

On Monday morning after his lecture D. M. intercepted me and invited me to afternoon tea. He got down to business straight away. He told me that after having listened to my two sermons he had come to the conclusion I had the makings of a popular preacher. Then, giving me one of his sharp looks, he added, 'provided you are prepared to subject yourself to vigorous and sustained discipline'. Somewhat taken aback I stupidly asked him in what sense I was indisciplined.

He answered, 'Well to begin with you use eye language instead of ear language.' I had never heard of this distinction so I asked him to explain. Rising from his chair he began walking round his study gesticulating vigorously, now and again stabbing a fore-finger in my

direction. 'Murdo Ewen eye language is essay language. From the day
we go to school we are indoctrinated into the essay style of writing.
The eye can take in a long, complex, convoluted sentence, not the ear.
If you are to become an effective preacher you have to learn a new
language, so to speak.'

At this point he sat down and, looking at me across the study, made
this very generous offer. He asked me to hand in to him every sermon
I wrote not later than Wednesday morning, promised to go over it
critically and discuss it with me over tea on Thursday afternoon. At
the end of three months I certainly knew the difference between eye
language and ear language.

On the shape of the sermon he was equally demanding and equally
helpful. He went out of his way to stress exegetical honesty, the
consulting of scholarly commentaries, but warned against overdoing
it. People do not come to church to listen to a learned seminar on
hermeneutics, he would say. The introduction he insisted must arrest
attention. It should be interesting and succinct. I think it was from
him I first heard of the perceptive old lady who caustically criticised a
preacher thus, 'He took so long to lay the cloth that I lost all appetite
for the meal'.

His advice on how to end a sermon was bang on. The conclusion
must on no account be an anti-climax. Again and again he would
emphasise that from start to finish a sermon is a dynamic unity. He
would say Amen to T. S. Eliot who wrote:

In my beginning is my end . . .
And the end of our exploring will be to arrive
Where we started
And know the place for the first time.

Good poetry and good homiletics.

D. M.'s comments on the use of illustrations I couldn't possibly
forget. The timing is all important, he would argue. In the
development of the sermon there is an exact position for the
illustration. Used too soon it is thrown away. Used too late it has
become redundant. All the great preachers he would claim had a
'feel', an intuitive sense of sequence.

The afternoon this gruelling commando course in homiletic came
to an end audibly I breathed a sigh of relief. D. M. must have heard

it for he gave me his sharpest look yet and said, 'Murdo Ewen now your conduct of public worship.' 'But Sir,' I expostulated, 'I never write my prayers.' And he reposted, 'That is very obvious. I have listened to you conducting worship at least six times and your prayers are marked by untidiness and repetitiveness.'

Rarely did D. M. indulge in irascibility but this time he did. 'Why are you Gaelic speakers, fed on the Bible, so stubbornly opposed to written prayers?' Reaching for his own Bible, he opened it at Psalm 51 and ordered me to read it aloud. I heard myself intoning, 'Have mercy upon me, O God, according to thy loving-kindness; according to the multitude of thy tender mercies blot out my transgressions.' At which point he interrupted and said, 'That is a prayer of confession. It is in the Bible and it is written.' He came over to where I was sitting, turned over the leaves and stopped at Psalm 103 and again ordered me to read aloud. 'Bless the Lord, O my soul; and all that is within me, bless his holy name. Bless the Lord, O my soul, and forget not all his benefits.' Another imperious interruption, 'Murdo Ewen that is a prayer of thanksgiving – a classic. It is in the Bible and it is written. What have you to say to that?' I didn't say anything. There and then I experienced a Damascus Road liturgical conversion. Ever since that afternoon in D. M.'s book-lined study I have meticulously written all my prayers, even more carefully than my sermons.

God does not bestow His benediction on extemporaneous garrulousness. He favours meaning, for meaning has authentic shape. The language of worship is the language of devotion and imagination. This can be nurtured from constant companionship with the psalms and familiarity with prayers of classic dimension.

Donald Baillie did not know Paul Tillich's book *Theology of Culture* for it was published after his death, but I am convinced he would have agreed with Tillich's analysis of the nature of religious language. Along with great music, great literature, great paintings, authentic religious language can open up a level of Reality which otherwise would have remained hidden.

Professor A. C. Cheyne (also a friend of D. M.) draws our attention to 'the beautiful simplicity of structure and language' which characterised all his sermons. No doubt this is a gift which defies analysis, but I suspect the innate gift was developed by his rigorous classical training in the Inverness Royal Academy. His headmaster was the celebrated W. J. Watson, a brilliant linguist who later became Professor of Celtic at Edinburgh University.

I agree with Alec Cheyne. Linguistic skill is a powerful preaching tool and in this special ability Donald Baillie had few if any equals. But along with enviable skill he possessed a finely honed pastoral skill. In one of his books Paul Tillich uses a memorable phrase. 'Without participation there is no communication.' More than most Donald Baillie participated in the human predicament. With rare sensitivity he could enter into the anxieties, the regrets, the longings and aspirations of his fellow humans. It was this gift of empathy along with lucidity of thought and clarity of style that made him such a superb communicator.

Donald Baillie was a unique person so it was not surprising to meet in him an intriguing coalescence of contrarieties. In a way he was a workaholic, but he could also relax with his friends. Stern and uncompromising on certain issues, he was on the whole charitable and non-judgmental. An ascetic in many ways, he was tolerant of the failings of others. A good raconteur, he had a highly developed sense of the absurd.

The parties he hosted in his house 'Crask', usually on a Friday night, were incomparably the best in the university. A splendid meal was followed by a few games, some irreverent exchanges, all sorts of stories, mostly apocryphal. He always insisted on my impersonating Professor Stout, Professor Blythe Webster, Professor Morrison, Professor Duncan, Professor Forrester, himself pronouncing the Benediction.

D. M. was a wonderful friend. After I was taken prisoner he tracked down the address of the camp I was in and without delay set things in motion. Through the Red Cross in Geneva he arranged to send me books. In Stalag Luft 3, thanks to him, I had a fine theological library. Sadly I had to leave it all behind when in January 1945 the Russians closed in and we had to march out in the middle of a snow storm.

After repatriation he invited me to say with him in St Andrews for a week. I was surprised that he was so intensely interested in the war. He wanted to know how I was treated as a prisoner of war. He had heard of the Great Escape and of the fifty who were executed. When I told him we had a fine German Commandant who treated me as a friend and that the military proper were not responsible for the murder of the escaped prisoners of war, he was visibly relieved.

D. M. was greatly pleased when I was called to St George's West in 1949 and insisted on introducing me. Known from the beginning as Free St George's, he had a special affection for it as he himself was born in a Free Church manse. That affection was considerably reinforced when he got to know Alexander Whyte, his Principal at New College.

A few days before he died John Baillie got his wife, Jewel, to phone me. She said simply, 'John wants to see you.' When I reached Whitehouse Terrace, she led me into his bedroom, left me with him and closed the door behind her. He looked very frail and I knew he didn't have long to go. Pointing to a bronze plaque on a table beside his bed he said, 'You have seen that often.' 'Oh yes', I said, 'That was the plaque Donald had on his desk at "Crask".' John went on to say that Donald had left it to him, but had instructed him to leave it to me in his Will. He asked me to hand it over to him and he read the Gaelic inscription aloud, apologising for his pronunciation. When I assured him his pronunciation was excellent he gave a little ghost of a smile and said, 'You Gaelic speakers are born flatterers.' The inscription is ancient and beautiful. It reads:

Thig crióch air
An T-saoghal
Ach mairidh
Gaol is ceól

'The world will come to an end but Love and Music will endure.'

I thanked him, picked up the plaque and turned to go as he looked so exhausted. I was opening the door when I heard his voice, hardly audible, 'Murdo Ewen come back please.' On reaching the bed he looked at me and said, 'Gaelic was the first language I heard prayer in. Will you give me a blessing in Gaelic?'

At one of the meetings of the Greek Club in Edinburgh, Reinhold Niebuhr was present as a guest. At the end of the evening John Baillie asked him if he wished to say something. I can still see him uncoiling himself from his chair. It was many years ago, but so impressed was I by what he said that I can quote him verbatim without any difficulty. 'Over the passing generation this little country of yours has produced theologians who have combined sound scholarship with authentic piety.' Whether he intended it or not, Niebuhr was giving an accurate description of John and Donald Baillie.

NOTES ON CONTRIBUTORS

Ray S. Anderson is Professor of Theology and Ministry at Fuller Theological Seminary, Pasadena, California. His publications include *On Being Human* (1982), *Theology, Death and Dying* (1986) and *The Gospel According to Judas* (1991).

Alec C. Cheyne was Professor of Ecclesiastical History in the University of Edinburgh (1964–86). His publications include *The Transforming of the Kirk* (1983) and *The Practical and the Pious: Essays on Thomas Chalmers* (1985)

Keith W. Clements was until 1990 Senior Tutor at Bristol Baptist College and is now Co-ordinating Secretary for International Affairs, Council of Churches for Britain and Ireland. His publications include *Lovers of Discord* (1988) and books on Dietrich Bonhoeffer and Ronald Gregor Smith. He is currently working on the biography of J. H. Oldham.

David A. S. Fergusson is Professor of Systematic Theology in the University of Aberdeen. His publications include *Bultmann* (1992).

Duncan B. Forrester is Professor of Christian Ethics and Practical Theology in the University of Edinburgh, Principal of New College and Director of the Edinburgh University Centre for Theology and Public Issues. His publications include *Theology and Politics* (1988) and *Beliefs, Values and Policies* (1989).

George B. Hall is a Senior Lecturer in Divinity at the University of St Andrews. Before moving to Scotland in 1973, he was Dean of Colgate Rochester Divinity School, USA.

George S. Hendry served as a parish minister in Bridge of Allan (1930–49) before becoming Charles Hodge Professor of Systematic Theology at Princeton Theological Seminary (1949–73). His publications include *The Holy Spirit in Christian Theology* (1956), *The Gospel of the Incarnation* (1958) and *Theology of Nature* (1980).

Jan Milič Lochman was Professor of Theology and Philosophy at the Comenius Faculty, Prague (1950–68). He is currently Professor of Theology at the University of Basel where he was also Rector Magnificus (1981–83). His publications include *Reconciliation and Liberation* (1980), *The Faith We Confess* (1984) and *The Lord's Prayer* (1990).

John C. Lusk is a minister of the Church of Scotland. He has served as a chaplain in the RAF, as a parish minister in Berwickshire and West Lothian, and as tutor at St Columba's College, Alice, Cape Province.

Murdo Ewen Macdonald held ministerial charges in Portree, Glasgow and Edinburgh before becoming Professor of Practical Theology at Trinity College, Glasgow (1964–84). His publications include *The Vitality of Faith* (1955), *The Need to Believe* (1959) and *The Call to Obey* (1963).

John McIntyre was Professor of Divinity in the University of Edinburgh (1956–86) and Moderator of the General Assembly of the Church of Scotland in 1982. His publications include *St. Anselm and His Critics* (1954), *The Shape of Christology* (1966) and *Faith, Theology and the Imagination* (1987).

Donald M. MacKinnon was Regius Professor of Moral Philosophy in the University of Aberdeen (1947–60) and Norris-Hulse Professor of Divinity in the University of Cambridge (1960–78). His publications include *The Problem of Metaphysics* (1974), *Explorations in Theology* (1979) and *Themes in Theology: The Threefold Cord* (1987).

George M. Newlands is Professor of Divinity in the University of Glasgow and Principal of Trinity College. He was formerly Dean of Trinity Hall, Cambridge and a University Lecturer in Divinity. His publications include *Hilary of Poitiers* (1978), *Theology of the Love of God* (1980), and *Making Christian Decisions* (1985).

Thomas F. Torrance was Professor of Christian Dogmatics in the University of Edinburgh (1952–79) and Moderator of the General Assembly of the Church of Scotland in 1976. His publications include *Theological Science* (1969), *The Trinitarian Faith* (1988) and *The Mediation of Christ* (1992).

James A. Whyte was Professor of Practical Theology and Christian Ethics in the University of St Andrews (1958–87) and Principal of St Mary's College (1978–82). He was Moderator of the General Assembly of the Church of Scotland in 1988.

BIBLIOGRAPHY OF PRINCIPAL WRITINGS

JOHN BAILLIE

Books

The Roots of Religion in the Human Soul (Hodder and Stoughton, London, 1926)

The Interpretation of Religion (T&T Clark, Edinburgh, 1929)

The Place of Jesus Christ in Modern Christianity (T&T Clark, Edinburgh, 1929)

And the Life Everlasting (Scribners, London, 1934)

A Diary of Private Prayer (Oxford University Press, London, 1936)

Our Knowledge of God (Oxford University Press, London, 1939)

Invitation to Pilgrimage (Oxford University Press, London, 1942)

What is Christian Civilization? (Oxford University Press, London, 1945)

What is Christian Civilization? Second Edition (Oxford University Press, London, 1947)

The Belief in Progress (Oxford University Press, London, 1950)

The Idea of Revelation in Recent Thought (Oxford University Press, London, 1956)

The Sense of the Presence of God (Oxford University Press, London, 1962)

Christian Devotion (Oxford University Press, London, 1962)

A Reasoned Faith (Oxford University Press, London, 1963)

Baptism and Conversion (Oxford University Press, London, 1964)

Books Edited

with H. Martin, *Revelation* (Faber, London, 1937)

God's Will in Our Time (SCM, London, 1946)

A Diary of Readings (Oxford University Press, London, 1955)

with J. T. McNeill and H. P. van Dusen, *The Library of Christian Classics*, 26 vols., (Westminster Press, Philadelphia, 1950–57)

K. Barth and E. Brunner, *Natural Theology* (Bles, London, 1946)

Essays and Articles

'The Subliminal Consciousness as an Aid to the Interpretation of Religious Experience', *The Expository Times*, 24, 1912/13, p. 353–358

'Belief as an Element in Religion', *The Expositor*, 9, 1915, pp. 75–92

'The Present Situation in Theology', *Auburn Seminary Record*, 16, 1920, p. 209–229

'The True Ground of Theistic Belief', *Hibbert Journal*, 21, 1922, pp. 44–52

'The Fundamental Task of the Theological Seminary', *Reformed Church Review*, 1, 1922, pp. 259–275

'The Idea of Orthodoxy', *Hibbert Journal*, 24, 1926, pp. 232–249

'The Meaning of Duty: A Plea for a Reconsideration of the Kantian Ethic', *Hibbert Journal*, 24, 1926, pp. 718–730

'"Happiness" Once More', *Hibbert Journal*, 26, 1927, pp. 69–83

'The Mind of Christ on the Treatment of Crime', *Expository Times*, 41, 1930, pp. 261–265

'The Psychological Point of View', *Philosophical Review*, 39, 1930, pp. 258–274

'The Logic of Religion', *Alumni Bulletin of Union Theological Seminary*, 3, 1930, p. 6–16

'The Predicament of Humanism', *Canadian Journal of Religious Thought*, 22, 1931, pp. 109–118

'The Young Minister and the Modern Situation', *Methodist Review*, 114, 1931, pp. 151–156

'Confessions of a Transplanted Scot', *Contemporary American Theology: Theological Autobiographies*, ed. Vermiglius Ferm (Round Table Press, New York, 1933), pp. 33–59

Science and Faith Today, with R. Boyd, D. MacKay, and D. Spanner, (Oxford University Press, London, 1935)

'The Theological Course as a Preparation for the Missionary', *International Review of Missions*, 28, 1939, pp. 535–548

'Does God Defend the Right?', *Christian Newsletter*, 53, 30 October, 1940.

'The Theology of the War', *Christian Century*, 60, 1943, pp. 354–356

The Prospects of Spiritual Renewal: (Closing Address to General Assembly, 1943) (Blackwood, Edinburgh, 1943)

The Mind of the Modern University (SCM, London, 1946)
'The Given Word: The Message of the Unvarying Gospel',
     International Review of Missions, 36, 1947, pp. 452–466
'Why I Believe in God', *Union Seminary Quarterly Review,* 3, 1948,
     pp. 3–6
'Beliefs About the Last Things', *Congregational Quarterly,* 28, 1950,
     pp. 206–218
The Human Situation (Longmans, London, 1950)
Natural Science and the Spiritual Life (British Association Lecture,
     London, 1951)
'Beware the Whitewash', *Christian Century,* 68, 1951, pp. 1248–1249
'The Theology of the Frontier', *The Frontier,* 6, 1952, pp. 212–226
'Faith and the Scientific Impulse', *Theology Today,* 9, 1952,
     pp. 304–305
'The World Mission of the Church: The Contemporary Scene',
     International Review of Missions, 41, 1952, pp. 161–169
'Some Reflections on the Changing Theological Scene', *Union
     Seminary Quarterly Review,* 12, 1957, pp. 3–7
'Donald: A Brother's Impression' in D. M. Baillie, *Theology of the
     Sacraments* (Faber, London, 1957) pp. 3–16
'Looking Before and After', *Christian Century,* 65, 1958, pp. 400–402
'Some Comments on Professor Hick's Article on "The Christology of
     D. M. Baillie"', *Scottish Journal of Theology,* 11, 1958,
     pp. 265–270
Liberalism in Theology, Eugene William Lyman Lecture (Sweet Briar,
     Virginia, 1959)

DONALD BAILLIE

Books
Faith in God and its Christian Consummation (T&T Clark,
     Edinburgh, 1927)
God Was In Christ (Faber, London, 1948)
To Whom Shall We Go? (St. Andrew Press, Edinburgh, 1955)
Theology of the Sacraments (Faber, London, 1957)
Out of Nazareth (St Andrew Press, Edinburgh, 1958)

Books Edited
Intercommunion (SCM, London, 1952)

Essays and Articles
'What is the Theology of Experience?', *Expositor,* 8, 1920, pp. 64–77
'Philosophers and Theologians: An Irenicon', *Expositor,* XXVI, 1923,
    pp. 61–79
'Recent Foreign Theology', *Expository Times,* 42, 1930, pp. 44–5
'The Christian Life', *Christian Faith and Practice VI* (Church of
    Scotland Committee on Publications, Edinburgh, 1932),
    pp. 129–192
'The Message of H. R. Mackintosh', *Life and Work,* August 1936,
    pp. 310–312
I Believe in God (Church of Scotland Publications, Edinburgh, 1937)
'Theologians and Philosophers: Changes of 50 Years', *Times Literary
    Supplement,* April 30, 1938, p. x
'The Justification of Infant Baptism', *Evangelical Quarterly,* 15, 1943,
    pp. 21–31
'Memoir', *David Cairns: An Autobiography* (SCM, London, 1950)
    pp. 9–37
'Philosophers and Theologians on the Freedom of the Will', *Scottish
    Journal of Theology,* 4, 1951, pp. 113–122
'The Christological Theory of William Sanday', *Expository Times,* 44,
    1953, pp. 236–239
The Meaning of Holy Communion (Iona Community Publishing
    Department, Glasgow)

INDEX

Aberlard, P., 119
Anscombe, E., 134
Anselm, 103, 115ff., 132, 278
Aquinas, T., 142, 157, 160, 164, 213
Aristotle, 116, 162
Athanasius, 278
atonement, 115ff., 132ff., 138
Auber, H., 103
Augustine, 103, 162, 257f., 278

Baillie, Annie Macpherson, 3, 5
Baillie, Florence Jewel, 4, 253, 265
Baillie, John (senior), 3, 5, 7, 253
Baillie, Peter, 3
Barth, Karl, 33ff., 87, 90, 98f., 123
    139ff., 143ff., 148, 149, 151, 153,
    158, 160ff., 202, 212f., 215ff.,
    221f., 224, 236, 244, 246, 253f.,
    255, 258, 264, 269f., 277f.
Beveridge, C., 221
Bishops' Report, 5, 191ff.
Blake, C., 100
Bliss, K., 217
Boff, L., 87
Bonaventure, 142, 256
Bonhoeffer, D., 34, 50f., 152, 246
Bosanquet, B., 12
Bradley, F. H., 12, 157
Brilioth, Archbishop, 197
Brunner, E., 33, 34, 90f., 137, 143ff.,
    153, 202, 208, 215, 221f., 236,
    244, 274, 278f.
Buber, M., 34, 72, 201
Buddhism, 129, 145
Bulgakov, S., 72, 75
Bultmann, R., 23, 87, 90, 98f., 158,
    279
Busch, E., 144

Cairns, David S., 21, 34, 260
Cairns, David, 137, 144

Calvin, J., 9ff., 213, 240, 254, 278
Campbell, John McLeod, 119
Carlyle, T., 30, 32
Carnell, E. J., 45, 53ff.
Celtic influences, 5ff.
Chalmers, T., 21, 128, 241
Cheyne, A. C., 43, 264, 283
Churchill, W., 236
Clark, G., 53
Coleridge, S. T., 174
Collingwood, R. G., 99f.
Commission for the Interpretation of
    God's Will in the Present Crisis, 5,
    182ff., 185ff., 218, 225ff., 235ff.,
    266
Cox, Harvey, 247f.
Craig, Archie, 191f.
Curtis, W. A., 15

Dalferth, I., 162ff.
Demant, V. A., 222
Dickie, E., 274, 283
Dilthey, W., 202
Dodd, C. H., 15, 91ff., 118
Dods, M., 11, 14
Dow, J., 176, 197
Dray, W. H., 100
Duncan, G. S., 274
Dyck, N. Van, 283

Ebner, 201
Eliot, T. S., 140, 146, 200, 202, 206,
    208, 211, 222, 240, 241, 247, 284
Ellul, J., 246

Fairbairn, A. M., 89
Farmer, H. H., 202
Fenn, E., 202, 204
Flint, R., 128
Forrester, D., 248
Forrester, I., 145, 197

Forrester, W., 274, 283
Forsyth, P. T., 119
Fox, George 49
Fox, R., 222f.
Fry, Christopher, 52, 64

Gardiner, P., 100
Gorman, J. L., 100
Graham, Gordon, 83-4
Grisebach, 201

Harkless, J., 16
Harnack, A., 24
Harvey, van A., 100
Hegel, 125f, 130, 137, 157, 160, 164
Heidegger, M., 141
Herrmann, W., 35, 46, 123f., 138
Hendry, G. S., 34, 144
Hick, J., 105ff.
Hocking, W. E., 141
Hodges, H. A., 202, 207, 215f., 218
Hodgson, L., 278
Honeyman, 274
Hopkins, G. M., 115
Hoskyns, E., 99
Hromadká, J. L., 277, 278, 280
Hügel, Von, 35

incarnation, 71ff., 75ff., 103ff., 115, 120, 131f., 137, 143, 194
Inge, D. R., 66
Irenaeus, 112

James, W., 29, 49
Jesus, history of, 90ff., 117ff., 131f., 276
Joyce, J., 140
Jüngel, E., 160, 166
Justin, Martyr, 35, 133

Kähler, M., 98
Kairos Document, 223f., 234
Kant, 12, 32, 46, 47, 124ff., 134, 157, 160

Kee, A. A., 249
Kelman, J., 11
Kempis, Thomas à, 103
Kennedy, H. A. A., 13
kenoticism, 89, 100, 115f., 120
Kierkegaard, S., 34, 49, 53, 91, 98, 198, 236, 244
Klee, P., 140
Klinefelter, D., 140, 141, 152, 215
Kuhn, T., 162

Leckie, J. H., 16
Lester, J., 274
Levick, B., 118
Lewis, H. D., 143
Lindbeck, G., 130
Lindsay, A. D., 221
Lonergan, B., 164
Löwe, A., 206
Luscombe, D., 119
Luther, M., 143, 162, 213

Mackay, J. A., 6, 152
Macaulay, A. B., 117
MacKinnon, D., 217
Mackintosh, H. R., 13, 18, 34, 73, 88f., 101f., 115, 279
Macintyre, A., 135
McIntyre, J., 75, 88, 96ff., 111ff., 143, 221
MacLeod, D., 120
MacLeod, G., 266
Macmurray, J., 213, 221, 222
Macquarrie, J., 75, 88, 96ff., 111ff., 143, 221
Mannheim, K., 159, 203, 206, 209ff., 217, 218
Mansell, 157
Mansfield, K., 202
Manson, W., 191
Maritain, J., 212ff.
Martin, A., 13
Mathers, D., 274
Maxwell, W. D., 266
mediated immediacy, 22, 141ff.

Meynell, A., 133
Millar, J., 140
Mitchell, B., 136
Moberly, R. C., 119
Moberly, W., 202f., 210, 218
Moffat, J., 16
Moltmann, J., 87, 160
morality, 30f., 45ff., 124ff.
Mott, J. R., 190
Munby, D., 247
Murray, G., 242
Murry, J. Middleton, 202, 207

Newbigin, L., 153
Niebuhr, Reinhold, 53, 147, 153, 202, 214, 221ff., 227, 231, 235, 239, 243f., 274, 277, 278, 287
Niebuhr, Richard, 221
Niebuhr, Ursula, 147
Nineham, D., 117f.

Oldham, J. H., 187, 190, 199ff., 207f., 217, 218, 222, 229, 235
Oldham, Mary, 203
Otto, R., 47

Pannenberg, W., 87, 112, 164, 166
paradox of grace, 77ff., 103ff., 276, 280
Pascal, B., 28, 256f.
Patocka, J., 280
Paton, W., 208
Paterson, W. P., 2, 12
Picasso, 140
Pittenger, N., 87, 112
Plato, 12, 31, 129, 153, 211, 271
Polanyi, M., 44
Pompa, L., 100
Power, W., 152
Proust, M., 140

Rahner, K., 87, 112, 160, 166
Rainy, R., 11
Rashdall, H., 119
religious doubt, 26ff., 41-64

resurrection of Jesus, 91, 120, 138
Ritschl, A., 31, 34f., 46, 126, 128f., 239, 248
Robertson, F. W., 30, 31
Robinson, J., 87, 267
Rushdie, S., 245

Sabatier, 157
sacraments, 8, 121, 186, 193ff., 240ff., 254
Sanders, E. P., 97f.
Santayana, G., 16, 160
Schillebeeckx, E., 87, 166
Schleiermacher, F. D. E., 112, 128, 162
Schlink, 153
Scott, E. F., 16
Scotus, John Duns, 115
Shakespeare, 10
Shaw, Gilbert, 210
Shaw, D. W. D., 43, 111
Smith, Donald C., 232
Smith, George Adam, 142
Smith, Ronald Gregor, 43, 201, 221, 269
Snaith, N., 272
Sobrino, J., 87
Sophocles, 118
Souček, J. B., 280
Spinoza, 160
Steiner, G., 160
Stevenson, R. L., 29, 48
Strachan, R. H., 16
Summers, J., 267

Tawney, R. H., 222, 229
Temple, W., 181, 221, 228f.
Templeton, E., 192
Tertullian, 237
theological education, 23ff.
Thompson, F., 50
Thomson, G. T., 264
Tillich, P., 94, 157, 222, 246, 283, 285f.
Torrance, T. F., 153, 162, 216f.

Trinity, doctrine of, 101f., 131f., 138, 150, 176
Tulloch, J., 128
Turnbull, R., 221

Vidler, A., 202, 209, 218
Visser t' Hooft, W. A., 222, 229

Walsh, W. H., 100
Watson, W. J., 286
Weil, Simone, 246

Weingard, R. E., 119
Westminster Standards, 5, 7, 15ff., 103, 124, 196, 227, 253, 264, 275
White, John, 183
Whitehead, A. N., 87
Whyte, Alexander, 12, 13, 14, 287
Whyte, James, 283
Wingren, G., 36, 153
Wittgenstein, L., 158
World Council of Churches, 4, 5, 144, 191ff., 200, 222, 253, 267, 280

SCHOLASTIC
ENGLISH SKILLS

Spelling and vocabulary
Workbook

Ages 9–10

SCHOLASTIC
ENGLISH SKILLS

Spelling and vocabulary

Scholastic Education, an imprint of Scholastic Ltd
Book End, Range Road, Witney, Oxfordshire, OX29 0YD
Registered office: Westfield Road, Southam,
Warwickshire CV47 0RA

www.scholastic.co.uk

© 2016, Scholastic Ltd

2 3 4 5 6 7 8 9   7 8 9 0 1 2 3 4 5

British Library Cataloguing-in-Publication Data
A catalogue record for this book is available from the British Library.

ISBN 978-1407-14191-6
Printed by Ashford Colour Press

Author
Sally Burt and Debbie Ridgard

Editorial
Rachel Morgan, Anna Hall, Jenny Wilcox, Red Door Media

Design
Andrew Scott, Neil Salt and Nicolle Thomas

Cover Design
Nicolle Thomas

Illustration
Dave Shephard/Beehive Illustration

Cover Illustration
Eddie Rego

Contents

4 | INTRODUCTION
How to use this book

5 | CHAPTER 1
Revisit and reinforce

17 | CHAPTER 2
Suffixes and prefixes

26 | CHAPTER 3
Word endings

35 | CHAPTER 4
Word families, roots and origins

53 | CHAPTER 5
Homophones and other tricky words

66 | CHAPTER 6
Improving your work

80 | PROGRESSION
Progress chart

How to use this book

● *Scholastic English Skills Workbooks* help your child to practise and improve their skills in English.

● The content is divided into topics. Find out what your child is doing in school and dip into the practice activities as required.

● Keep the working time short and come back to an activity if your child finds it too difficult. Ask your child to note any areas of difficulty. Don't worry if your child does not 'get' a concept first time, as children learn at different rates and content is likely to be covered at different times throughout the school year.

● Check your child's answers at www.scholastic.co.uk/ses/spelling.

● Give lots of encouragement, complete the 'How did you do' for each activity and the progress chart as your child finishes each chapter.

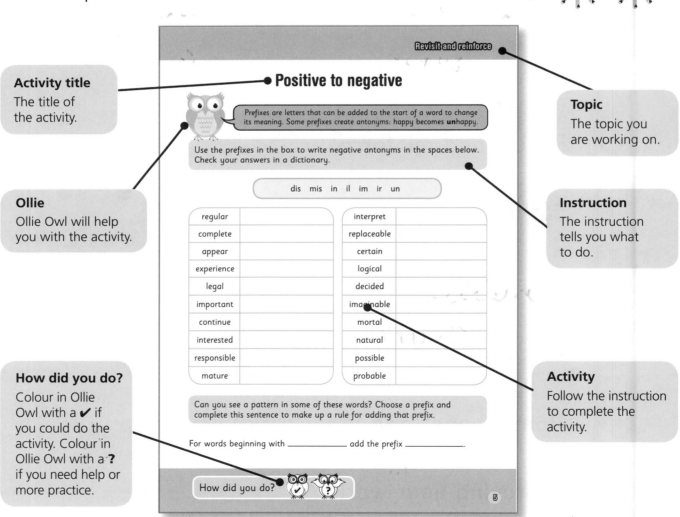

Activity title
The title of the activity.

Ollie
Ollie Owl will help you with the activity.

How did you do?
Colour in Ollie Owl with a ✔ if you could do the activity. Colour in Ollie Owl with a **?** if you need help or more practice.

Topic
The topic you are working on.

Instruction
The instruction tells you what to do.

Activity
Follow the instruction to complete the activity.

Revisit and reinforce

Positive to negative

Prefixes are letters that can be added to the start of a word to change its meaning. Some prefixes create antonyms: happy becomes **un**happy.

Use the prefixes in the box to write negative antonyms in the spaces below. Check your answers in a dictionary.

dis   mis   in   il   im   ir   un

regular	
complete	
appear	
experience	
legal	
important	
continue	
interested	
responsible	
mature	

interpret	
replaceable	
certain	
logical	
decided	
imaginable	
mortal	
natural	
possible	
probable	

Can you see a pattern in some of these words? Choose a prefix and complete this sentence to make up a rule for adding that prefix.

For words beginning with _____ add the prefix _____.

How did you do?

If you need help, ask an adult!

Positive to negative

Prefixes are letters that can be added to the start of a word to change its meaning. Some prefixes create antonyms: happy becomes **un**happy.

Use the prefixes in the box to write negative antonyms in the spaces below. Check your answers in a dictionary.

dis   mis   in   il   im   ir   un

regular	irregular
complete	incomplete
appear	disappear
experience	inexperience
legal	illegal
important	unimportant
continue	discontinue
interested	disinterested
responsible	irresponsible
mature	immature

interpret	misinterpret
replaceable	irreplaceable
certain	uncertain
logical	illogical
decided	undecided
imaginable	unimaginable
mortal	immortal
natural	unnatural
possible	impossible
probable	improbable

Can you see a pattern in some of these words? Choose a prefix and complete this sentence to make up a rule for adding that prefix.

For words beginning with _____ r _____ add the prefix _____ ir _____.

How did you do?

5

Prefixes sorted

Use a dictionary to find the meaning of the following prefixes.

Understanding the meaning of prefixes will help you with the meaning and spelling of many other words.

Prefix	Meaning
sub	Below.
super	Placed above or over.
re	indicating return to a previous condition.
anti	Against something
inter	
auto	

Add one of these prefixes to the words in brackets to show the correct meaning in each sentence.

1. After the earthquake, they had to (build) _rebuild_ the town.

2. The hero used his (natural) _supernatural_ powers to save the day.

3. Our (net) _internet_ connection is very slow today.

4. They didn't like his (social) _antisocial_ behaviour.

5. In winter, temperatures drop to (zero) _minuszero_ degrees.

6. The (pilot) _autopilot_ helped fly the plane to safety.

How did you do?

Get on board

Suffixes are letters that can be added to the end of a word to change its meaning. Sometimes the spelling of the word changes when you add a suffix.

ed	ing	er	ous

Choose a word from the box below and add an appropriate suffix from the train. Does the spelling of the word change? Write the new word in the correct train carriage. Check your spelling in a dictionary.

begin   prefer   consider   danger   poison
forget   mountain   occur   answer

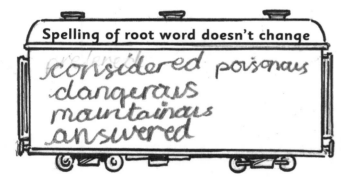

Spelling of root word doesn't change

considered poisonous
dangerous
mountainous
answered

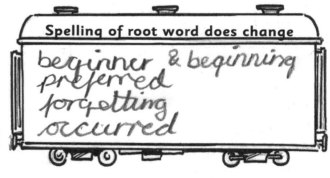

Spelling of root word does change

beginner & beginning
preferred
forgetting
occurred

Cross out the incorrect words to complete this rule.

Double the final consonant if the root word
ends with ~~one~~/two/three consonant(s),
has more than one/~~two~~/three syllable(s),
and the **first**/~~final~~ syllable is stressed.

How did you do?

Make the change

Some words change their word class when you add a suffix. The suffix **ation** can change a verb to a noun. The suffix **ly** can change an adjective to an adverb.

Add **ation** or **ly** to these words and write them in the correct box.

inform   complete   confirm   different   interpret   extreme   famous
consider   important   continue   natural   relax   experiment   recent
imagine   import   converse   special   observe   strange   certain

Nouns with ation	Adverbs with ly

How did you do?

Shhh!

The suffixes **tion, sion, ssion** and **cian** all have the /**sh**/ sound.

Identify the root words and suffixes and fill in the boxes below.

Word	Root word	Suffix
tension	tense	sion
discussion		
subtraction		
musician		
completion		
comprehension		
description		
opposition		
magician		
possession		
regulation		
separation		
punctuation		
electrician		
extension		
expression		

How did you do?

Hear the buzz

Complete the crossword using words from the honey pot that end with **sion** but sound like /**zhun**/.

Down

1. Convincing your friends
2. A crash
3. When an army attacks
4. What you use your eyes for to see
6. Being unsure

Across

5. Watching over someone
7. Sharing
8. A device providing entertainment
9. Going over work for a test

revision   division

invasion   confusion
television   vision

persuasion   supervision
supervision   collision

How did you do?

Apostrophes make sense

Apostrophes can be used to show something belongs to a person or thing, or lots of people or things.

Underline the possessive plural words in these sentences.

1. The dads rushed to buy the men's clothing.

2. The toddlers unpacked the box of children's toys.

3. Babies' bottles were given to all the new mothers.

4. Some schools provide kids' and teachers' meals.

Write a possessive plural for each statement.

5. Tools for dads _____

6. Cakes for bakers _____

7. Dresses for mums _____

8. Files for teachers _____

9. Wool for sheep _____

Plurals that don't end in **s** are known as irregular plurals.

Complete the table showing the apostrophe of possession.

Singular	Possessive	Plural	Possessive
boy	boy's	boys	
lady		ladies	
child		children	
sheep		sheep	

How did you do?

Plural apostrophe

The possessive apostrophe is added after the plural form of the word. Add **s** if the plural does not end in **s**. Do not add **s** if the plural already ends in **s**.

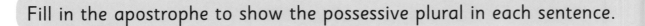

Fill in the apostrophe to show the possessive plural in each sentence.

1.   The rain wet all the bridesmaids hair.

2.   The children laughed at the clowns act.

3.   The teachers enjoyed the students presentation.

4.   The owners animals enjoyed the pet show.

5.   Don't forget to clean the mices cage.

6.   She dressed up in both her sisters clothes.

7.   Today is my parents anniversary.

8.   Please use the girls bathroom.

9.   The geeses feathers covered the ground.

10. The elves hats were red and white.

11. All the statues plaques need replacing.

12. The deers natural environment is being destroyed.

How did you do?

See the sea

Circle the correct homophones in the following story.

Last week / weak we went to the seaside four / for a short, summer break / brake . The weather / whether looked fine and it was great / grate to get out of town.

The see / sea was a beautiful blue / blew and the sand felt hot and soft under our feet / feat . We lay happily on our towels / tiles and ate / eight all our / hour bread rolls / roles . But we soon began to feel bored / board .

I / eye suggested a walk on the peer / pier , witch / which seemed like a good idea sew / so off we went. The son / sun was shining weakly / weekly. We were gone for / four about an hour / our when the wind picked up and the air / heir became chilly. The seen / scene soon changed as we raced back to / two / too pack up our things.

How did you do?

Sniff it out

Circle the mistake in each sentence. Then write the words correctly in the boxes below. The first one has been done for you.

1. It's a lovely day to go swimming in the (see).

2. The dog left it's bone in the ground.

3. Everyones' cars were damaged in the hail storm.

4. She is a very ilorganised person.

5. The chefs' hat fell off his head.

6. He sore what she did.

7. If you tuch the ball you're out.

8. I am very gratefull for your help.

9. The playful children need lots of supervition.

10. You must que for your tickets.

Tricky sound	Homophone	Punctuation	Prefix/suffix
	sea		

How did you do?

Adding ly

Complete the table below.

When **ly** (or **ally**) is added to an adjective, it becomes an adverb.

Adjective	Adverb	How did the words change?
complete hopeful final		
steady noisy happy		
sensible wriggle gentle		
basic frantic dramatic		

Write synonyms that end in **ly** or **ally** for each adverb. Use a thesaurus to help you.

quietly   s_____   strangely   o_____

fortunately   l_____   joyfully   h_____

carefully   g_____   crossly   a_____

How did you do?

Describe with ous

Change these words into adjectives by adding the suffix **ous**.

| poison | _poisonous_ | mountain | _____ |

| glamour | _____ | humour | _____ |

| courage | _____ | outrage | _____ |

| curiosity | _____ | courtesy | _____ |

Write the words above in the correct rule boxes below. An example has been provided for each rule.

Rule	Words
When the root word is obvious and ends with a single consonant, it stays the same before adding **ous**.	danger – dangerous
Change **our** to **or** before adding **ous**.	vigour – vigorous
Keep the final **e** of the root word if the **g** has a /**dz**/ sound.	advantage – advantageous
If there is an /**i**/ sound before the **ous** ending, it is usually spelled with an **i** but some words use **e**.	serious, spontaneous

How did you do?

Verb that noun

This machine makes verbs by attaching suffixes on to nouns. Put each noun through the machine. Write new verbs in the correct boxes.

The machine doesn't work for all nouns, some get rejected! Check your verbs using a dictionary.

computer   priority   solid   ceiling   captive   glory   truck   quantity
scrutiny   vaccine   apology   chair   person   caffeine   carpet

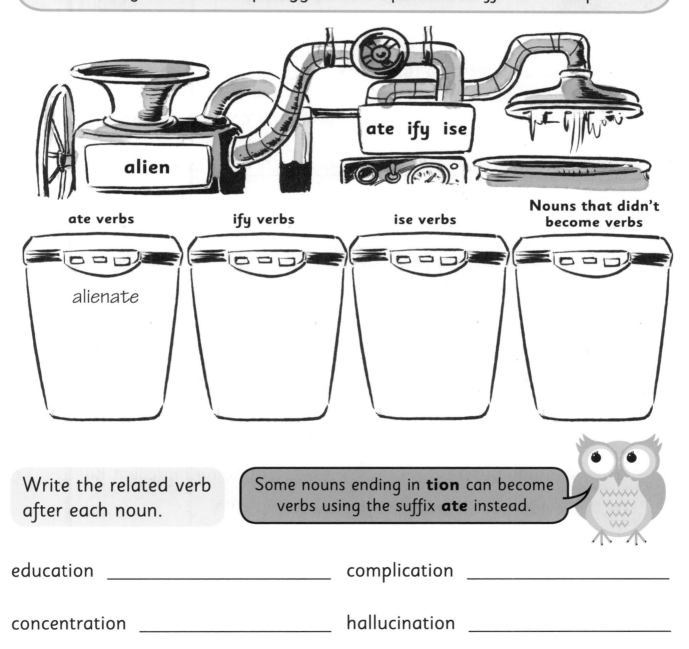

alien

ate   ify   ise

ate verbs   **ify verbs**   **ise verbs**   **Nouns that didn't become verbs**

alienate

Write the related verb after each noun.

Some nouns ending in **tion** can become verbs using the suffix **ate** instead.

education _____   complication _____

concentration _____   hallucination _____

Adjectives get active

Change the adjectives in brackets into verbs by adding one of the super suffixes to complete each sentence.

Super suffixes

ate   en   ise   ify

1.   The principal wanted to (modern) _____ all the classrooms.

2.   Jonah (ample) _____ the sound by connecting larger speakers.

3.   Make sure you (sharp) _____ your pencil before the test.

4.   The council decided to (wide) _____ the road next year.

5.   The nurse explained how to (sterile) _____ the baby's bottle.

6.   "(Initial) _____ rocket launch take-off protocol!" ordered the controller.

7.   "Those puppies are cute enough to (glad) _____ anyone's heart," sighed Gran.

8.   "How can you (just) _____ finding my client guilty on this evidence?" demanded the lawyer.

9.   Click on the link to (active) _____ your membership.

10. Please can you (simple) _____ the instructions because they are too complicated.

How did you do?

Give me a clue

Complete the crossword, adding a suffix to each word to create the verb.

Some words change more than their ending when they become a verb.

Across

3. white
5. mad
8. hypnosis
10. electric
11. clarity
12. glamour

Super suffixes
ate   en   ise   ify

Down

1. live
2. terror
4. pure
6. dictation
7. pacification
9. maximum

How did you do?

Perplexed prefixes

Write the correct verb next to each mistake.

These prefixes are a bit perplexed – they have joined up with the wrong root verbs.

overallow _____

misrail _____

recome _____

disturn _____

dehandle _____

relike _____

overbound _____

diswork _____

These prefixes are lonely and want to join a root verb.

Join a prefix to each verb to form new verbs.

MIS HANDLE

Prefix

re   mis   de   dis   over

mis handle _____continue _____bug

_____shoot _____carry _____burden

_____lead _____hear _____select

_____wind _____embark _____centralise

_____excite _____simplify _____arm

How did you do?

20

Prefix fact file

More than one new verb can sometimes be created by adding different prefixes to a single root verb.

Complete the table below to create a prefix fact file.

Root verb: charge	Definitions
discharge	to allow to leave
recharge	
overcharge	
Root verb:	**Definitions**
return	
overturn	
Root verb:	**Definitions**
misdirect	
redirect	
Root verb:	**Definitions**
misprint	
reprint	
Root verb:	**Definitions**
restock	
overstock	

Which prefix can be attached to the most verbs?

_____

How did you do?

Prefix with meaning

Add a prefix to create a new verb to make sense of each sentence below.

Use the prefix pack at the bottom of the page.

1. Please help me ____**lodge** the stone that is stuck in my shoe.

2. The boys crept round the field to avoid ____**raging** the bull.

3. The RSPCA helps to protect animals that have been ____**treated**.

4. Mrs Arbuthnot decided to ____**clutter** her house with a big clear out.

5. "Don't ____**indulge** in cake at the party or you'll get a bad stomach!"

6. Percy was ____**trusted** with an important note for the head wizard.

7. The fishmonger ____**boned** the fish for Mrs Patel before wrapping it up.

8. The king finally ____**gained** his throne after the long civil war.

9. The dentist ____**infects** all the instruments before seeing each patient.

10. I keep ____**living** the moment I walked on stage to collect my prize.

11. The drains ____**flowed** because they were blocked by tree roots.

12. I totally ____**judged** our new teacher at first; she is great!

mis   re
over   de
en   dis

How did you do?

Hyphens help

Hyphens can help us work out how to pronounce words, especially when a prefix ends in a vowel and the root word begins with a vowel. The hyphen creates a syllable break. So co/op/er/ate rather than coo/per/ate.

Mark a line between the syllables of each word. Then rewrite the word using a hyphen. The first one has been done for you.

c o/o w n	co-own	p r e e m i n e n t	
r e i n f e c t		c o o p t	
d e a c t i v a t e		r e i n s u r e	
r e a s s e m b l e		d e i n k	
r e a r m		d e i o n i s e	
r e a c c u s t o m		c o i n h a b i t	
c o e d i t		r e e n c o d e	
r e a s s e s s		r e e m b a r k	

Write three sentences using hyphenated words. Pick ones you are unfamiliar with and use your dictionary to check the meanings first.

1. _____

_____

2. _____

_____

3. _____

_____

How did you do?

Double trouble

Sometimes adding a prefix creates a double letter. A hyphen can show where to split the word.

dis over

mis

Choose a prefix to add to each root word.
Write out the new word using a hyphen.

step _____   react _____

ripen _____   shapen _____

select _____   reach _____

send _____   ride _____

satisfy _____   run _____

Study the words below and underline the letter combination that could cause you to mispronounce the word.

mishandle   mishear

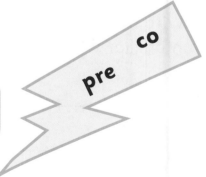

pre co

Unjumble these mixed-up words. Then write each one out with a hyphen to mark off the prefix.

rpx**e**niamee _____pre-examine_____   rctsoa _____

gerrparnea _____   xictsoe _____

ngsoci _____   ycpucorep _____

dporeerr _____   dancroteoi _____

How did you do?

24

Spot the difference

Choose five words from the word cloud. For each word, write a sentence that shows what it means with and without a hyphen.

The prefix **re** means again or anew. If adding **re** makes a word that already exists, add a hyphen to avoid confusion.

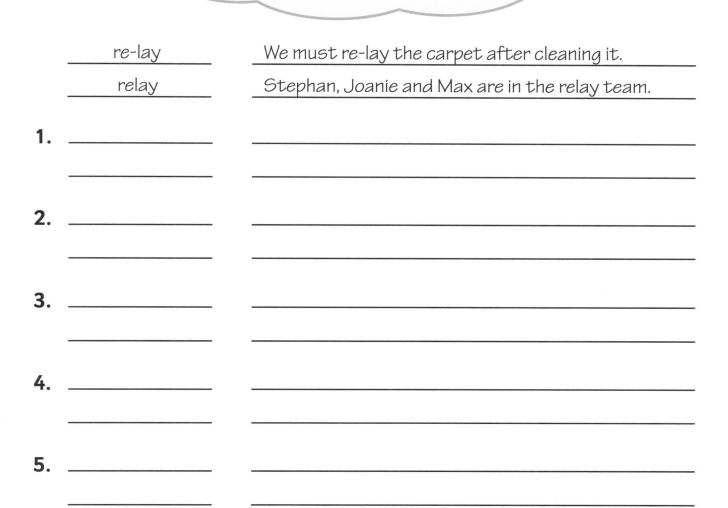

re-sound   re-pose
re-strain   re-sort   re-dress
re-lease   re-store   re-sent

| re-lay | We must re-lay the carpet after cleaning it. |
| relay | Stephan, Joanie and Max are in the relay team. |

1. _____

2. _____

3. _____

4. _____

5. _____

How did you do?

cious and tious

Complete the crossword using adjectives from the word box and the synonyms provided.

The suffixes **cious** and **tious** sound the same. They generally change words into adjectives.

Across

3. bold
4. irritable
8. tasty
9. aware
10. diligent
11. greedy

Down

1. violent
2. catching
5. awful
6. fearful
7. cruel

vicious
fractious
avaricious
audacious
superstitious
delicious
conscious
atrocious
malicious
infectious
conscientious

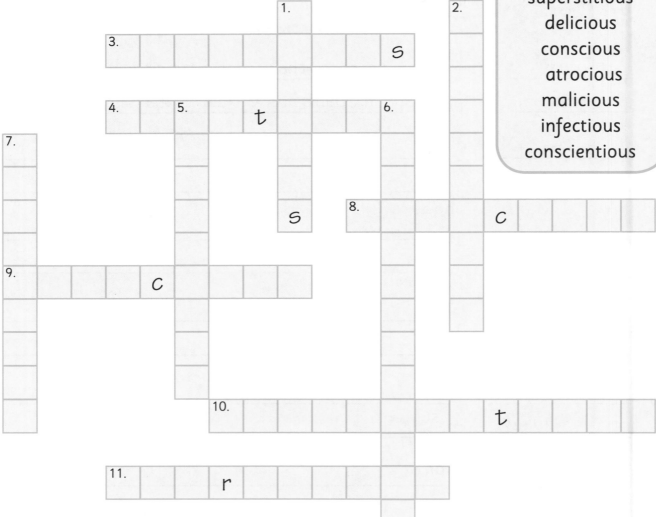

How did you do?

cious or tious?

> Words that end with **ce** or **city** usually have the **cious** suffix.
> Words that end with **tion** usually have the **tious** suffix.

Choose the correct root word from the box to match each sentence.
Change it to an adjective using the correct suffix and write in the space.

space	repetition	office	infection	~~suspicion~~
auspice	contention	nutrition	caution	vice

1. The detective thought the suspect had a ___suspicious___ face.

2. The doctor warned that her patient was _____.

3. The inside of the spacecraft was definitely not _____.

4. The _____ attack left many people injured.

5. We found the revision very _____.

6. The _____ police officer approached the scene.

7. _____ leadership is not always the best approach.

8. Many schools provide _____ meals for students.

9. The _____ subject matter was handled sensitively.

10. Her graduation was an _____ occasion.

How did you do?

27

cious and tious exceptions

Use a dictionary to find the correct suffix to complete each word. Write a sentence to show you know what it means.

These words don't stick to any rules – you just have to get to know them!

1. cons_____ _____

_____

2. ficti_____ _____

_____

3. conscien_____ _____

_____

4. face_____ _____

_____

5. scrump_____ _____

_____

How did you do?

Finding cial and tial words

There are 11 words that end with **cial** or **tial** in this word shell. Identify them by separating them with a line.

The word endings **cial** and **tial** (pronounced /**shul**/) mean 'having the quality of'. They make adjectives.

Write five sentences using two **cial** or **tial** adjectives in each sentence.

1. _____

_____

2. _____

_____

3. _____

_____

4. _____

_____

5. _____

_____

How did you do?

Sorting cial and tial

Match these word beginnings with their endings.
Write the words in the correct bucket.

par   mar   so   residen   judi   poten
torren   sequen   impar   offi   sacrifi
confiden   essen   artifi   substan   cru

If word beginnings end with a vowel add **cial**.
If word beginnings end with a consonant add **tial**.

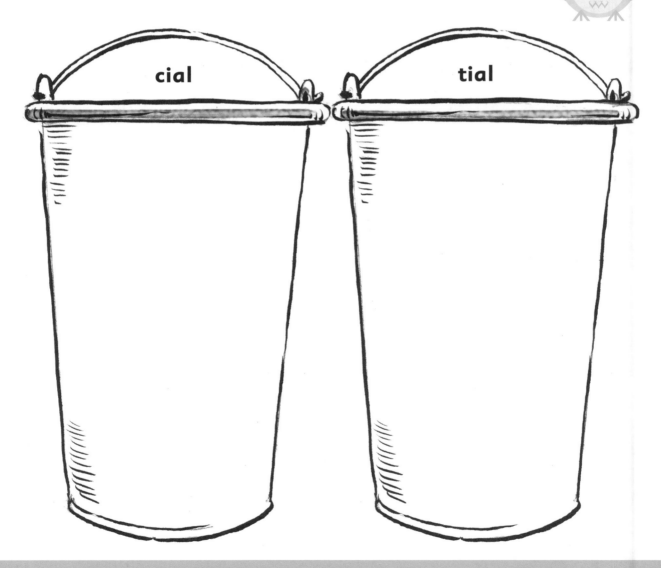

cial

tial

How did you do?

Find the exception

Circle the word in each list that has an incorrect suffix. Then write the words correctly on the lines.

Watch out! These words do not follow the rules.

1. torrential, finantial, presidential, residential _____

2. official, sacrificial, facial, inicial _____

3. commertial, partial, martial, sequential _____

4. judicial, crucial, palacial, social _____

5. benefitial, confidential, substantial, essential _____

6. impartial, influential, preferential, provintial _____

Use some of the corrected words to complete the following sentences.

7. The _____ team worked hard to deliver the report.

8. Keeping fit and healthy is a _____ lifestyle choice.

9. The party will take place in her _____ residence.

10. A community market is a great _____ opportunity.

How did you do?

Ant adjectives

Look inside the ants' nest for word beginnings you can use to make five adjectives that end in **ant**. Write them in the boxes.

Some words end with **ant** and some with **ent**.

opul   abund

ignor   differ   import   excell

depend   hesit

Use the **ant** adjectives to complete the sentences below.

1. There was an _____ supply of fruit at the market.

2. She thought the shopkeeper was rude and _____.

3. You must complete this _____ homework.

4. As a _____ teenager he relied on his weekly allowance.

5. The _____ boy peered into his new classroom.

How did you do?

Making words with ance, ancy, ence, ency

Find example words from the box to match the rules. The first one has been done for you.

~~elegance~~ appearance recent agent frequent reliance payment ~~significance~~ vacancy insurance confidence reference interference

ant, ance, ancy	Example words
After a hard **g** or **c**	elegance significance
If the root word ends in **y**, drop the **y** and add **i**	
If the word ends with **ation**, replace with **ance** or **ancy**	
If the word ends with **ure**, drop the **e**	
If the word ends with **ear**, simply add **ance** or **ancy**	

ent, ence, ency	Example words
If the word ends with a soft **c**, soft **g** or **qu**	
If the syllable before is **id**	
If a word ends with **ere** or **er**	
If a word ends with **ment**	

How did you do?

Spot the difference

The prefix **re** means again or anew. If adding **re** makes a word that already exists, add a hyphen to avoid confusion.

Change the nouns to adjectives and change the adjectives to nouns. Use **ant, ance**, **ancy** or **ent**, **ence**, **ency** to complete the crossword puzzle.

Across

4. fragrant (adj)
5. frequency (n)
6. absence (n)
7. vacant (adj)
9. excellent (adj)
10. elegant (adj)

Down

1. radiance (n)
2. proficient (adj)
3. distance (n)
8. obedience (n)

How did you do?

Word builder

Remember the spelling rules!

Create new words by adding suffixes. Beware, not all the root words take all the suffixes – only make words that make sense.

Root word	er	est	ly	ness
smart	smarter	smartest	smartly	smartness
lazy				
sturdy				
tall				
funny				
gentle				
happy				
mean				
mad				
heavy				
wet				
early				

Write the root word next to each group of words. Remember that the root may have been altered in some words because of a spelling rule.

blockage   un**block**   **block**ed   _____

likely   unlikely   likelihood   _____

politeness   politest   impolite   _____

scales   scaly   descale   _____

imagined   imagination   imaginary   _____

freest   freed   freedom   _____

How did you do?

Add and change

Match each clue to a prefix and suffix pair from the box. Then use these to complete the crossword.

Try adding each prefix and suffix pair to each word in turn. When you find one that works, cross it out and write in the answer.

un___ment   dis___ed   anti___wise   under___ed   in___ity

un___ed   in___ly   un___ful   im___al   ir___ible

Down

1. satisfy
2. believe
3. clock
4. success

5. employ
6. sincere
7. response

Across

8. person
9. sufficient
10. rate

How did you do?

Writing rules

Write rules to help you remember how to spell these groups of words.

picnic – picnicking   traffic – trafficking   mimic – mimicking

My rule: _____

_____

happy – happiness   beauty – beautiful   fury – furious   plenty – plentiful

My rule: _____

_____

hope – hoping   wake – waking   ride – riding   write – writing

My rule: _____

_____

skill – skilful   full – fulfil   well – welcome   will – wilful

My rule: _____

_____

bitter – biting   dinner – dining   latter – later   hopper – hoping

My rule: _____

_____

How did you do?

Spot the errors!

Read the passage below and circle seven more prefix or suffix mistakes.

Cinderella was the (prettyest) girl in all the land but her beauty was hidden behind the scruffiest clothes and the sadest of faces. Her unhappiness was due to her ugly sisters' laziness which meant that poor Cinders worked from dawn to dusk to keep their house cleanner and tidier than any other.

When Cinderella heard that the Prince was holding a ball, she was hopefull that she might be allowed to go. Dreaming of danceing in the moonlight kept her going while sweepping, polishing and scrubbing.

It was an inescapeable fact that she had no fine dress to wear, but she kept hoping for a miracle. Luckyly her fairy godmother came to the rescue.

Complete the table below. For each mistake, write the correct spelling and the rule for adding the prefix or suffix.

Correct spelling	Rule
prettiest	y changes to i when adding a suffix beginning with a vowel

How did you do?

Plural patterns

Follow the pattern and write the plural of these nouns.

Words ending in **fe** and **f** (but not **ff**) replace with **ves**.

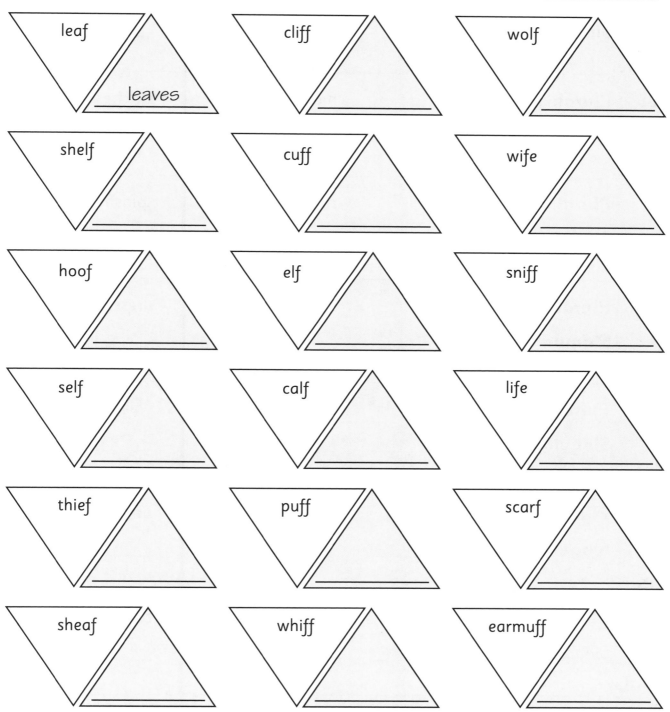

leaf — leaves

cliff

wolf

shelf

cuff

wife

hoof

elf

sniff

self

calf

life

thief

puff

scarf

sheaf

whiff

earmuff

How did you do?

More plural patterns

Look at the groups of **plural** nouns. Write out the **singular** nouns for each group. Then write the rule underneath.

1. **Plural:**   boxes   hoaxes   reflexes

    Singular: _____   _____   _____

Rule: _____

2. **Plural:**   churches   matches   stitches

    Singular: _____   _____   _____

Rule: _____

3. **Plural:**   wishes   radishes   splashes

    Singular: _____   _____   _____

Rule: _____

4. **Plural:**   kisses   compasses   dresses

    Singular: _____   _____   _____

Rule: _____

5. **Plural:**   essays   delays   valleys

    Singular: _____   _____   _____

Rule: _____

6. **Plural:**   studios   embryos   patios

    Singular: _____   _____   _____

Rule: _____

7. **Plural:**   volcanoes   heroes   torpedoes

    Singular: _____   _____   _____

Rule: _____

How did you do?

Exceptional plurals

Follow the rules to find the plural for each word on the scroll. Find and circle them in the word search below.

Change word endings **um** and **on** to **a**
Change word endings **ix** and **ex** to **ices**
Change word ending **is** to **es**
Change word ending **us** to **i**
Change word ending **a** to **ae**

Not all plurals follow standard rules. Some words originally from another language follow plural rules from the root word language.

podium	medium	diagnosis	parenthesis
formula	nucleus	stimulus	crisis
bacterium	phenomenon	octopus	thesis
stadium	datum	ellipsis	oasis
larva	fungus	index	vertebra
criterion	cactus	curriculum	appendix

e	s	t	i	m	u	l	i	d	a	t	a	p	b	f	o	m	s
j	a	u	p	v	p	e	a	g	a	k	a	a	l	o	a	a	e
u	n	p	c	e	h	b	j	a	n	i	e	r	s	r	s	y	s
d	q	o	r	a	e	i	w	h	d	u	o	e	y	m	e	i	o
c	w	d	i	k	n	s	j	a	i	s	f	n	g	u	s	y	n
r	r	i	t	e	o	o	t	i	h	t	g	t	a	l	j	s	g
i	a	a	e	w	m	s	w	f	q	h	k	h	t	a	a	e	a
s	v	e	r	t	e	b	r	a	e	e	u	e	h	e	m	c	i
e	b	h	i	p	n	z	n	q	j	s	d	s	w	n	d	i	d
s	t	m	a	h	a	v	k	s	k	e	m	e	d	i	a	d	e
c	u	r	r	i	c	u	l	a	a	s	b	s	n	l	j	n	a
a	e	k	p	t	a	e	h	i	z	i	e	l	c	u	n	i	v
c	w	s	e	s	p	i	l	l	e	a	f	s	k	l	v	q	r
t	n	h	w	a	a	p	p	e	d	i	c	e	s	p	y	k	a
i	p	o	t	c	o	a	i	o	a	i	r	e	t	c	a	b	l

How did you do?

Word magic

Use a bit of magic to create a list of compound words. Match words from above each bag to make the new words. List the words in alphabetical order.

Write the words on a separate sheet first. Then copy them on to the list in alphabetical order.

pepper sun

brain lip   wheel

jig eye hedge

rain scare jack

leap super

tooth high

sauce earth

black snow

blackmail

hog mint stick

dial bow mail

frog ball pot

crow quake

chair pan

market saw

witness way

storm pick

How did you do?

Compound word chain

Complete this chain of compound words by choosing words to complete the links. The second part of each compound word becomes the first part of the next one.

Some words may fit with more than one partner but you need to find the right partner to complete the chain!

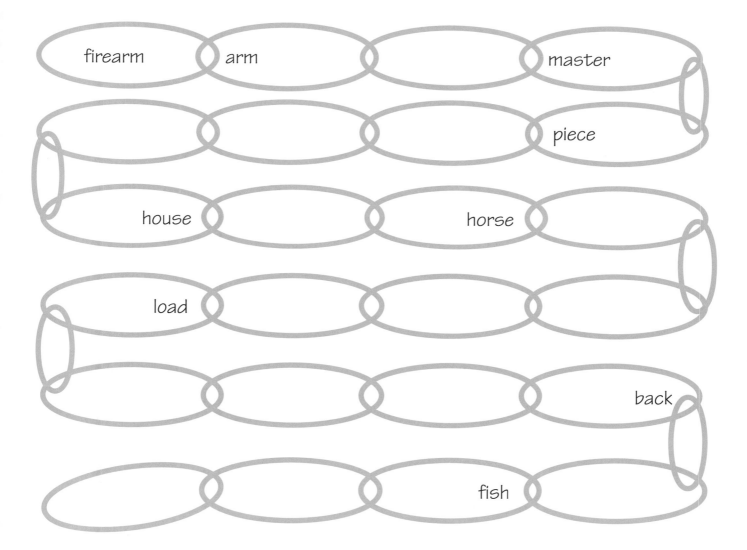

firearm — arm — — master

piece

house — horse

load

back

fish

~~arm~~   ~~master~~   ~~back~~   ~~piece~~   meal   time   ware   paper
work   ~~horse~~   eye   band   ground   table   bone   nut
~~fish~~   ~~load~~   case   stone   ~~fire~~   ~~house~~   ball   wall   play

---

How did you do?

Head of the family

Write the root word acting as the head of each word family.

1. _____ ➔ considerable considerate consideration reconsider considerably inconsiderate

2. _____ ➔ imaginative imaginable imagination unimaginable imaginary unimaginably

3. _____ ➔ pleasure unpleasant displeasure pleasant displease pleasantly unpleasantly pleasing pleasurable

4. _____ ➔ known knowledge unknown knowing knowledgeable knowingly unknowingly knowledgeably

5. _____ ➔ personal personality impersonal personalise personify personally personable personification

Write all the words in the correct word class box.

Noun	Verb	Adjective	Adverb
consideration	consider reconsider	considerable considerate inconsiderate	considerably

How did you do?

Family trees

Find family members for each word and fill in the word family trees.

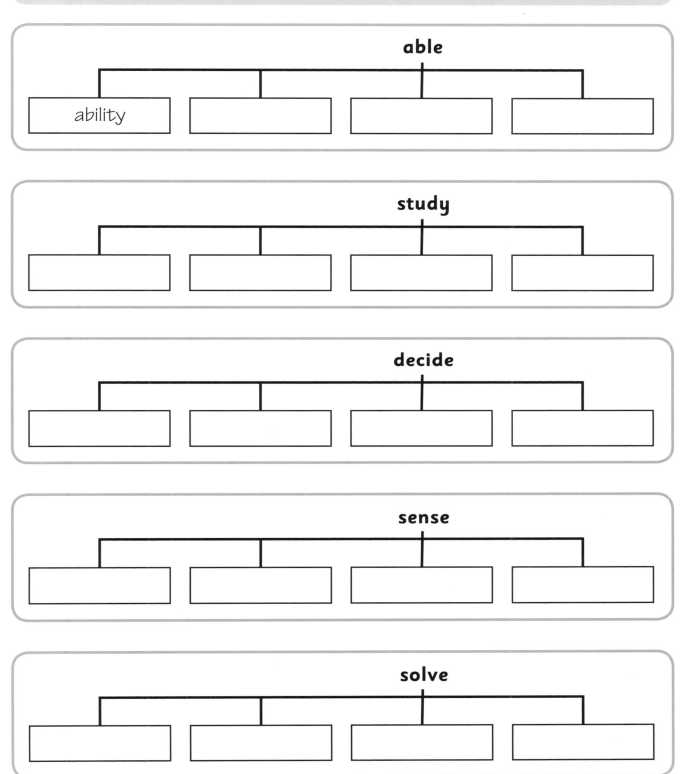

able

| ability | | | |

study

decide

sense

solve

How did you do?

The produce family

Write sentences using each word in this word family to show its meaning.

produce _____

_____

producer _____

_____

product _____

_____

production _____

_____

productive _____

_____

productively _____

_____

unproductive _____

_____

reproduce _____

_____

reproduction _____

_____

counterproductive _____

_____

How did you do?

Prefix work

Look at the list of prefixes and their meanings. Write another word using the same prefix in the last column.

Use a dictionary to help if you get stuck!

Latin or Greek prefix	Meaning	Example	Your own example
tele	far away	telescope	
bene	good	benefit	
aqua	water	aquatic	
com	together, with	combine	
contra	against	contradict	
micro	small	microphone	
super	above, over, bigger	superlative	
sub	below, under	submarine	
hydro	water	hydrogen	
hyper	too much, excessive	hypertension	
trans	across, through	transmit	
mono	one	monotone	
inter	between, among	interrupt	

Use some of your examples in sentences.

_____

_____

_____

_____

How did you do?

Suffix work

Look at this list of suffixes and their meanings. Write another word using the same suffix in the last column.

Suffix	Meaning	Example	Your example
graph	draw, write	autograph	
logue	speech	dialogue	
phobia	fear of	hydrophobia	
oid	shaped like, resembling	humanoid	
ism	belief	patriotism	
ist	follower or profession	violinist	
al	relating to, belonging to	economical	
ous	state or condition	dangerous	

Use some of your examples in sentences.

_____

_____

_____

_____

_____

_____

_____

How did you do?

Suffix matching game

If suffixes originate in an ancient language, such as Latin or Greek, they can help you decode the meaning of an unfamiliar word.

Read the definitions in the suffix table. Then use these to help you match the vocabulary words to their definitions. Draw lines to match the pairs.

Suffix	Meaning
ist	practising or following a particular skill or study
gram	written or drawn
graph	instrument for writing, drawing or recording
logue	speech
oid	like/resembling, shape/form (forms adjectives and nouns)
phile	one that loves/has a strong affinity for, loving
arium	a place for

Vocabulary	Definitions
humanoid	drawn record of heartbeats
xenophobia	person who loves and collects books
seismograph	glass-sided tank where water animals are kept
monologue	like a human
psychologist	device for recording the size of an earthquake
cardiogram	speech or play for one actor
bibliophile	person who studies behaviour
aquarium	fear of foreigners or strangers

How did you do?

Greek and Latin roots

Work out the missing words using the Greek or Latin root and the definitions. Write the word in the space provided.

micro from mikros, meaning small

_____ a tiny organism

_____ a very small aircraft

_____ too small to be seen with the naked eye

dec from deko, meaning ten

_____ ten years

_____ a ten-sided shape

_____ an athletic sport with ten events

geo, meaning earth

_____ a rock with crystals inside it

_____ the study of rocks and similar substances

_____ the study of the Earth's natural features and population

naut/naus, meaning ship

_____ relating to ships, the sea and navigation

_____ a warm-water mollusc with spiral shell

_____ a feeling of sickness (like feeling seasick)

How did you do?

Ancient word roots

Many root words that came from ancient languages, such as Latin or Greek, are not whole words. Use these ancient word roots to find some commonly used words today. Look up the meanings of the words in a dictionary and write them in the boxes.

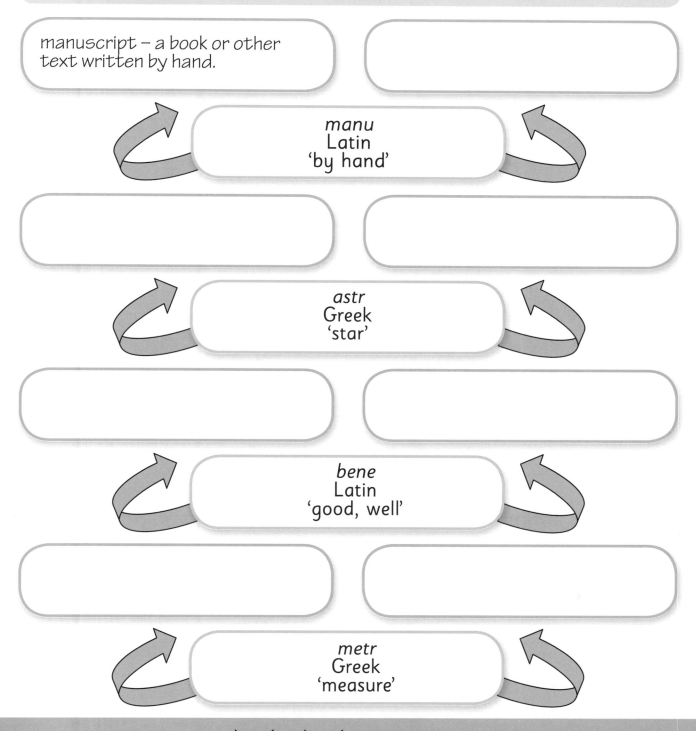

manuscript – a book or other text written by hand.

manu
Latin
'by hand'

astr
Greek
'star'

bene
Latin
'good, well'

metr
Greek
'measure'

How did you do?

Borrowed roots

Each word below shares the common root, **facile**, which means easy in French.
Use each of the related words in a sentence.

Use a dictionary to help if you get stuck!

facile _____

_____

facilitate _____

_____

difficult _____

_____

Explain why you think these words share the root **facile**.

_____

_____

Unscramble these words with Old English roots.

lowdegken   _knowledge_   oersh   _____

ssietr   _____   afrhte   _____

ohtmn   _____   eseph   _____

hvorbaeui   _____   nos   _____

tboehre   _____   tomhre   _____

getuadhr   _____   shgto   _____

reaht   _____   dchli   _____

How did you do?

Homophone signs

Choose one word from each pair of homophones and draw a picture to illustrate your chosen word's meaning.

see / sea	four / for	bruise / brews
time / thyme	through / threw	sight / site
aisle / isle	heard / herd	dessert / desert
pore / poor	male / mail	sew / sow
rain / reign	ate / eight	draft / draught

Test your drawings on someone else to see if they can match the correct homophone to each picture.

How did you do?

Write it right

Read through the following story and correct the errors. Use the space available to write the correct word above each error.

Last weak we went to the coast for a short brake. My uncle has a knew

motorcar sew he was keen to take the for of us on it's maiden voyage!

However, with only too doors and a tiny boot, their was know room four

all hour luggage. Since the whether was looking good, it seamed fare two

leaf behind sum luxuries such as umbrellas and reign coats! Oh buoy! If

only weed herd the forecast that mourning! Buy the thyme we were half

way their, it was bucketing down and

didn't stop for the hole weekend.

Fortunately, I had lots to reed and my

ever-helpful stationary box so I could

right the first draught of this storey.

How did you do?

Homophone search

Use the word search to find a homophone for each word in the box.
Write the words out in the spaces below each word.

lead	passed	would	allowed	altar
_____	_____	_____	_____	_____
guessed	ascent	bridle	complement	cereal
_____	_____	_____	_____	_____

f	w	r	y	k	a	w	o	o	d	m	s
s	x	j	p	a	d	k	w	c	j	a	e
g	a	r	h	e	s	q	z	v	a	l	r
q	u	a	l	a	b	s	w	v	i	o	i
h	a	e	d	h	r	s	e	a	y	u	a
u	h	i	s	e	i	s	k	n	c	d	l
n	c	h	t	t	d	s	p	s	t	a	o
e	s	l	a	h	a	k	n	a	a	h	g
a	a	a	j	k	l	a	l	h	s	w	v
h	c	o	m	p	l	i	m	e	n	t	a
o	d	h	d	f	h	k	b	w	k	f	b
l	g	n	a	k	l	x	a	d	n	g	b

How did you do?

Near homophones

Circle the correct word for each definition.

1.	To tell someone what to do	**advise / advice**
2.	To feel suspicious	**wary / weary**
3.	To have a disagreement	**descent / dissent**
4.	To leave without warning	**desert / dessert**
5.	To go on	**precede / proceed**
6.	To make a plan	**devise / device**
7.	To cause a change	**affect / effect**
8.	To leave something out	**except / accept**
9.	The opposite of rich	**poor / paw**
10.	Belonging to us	**are / our**
11.	Untidy writing	**eligible / illegible**
12.	A low dam	**wear / weir**
13.	To be certain	**insure / ensure**
14.	Money	**sense / cents**

How did you do?

Apostrophe catastrophe

Draw lines to match the words that sound similar but have different meanings.

he'll	wear
we're	your
they're	heel
I'll	their
you're	isle

it's	whose
we've	wheel
who's	were
we'll	its
we're	weave

Choose the correct word to complete each sentence.

1. The sports fans bought **there / their / they're** tickets early so **there / their / they're** definitely going to the game.

2. If **we're / wear / weir** going to the party I need to know what to **we're / wear / weir**.

3. **Heel / Heal / He'll** want his **heel / heal / he'll** to **heel / heal / he'll** before the match.

4. **It's / Its** managed to get a thorn in **it's / its** foot.

How did you do?

Colour sense

Use each word in a sentence to show what it means. Colour the key words according to how you use them — nouns in blue, verbs in red and adjectives in orange.

loose: _____

_____

lose: _____

_____

dessert: _____

_____

desert: _____

_____

assent: _____

_____

accent: _____

_____

breathe: _____

_____

breath: _____

_____

How did you do?

Silent jumble

Unjumble the letters in each word. Look out for the silent letter.

nitk __ __ __ __

chlo __ __ __ __

leis __ __ __ __

mnhy __ __ __ __

secatl __ __ __ __ __ __

lmab __ __ __ __

mlpa __ __ __ __

tagn __ __ __ __

Write the words in the correct boxes. Then add your own examples.

Silent k	Silent c	Silent s	Silent n

Silent t	Silent b	Silent l	Silent g

Circle the words in the cloud that have silent letters. Add them to the correct boxes above.

subtle   jewel   fasten   column   plastic   viscount
foreign   bicycle   knuckle   muscle   library

How did you do?

59

Silent letter match

Match the words that contain the same silent letters.

knew	sovereign
rhyme	column
muscle	stomach
foreign	whistle
island	knight
solemn	crumb
listen	ancient
doubt	debris
knuckle	rhythm
vehicle	viscount
yacht	daughter
neighbour	conscience
aisle	knit

How did you do?

I can't hear you

Use each word in a silly sentence to help you remember the spelling.
The first one has been done for you.

1. **debris** _Throw all the debris away but keep the 's' at the end._

2. **knight** _____

   _____

3. **vehicle** _____

   _____

4. **conscious** _____

   _____

5. **through** _____

   _____

6. **column** _____

   _____

7. **calm** _____

   _____

8. **castle** _____

   _____

9. **muscle** _____

   _____

How did you do?

No stress

Place the word beginnings in the correct box to show which word ending they have. Then add some of your own.

amat	cemet	definit	diction
equipp	especi	categ	should
interfe	appar	restaur	awkw

re	**ent**	**ely**	**ard**

ally	**ant**	**er**	**eur**

ory	**ery**	**ed**	**ary**

Circle the words that are incorrect. Correct the unstressed word endings and write them in the correct boxes above.

literely   personally

sincerally   strangely   solitery   temporory

stationary   contrery

How did you do?

Sounding syllables

Syllables from the words below have been mixed up. Match syllables from each column to recreate the words.

First syllable	Second syllable	Third syllable	Full word
de	quent	tee	
com	taur	ture	
fre	cu	rass	
sig	ve	py	
res	bar	ly	
oc	mit	ant	
em	na	lop	

Mark a line between the syllables in these words. Write down the number of syllables in each word.

1. queue

2. privilege

3. explanation

4. bruise

5. accommodation

How did you do?

Can you hear it?

Circle the words in each line that have the /z/ sound (as in **zip**).

1. conscious, fleas, fleece, trees

2. aggressive, recognise, precise, disastrous

3. persuade, physical, leisure, physician

4. exaggerate, excellent, explanation, existence

Circle the word in each line that does not have the /ch/ sound (as in **chop**).

5. achieve, attach, yacht, arch

6. chin, stomach, chop, chime

7. loch, cherry, patch, scratch

8. ache, archery, chimney, artichoke

Circle the word in each line that has the /ee/ sound (as in **bee**).

9. sly, especially, try, why

10. ancient, sieve, believe, promise

11. pear, relevant, vegetable, appreciate

12. leisure, neighbour, sleigh, caffeine

13. guarantee, environment, system, relevant

How did you do?

Dictionary delve

Choose four tricky words that you often misspell. Write them below.
Use your dictionary to complete the information.

Word: _____

Tricky sound: _____

Class: _____

Meaning: _____

_____

Page: _____

Word: _____

Tricky sound: _____

Class: _____

Meaning: _____

_____

Page: _____

Word: _____

Tricky sound: _____

Class: _____

Meaning: _____

_____

Page: _____

Word: _____

Tricky sound: _____

Class: _____

Meaning: _____

_____

Page: _____

How did you do?

Correct that spelling

Use a dictionary to check the spelling of these words. Underline the mistakes and write the correct spellings in alphabetical order.

mischeivous pronounciation marvelous neiyghbour exsellant

goverment awkw<u>o</u>rd restorant embarress interupt privelige ocurr

forein hindrence cemetary parliamant exagerration comunicate

Alphabetical word list

awkward _____   _____

_____   _____

_____   _____

_____   _____

_____   _____

_____   _____

_____   _____

_____   _____

Choose three of the words and use them in sentences.

_____

_____

_____

How did you do?

Dictionary entries

Complete the dictionary entry cards, following the example.

n (noun)   **v** (verb)   **adj** (adjective)   **adv** (adverb)

controversy _____ _____ **C**
_____

environment _____ _____ **E**
_____

guarantee _____ _____ **G**
_____

nuisance _____ _____ **N**
_____

profession _____ _____ **P**
_____

sacrifice _____ _____ **S**
_____

sufficient _adj_ _____ enough for a specific purpose **S**
_____ The teacher bought sufficient food for the whole class.

How did you do?

Interesting synonyms and antonyms

Use a thesaurus to find more interesting synonyms and antonyms for each of these overused words. The first has been done for you.

Remember to choose synonyms and antonyms in the same word class and form as the root word: **stroll, amble, stride** not **stroll, ambled, striding**. Be bold!

fine *adj*

synonym	antonym
acceptable	unsatisfactory

awkward *adj*

synonym   antonym

definitely *adv*

synonym   antonym

excellent *adj*

synonym   antonym

gives *v*

synonym   antonym

good *adj*

synonym   antonym

liked *v*

synonym   antonym

really *adv*

synonym   antonym

scary *adj*

synonym   antonym

sometimes *adv*

synonym   antonym

well *adv*

synonym   antonym

cross *adj*

synonym   antonym

How did you do?

Increase the effect

Order these thesaurus entries according to strength of meaning, for example: **nibble**, **eat**, **gobble**, **gorge**. Then complete the box.

woeful
sad
despondent
gloomy

1.——————
2.——————
3.——————
4.——————

Word class:
adjective
Most interesting antonym:
merry

ecstatic
happy
blissful
jovial

1.——————
2.——————
3.——————
4.——————

Word class:
——————
Most interesting antonym:
——————

enraged
fractious
cross
incensed

1.——————
2.——————
3.——————
4.——————

Word class:
——————
Most interesting antonym:
——————

munificent
kind
magnanimous
benevolent

1.——————
2.——————
3.——————
4.——————

Word class:
——————
Most interesting antonym:
——————

dreary
tedious
boring
humdrum

1.——————
2.——————
3.——————
4.——————

Word class:
——————
Most interesting antonym:
——————

How did you do?

Freshen up your writing

Read the paragraph below. Use a thesaurus to choose more interesting synonyms for the words in brackets.

Try to replace groups of words with single words that say the same thing, but are more precise and descriptive.

"Oh no! It's raining again," Jack [said in a depressed way] _____, [sitting down heavily] _____ on the beanbag.

"Why are you [looking so cross] _____?" his twin Melody [asked in a cheerful voice] _____. "If it's raining then maybe it's a [good] _____ time to go up to the attic. You know you are [very interested] _____ to [look around in it] _____. We would have to [go up quietly without asking] _____ though, as mum is bound to [say no] _____ if we ask – even if we say we want to [very much] _____."

"Ok," John replied [in a way that did not sound very keen] _____, following his sister to the back staircase.

Even though they [went slowly and quietly] _____ up the stairs, the stairs [made a loud sound] _____ which made the twins [stop absolutely still] _____ to check if their mother had heard.

It was [very dark] _____ inside the attic. "Have you [got] _____ your torch?" [said] _____ Melody as she [carefully] _____ pushed up the flap.

"Of course," said Jack. "Here!" He [gave] _____ his pocket torch to Melody. "Hurry up," he said [in an excited way] _____.

Melody [slowly moved] _____ the torch around the attic and came face to face with eyes [shining in the light] _____…

How did you do?

Proof your spelling

Use your proofreading skills to correct the spelling and word choices in this letter. Circle as many mistakes as you can in 10 minutes.

Focus on homophones, apostrophes, double and single consonants, graphemes and word endings.

Colethatch Cottage
Lane End
Peterborough
25 Janury

Dear Councillor Smithson

We have started a organic vegtable gardin at our school with a spetial worm farm witch helps us make compost.

We realised it would be benefitial after watching a programe on hleathy eating, espetially the importence of fresh food. The hole comunity is volanteering just an our each week in exchange for serplus produse. It turns out that fresh broccolli and sallad is delitious as well as nutricious.

It was a bit disastrous at first because sluggs and snales wouldnt stop nibling our cabagge and lettis. We lernt that slugs and snails are gastropods (which means stummach foot). We took a vote and decided not to kill them as they can be usefull in the right plaice. We take turns patroling the garden and scoopping them up to relaocte them to the compost heap. Theyr'e brillient their.

We wood like to invite you to hour special event to cut the gient green ribon declaring our garden oficialy open.

Yours sincerly

Tarryn Marx
Class 5
Hazlewood Primary

How did you do?

Rewrite and make it right!

Rewrite each sentence with the correct punctuation and capital letters.

1. drat ill have to rewrite the entire letter moaned marvin

_____

_____

2. joanie whispered dont worry well do it together

_____

_____

3. what do you think youre doing shrieked mum thats not allowed

_____

_____

4. a voice quavered out of the darkness murmuring whos there

_____

_____

5. mr lawrence marked jonass maths exam he passed

_____

_____

6. dont let the dogs out shouted the janitor they bite

_____

_____

How did you do?

Be a spelling and grammar checker

Martin's spelling and grammar checker stopped working on his email. Underline his spelling errors in red and any other mistakes in green. Then rewrite his email below.

Focus on spelling, grammar, missing words and layout.

hi arthur thanks for emale asking me to go wiht you too the foot ball final its some thing ive always wanted to do ill meat you at wembley under ground tube stashun at 3 oclock will you bring the to tikkets with u im going to lend ashleys rain coat as the whether forcast sayz itmite reign thanks amillion jasper

How did you do?

That's not nice!

Unjumble each of these ambitious and descriptive synonyms for the word nice. Choose four to use in sentences of your own.

Check the words in a thesaurus.

bgretahtkina, cmhaingr, cnhannetig, rreenhifsg, taelegn, gmtcanfieni, doniersatce, ppprriaatoe, lciorda, rxgeainl, stogohin, pagspetiin

_____ _____ _____

_____ _____ _____

_____ _____ _____

_____ _____ _____

1. _____

2. _____

3. _____

4. _____

How did you do?

Applying ambitious vocabulary

Replace the existing verb with a more powerful choice to improve each sentence. Then add descriptive detail by adding ambitious adjectives and astounding adverbs.

1. The dog <u>ran</u> across the road.

   Impulsively, the excitable dog scampered across the busy road.

2. The boy opened his present.

   _____

   _____

3. The man dropped his mug.

   _____

   _____

4. Alice looked at the monument.

   _____

   _____

5. Teju tore up his raffle ticket.

   _____

   _____

6. The weather was bad.

   _____

   _____

7. The troll shouted at the goats.

   _____

   _____

8. The girl told her teacher she had not done her homework.

   _____

   _____

How did you do?

Which words can you improve?

Marian has finished the first draft of her story. Help her edit her work by underlining at least 20 words you think could be improved.

Suggest a more ambitious replacement for each underlined word.

Everyone had heard about the old shipwreck. No one had ever seen the old wreck but everyone knew of it. Mothers warned small children to stay away from the empty beach when it got dark. But the story was still told quietly, from child to child, getting scarier, madder and more unlikely at each telling.

Maya had heard the scary story from her naughty cousin, Tom. Tom should not have told Maya because he knew she was too young and too easily scared, but he couldn't stop himself. It was so much fun to see her scream and run out of the room with her small hands placed over her ears. This time though Maya didn't just run and hide under her creaky, old bed with her eyes shut very tight. This time, Maya ran straight out of the house and down the narrow lane and out onto the empty beach.

She stopped, breathing heavily, and looked around in a worried way. She was cold and a light rain was beginning to fall. She couldn't see the entrance to the lane anymore as it was beginning to get dark. Very dark. Too dark to be out alone on the beach. Maya looked about and in the dim light saw what looked like a hut, with a faint light shining in the window. She ran over to knock on the door to ask the way home, but there was no door and it certainly wasn't a hut…

How did you do?

Grab attention using attention-grabbing words!

> Choose stimulating vocabulary to entice someone to read.

Rewrite these simple story starters. On each new line, replace or add new words or groups of words.

1. The girl opened the door.

The girl tentatively unlocked the door.

The frail girl tentatively unlocked the door before

_____

2. A crab moved quickly over the sand.

_____

_____

_____

3. The apple tree had been there as long as the house.

_____

_____

_____

Swap your story starters with a partner. Make suggestions to improve each other's word power even further.

How did you do?

Words that just need to be learned

Some words do not follow spelling rules and some are just hard to spell. Practise spelling these words by filling in the gaps.

Use the definition and a dictionary to check if you are unsure.

acco_ _ _ _ate	have room for	def_ _ _te	clear, fixed, obvious
ac_ _ _pany	go or travel with	desp_ _ _te	needing or wanting something very much
ac_ _ _ding	as reported or stated by	dev_ _ _p	grow or change, become more advanced
ach_ _ _e	gain with effort	dicti_ _ _ry	reference book of words and meanings
ag_ _es_ _ve	behaving angrily or violently	disas_ _ _us	extremely bad
ama_ _ _r	doing something as a hobby not a job	embar_ _ _s	make someone feel ashamed or shy
anc_ _ _t	very old	eq_ _ _ment	tool or object used for a particular purpose
ap_ _ _ent	obvious, easy to notice	espe_ _ _lly	more than usual
ap_ _ _ _ iate	be grateful for	exag_ _ _ate	make something more than it is
av_ _ _ge	usual, most common	ex_ _ _lent	of highest quality
at_ _ _hed	joined, close to	exist _ _ _ e	state of existing
ava_ _ _ble	ready to use or get	fami _ _ _ r	well-known
a_ _ _ard	difficult, inconvenient	f _ _ _ _ y	the number 40
bar_ _ _n	sold for less than usual	freq _ _ _ tly	often
br_ _ _e	soft tissue injury mark	gov _ _ _ ment	the people or process of governing a country
cat_ _ _ry	things of similar type	g _ _ _ _ antee	promise that something is true or will happen
contr_ _ _ sy	disagreement, argument	ha _ _ _ s	continually annoy or upset someone
conve_ _ _nce	quality of being easy to use or get to		
cor_ _ _pond	communicate via writing		
crit_ _ _se	find fault with		
curi_ _ _ty	something strange/ unusual		

How did you do?

hindr _ _ _ e	anything delaying or preventing something
iden _ _ _ y	who someone is
immed _ _ _ ely	without delay
inte _ _ _ re	get involved or in the way of
inter _ _ _ ted	stopped temporarily
lang _ _ _ e	communication usually in words
le _ _ _ re	time for relaxation
lig _ _ _ ing	a flash of light in the sky during a storm
marve _ _ _ us	extremely good
misc _ _ _ vous	playfully naughty
mu _ _ _ e	element of body that enables movement
nece _ _ _ ry	absolutely essential
n _ _ _ hbour	person living near another
n _ _ _ ance	bothersome person or thing
o _ _ _ py	live in, keep busy with
oc _ _ _	happen, come to pass
op_ _ _ tunity	possibility that arises
parl _ _ _ ent	people responsible for passing laws in a country
per _ _ _ de	make someone agree to do or think something
ph _ _ _ cal	relating to the body
pre _ _ _ ice	prejudgment, forming an opinion not based on facts
priv _ _ _ ge	special advantage
profe _ _ _ on	occupation requiring special education

progra _ _ _	plan of events or activities with a set purpose
reco _ _ _ nd	suggest something be done
rel _ _ _ nt	important, related
resta _ _ _ nt	place where people eat
r _ _ _ e	words sounding the same
rh _ _ _ m	repeating pattern of sound
sacr _ _ _ ce	give up, kill or destroy
sec _ _ _ ary	someone working in an office doing administration
sh _ _ _ der	part of body between neck and upper arm
sign _ _ _ re	handwritten name
sin _ _ _ e	open and genuine
sol _ _ _ r	member of an army
st _ _ _ ch	body part that digests food
suff _ _ _ ent	enough to fulfil a need
su _ _ _ st	propose an idea or plan
s _ _ _ ol	image or object that represents something else
s _ _ _ em	method of doing things
temp _ _ _ ture	degree of hotness or coldness
thor _ _ _ h	very careful and accurate
tw _ _ _ th	position after eleventh
var _ _ _ y	many different types
ve _ _ _ able	edible plant
ve _ _ _ le	item of transport
y _ _ _ t	sailing boat

How did you do?

Progress chart

Tick () Ollie when you have completed the chapter.

1 Revisit and reinforce

2 Suffixes and prefixes

3 Word endings

4 Word families, roots and origins

5 Homophones and other tricky words

6 Improving your work

Well done! You have now completed the Spelling and vocabulary workbook for ages 9–10.